HOW TO WRITE NON-FICTION THAT SELLS

HOW TO WRITE NON-FICTION THAT SELLS

F. A. ROCKWELL

cbi Contemporary Books, Inc.
Chicago

Contents

Note to the Reader

This book is not guaranteed to make you a great writer. No book can do that, for, as Euclid said, "There is no royal road to learning." But I have put into it much time, energy, study, and experience gleaned from professional writing and teaching to steer you in the right direction.

I have read more than 3,000 articles and books in order to try to point out what editors and publishers want and, more important, to try to instill in you a love of reading and the desire to increase your knowledge and awareness. It is my hope that each quotation, excerpt, and reference will serve as an appetizer, making you hungry to learn more about the authors and writings quoted.

All of the titles in the following pages have been published. Do not use any of them. Their purpose, if I have done my job successfully, is to inspire your own original ideas. The three aims of this book, then, are (1) to kindle your love of reading, listening, and experiencing life, (2) to stimulate new thoughts and eagerness to convey them in writing, and (3) to show you how to "bale the hay"—the construction or craft that is as important as the art of writing nonfiction.

Confucius was on target in 500 B.C. when he wrote: "He who remembers from day to day what he has learned already, may be said to have a love of learning."

May you enjoy the multiple successes achieved by my thousands of students who have been and still are profiting from the following techniques!

F. A. Rockwell

Preface

$ucce$$ $hortcuts to Nonfiction Writing

You are about to be initiated into a success secret that is as new as next month's news and as old as the word NEWS, a word that represents the four directions of the compass: North, East, West, and South. The old trick of forming a time-saving, easy-to-remember word from the first letters of other words, the principle of the acronym or acrostic, is increasing in popularity in our "instant" society.

The first man was identified by an acronym. The name ADAM, like the word NEWS, represents the four directions in Greek: *Arktos* (North), *Duses* (West), *Anatole* (East), and *Mesembria* (South).

Adam's descendants will probably always use acronyms, just as they have recently concocted RADAR (Radio Detecting and Ranging), LASER (Light Amplification Simulated Emission of Radiation), MASER (Microwave Amplification by Simulated Emission of Radiation), and LEM (Lunar Excursion Module). Aquanauts escape earth problems via SCUBA (Self-Contained Underwater Breathing Apparatus), and underocean scientists live for days in SPID (Submerged Portable Inflatable Dwelling).

Acronyms pop up in everyone's life. Housewives join FIT (the consumer Fight Inflation Together movement). High school students earn money thanks to COY (Career Opportunities for Youth). Children of working parents learn to care for younger siblings from BAT (Basic Aid Training).

Social improvements are sought by PET (Parent Effectiveness Training), TET (Teacher Effectiveness Training), TEACH (Therapeutic Education and Child Health), and the television-monitoring group LOP (Least Objectionable Programming). Nonsmokers ban together to fight for their rights through GASP (Group Against Smokers' Pollution), ASH (Action on Smoking and Health), and IQ (I Quit). Drug control is helped by TIP (Turn in Pushers) just as this same acronym TIP (To Insure Promptness) has long remunerated waiters and guides.

Acronyms have become so popular that a *New Yorker* cartoon depicts a door marked:

A. C. R. O. N. Y. M.
Aroused Citizens
Representing Oppressed
N.Y. Minorities

Many people in the U.S. cheer VIVA (Voices in Vital America), which is patriotically active, but condemn IDA (the International Development Association), a huge foreign aid program financed mostly by American taxpayers. But people all over the world benefit from ERTS (the Earth Resources Technology Satellite), which, while orbiting earth every 103 minutes on a polar route, has discovered ground water resources, unknown lakes, and mineral deposits, as well as detecting pollution sources and charting ice movements and river floodings.

More and more organized groups have acronym names—even prostitutes—for example, there's the 3,500-member COYOTE (Call Off Your Old Tired Ethics), ASP (Associated Seattle Prostitutes), and PONY (Prostitutes of New York).

The list of acronyms in current use could fill many pages; in fact, the 211-page *Acronyms Dictionary* attempts to list those most commonly used. These acronyms are used by almost all professional groups, including writers.

You can insure steady success in selling your nonfiction by using the acronym secret in the following pages to remind you to include vital ingredients in the various types of articles editors are buying today.

For the exposé feature:

E = Evidence that the evil exists
X = X-plus research that X-rays through surface facts
P = Personal involvement
O = Objectivity—give opinions and observations of others
S = Seeds of motivation and the set-up that stimulates the evil
É = Examples of remedies to rectify the situation

For the travel article:

T = Timeliness and titular radiance
R = Reader rapport and research
A = Angle and anecdotes
V = Visualization and verisimilitude
E = Emotional enthusiasm and expenses
L = Location and luring lead

For the historical piece:

H = Human interest
I = Identification
S = Seasonal specialties
T = Timely tie-up to today
O = Originality and organization
R = Research
Y = Yeasty yarns of yesterday

The techniques detailed in the following chapters should bring you *marvelous* results. Then you will be able to shout Captain Marvel's "SHAZAM!"—which is an acrostic or acronym made up of traits that will help your writing:

S = Solomon—Wisdom
H = Hercules—Strength
A = Atlas—Stamina
Z = Zeus—Power
A = Achilles—Courage
M = Mercury—Speed

The Hows and Whats of Ideas

"In many ways ideas are more important than people—they are much more permanent."—Charles F. Kettering

"Getting an idea should be like sitting down on a tack: it should make you get up and do something about it."—Herbert V. Prochnow

Salable nonfiction = good ideas + correct timing and timeliness + right slant + professional development.

Where do we get good ideas? From everyone, everything, and everywhere. You can and should pick up many in any twenty-four hours of your life just working, living, reading, listening, observing, fantasizing about, and studying every aspect of your environment. The most likely sources are: (1) people; (2) reading; and (3) experience.

People as Idea Sources

Somerset Maugham became a famous author by training his powers of observation and his skills by going to his room and writing after talking to a stranger for a half hour. He said, "If I can't give a distinctive picture of a person in 2,000 words after I've been with him for 30 minutes, I shouldn't be in the writing game."

Your article ideas can come from what someone says, does, or even wears.

People are not only a writer's most important source as far as material is concerned, but they are also his customers. Thus, it will pay you to become a people-studier and an idea-seeking listener, questioner, and participant in discussions with persons of contrasting backgrounds, ages, races, and nationalities. Instead of driving your car, take a bus once in awhile and chat with someone new. Listen attentively to talk shows on radio and television, and study human interest angles in commercials. Attend classes and lectures, join activity groups, go to parks, museums, historical societies, concerts, airports and depots, plays, little theatres, even cemeteries on holidays—wherever the people are!

Hemingway warned that "if a writer quits observing, he is finished!" Balzac developed observation into intuition. It's even more important for nonfiction writers to keep audio antennae tuned in and optical perceivers honed.

Reading as an Idea Source

Become what H. L. Mencken called a bibliobibulus—a reading addict. In your quest for ideas, you should read everything: daily and weekly newspapers (including ads and the classifieds), magazines, directories, and telephone books (especially the yellow pages). There are ideas lurking even in junk mail. I just picked up a minor mail-order catalogue that advertises:

> Rebuff!: The perfect weapon for women who have to be out at night, or who live or travel alone. One squirt . . . gives attacker the feeling that his face is burned . . . He's completely disabled . . . Can't harm you . . . No permanent damage. Keep 1 in purse, glove compartment, on nightstand.
> *Not shipped in California.*

Why not? Look up California laws and statistics. You'll probably find more women there living alone, working nights, and needing protection but denied it. Why?

Even comedy writers read several newspapers every day and about twenty magazines every month. In a *Writer's Digest* interview, Pat McCormick stated that "one characteristic of most good writers is that they keep abreast with a lot of input on the way of the world around us; you've got to keep pumping it into your subconscious so that you are an aware person."

Read everything is your idea search. Your best aid will probably be the world's greatest credit card, which everyone can afford (and no writer can afford to be without). There are no bills at the end of the month, except perhaps a few pennies' tax for forgetfulness. This credit card is your free ticket to our "fact and thought centers"—the public libraries. Every nonfiction writer should be familiar with:

REFERENCE BOOKS including: almanacs *(World Almanac, Information Please Almanac,* etc.); encyclopedias *(Britannica, Americana, Collier's, Compton's, Encyclopedia International, World Book,* etc.); fact books *(Familiar First Facts, More First Facts, Guiness Book of World Records,* etc.); biographical books *(Marquis' Who's Who, Who's Who in America, International Who's Who, New Century Cyclopedia of Names, Dictionary of National Biography, Dictionary of American Biography,* etc.); and the numberless gazetteers and dictionaries. For reference books in specific fields, Constance Winchell's *Guide to Reference Books,* published by the American Library Association, is an invaluable guide.

THE READERS' GUIDE TO PERIODICAL LITERATURE. These greenbound compilations of nonfiction published in 125 American magazines yield a wealth of ideas and research matter for your chosen subject. They are arranged chronologically by years; then each volume has alphabetical listings of topics and authors.

NEW YORK TIMES INDEX and NATIONAL GEOGRAPHIC INDEX help you locate specific subjects and features in those publications.

SUBJECT GUIDE TO BOOKS IN PRINT. This lists more than 180,000 books under about 45,000 subjects.

THE CARD CATALOGUE. The small drawers of the cabinets in this section contain 3″ = 5″ index cards listing all the books in that particular library, cross-filed according to title, subject, and author.

STEEL FILES (usually near the reference desk). These are filled with up-to-date federal and state government pamphlets on a plethora of subjects.

Also ask in the Consumer Division for booklets on all types of consumer affairs. Here you'll find marvelous ideas on a variety of subjects from counseling and home and auto repairs to how to buy insurance, used cars, or almost anything. Make friends with librarians in both the adult and juvenile sections. They are there to help you, and, when it's impossible to go there for specific information, you can often get help on the phone.

Be sure to gather five times as much material as you will use to prop up and professionalize your finished article.

Always keep a detailed bibliography, stating the source of your facts. The brilliant reporter Harrison Salisbury may well have lost the 1967 Pulitzer Prize to R. John Hughes because he failed to document sufficiently his information about North Vietnam.

An ancient Chinese proverb warns:

> Unplowed fields make
> Hollow bellies.
> Unread books make
> Hollow minds.

To which you can add: "Unresearched nonfiction causes dejection due to rejection slips or miniscule checks."

Experience as an Idea Source

Experience is a great idea source, as well as the best teacher. No matter how much people-studying, interviewing, and research you do, the resulting article can be as cold and impersonal as a mannequin's smile. To breathe pulsating life into your material and cop a four-figure check, it's wise to try to get some personal experience related to what you're writing about. Good advice is: *"Write about what you know or know about what you write!"*

Successful scribes have done almost anything to get the ring of authenticity into their works. They've joined gangs, rumbles, motorcycle scrambles, police forces, and sex therapy groups; engaged in affairs, crimes, and criminal chases; gone to jail or foreign lands; taken jobs in industries they want information about or worked in hospitals to write factually about transplants, natural childbirth, specific surgeries, hospital inefficiencies, or other medical subjects. They've allied themselves (temporarily) with racketeers, pushers, and phoneys, participated in riots, and become smokejumpers, skydivers, skindivers, spacewheelers, parasailers, and you-name-it to get an authentic feel of the subject and give readers the facts.

Of course you don't have to have wild, weird experiences to sell nonfiction to top markets. Joan Mills sold five features to *Reader's*

Digest in one year by writing on down-to-earth domestic subjects, just as Jean Kerr, Marjorie Holmes, and Erma Bombeck do. They all use the vital techniques you will find in this book. Mrs. Mills is an English major, a voracious reader, and a word-lover who worked as a columnist and woman's editor on a country newspaper *(The Berkshire Eagle)* while her children were in camp and school. Your best subjects, like hers, may be your family, your own or your spouse's workshop, or other aspects of ordinary life with which the reader can identify— preferably with a solution to an interesting problem and an inspiring premise.

Start your own files based on your experiences:

Jobs, places, and people you know well.
Sports, hobbies, and games you are familiar with.
Beliefs and philosophies you cherish.
Pet peeves and what you think should be done about them.
Your happiest moments.
Your most embarrassing, shocking, or worst times.

Refer to these files often, and apply the following techniques to writing about your experiences. As you have ideas or experiences along these lines, capture them on paper while they're fresh and slip these "particles" into the proper file. Keep augmenting until you have enough rich material for an article—or perhaps even a book.

This is the secret of many successful authors. H. G. Wells kept huge barrels around his house, each marked with a different subject or category. "When the barrels are full," he used to say, "I know I have enough material for a book."

In seeking big ideas, don't overlook charming little ones. Henry Ward Beecher wrote:

To make much of little, to find reasons of interest in common things, to develop a sensibility to mild enjoyments, to inspire the imagination and to throw a charm upon homely and familiar things will constitute a man master of his own happiness.

Now that you have an idea—big or little—that you have a strong feeling about, remember: *Ideas won't work unless you do!*

Give Your Ideas the Acid Test

After you have selected an idea, put it to the test by asking these questions:

(1) Is it exciting, with impact, drama, and relevance?

(2) Is it of interest to a specific readership—men, women, or children, or a certain age or race—so that you can slant it to a particular market? Does that magazine use pictures, charts, tables, or artwork? If so, can you obtain good ones?

(3) What has already been written about your subject? Check it and related topics in *Readers' Guide,* the card catalogue, and the reference works listed above. What is the premise and angle of each published work? Can you add new dimensions of knowledge? What will be your specific approach?

A successful article presents a *narrow* view of a *broad* subject. After aerially photographing the area, you must concentrate on a target. For example, astrology is "in," with millions of people all over the world consulting horoscopes as their guidelines. On recent trips to Europe and the Orient I found astrology columns in every foreign newspaper.

Astrology, then, is a popular, *broad* subject. Your *narrow* approach would be your *angle.* Here are a few that have been used: Astrology for Skeptics . . . for Lovers . . . for Investors; Astrological Approach to the Stock Market; Astrological Cookbook; Your Pet's Horoscope; How Your Horoscope Can Help You Start the Day in a Good Mood; Your Horoscope Can Show Who You Were in Previous Lives; Horoscope for Sleepers; Your Horoscope Tells How to Handle an Emergency; Astrology Can Help You Stop Smoking . . . Lose Weight . . . Get a Better Job . . . Make a Killing in Nevada . . . Be Healthier; Care of Hair Astrologically—and a satirical reverse angle that points out all the unfortunate things about each sign: *You Were Born on a Rotten Day!*

(4) Will your article inform, instruct, inspire, or entertain the reader, therefore serving a purpose not just fulfilling your personal need for writing it?

(5) Will it pass the Rotary International 4-Way Test?

> First—Is it the truth?
> Second—Is it fair to all concerned?
> Third—Will it build good will and better friendships?
> Fourth—Will it be beneficial to all concerned?

Outline Your Idea

After your idea has passed these tests, organize your accumulated material into a firm outline. There are two excellent ones: (1) the HEY! YOU! SEE! SO! YOU! and (2) the ABCs of Articles. Remember: You *must* plan ahead (outline before writing your article); after all, it wasn't raining when Noah built the ark.

Hey! You! See! So! You!

One of the mány techniques for outlining your idea is summarized in the following table:

HEY! = Startle the reader.
YOU! = Involve the reader.
SEE! = Inform the reader of all the facts; 1, 2, 3, 4, etc.
SO! = Inspire your reader with a premise-conclusion.
YOU! = Urge the reader to action

The following is an example of an often-written-about subject as it would be outlined under the HEY! YOU! SEE! SO! YOU! method.

"Backaches" by Ellen Switzer (*Vogue)*

HEY!   A montage of situations involving sudden, excruciating back pains resulting from lifting heavy packages, stretching to wallop a tennis ball, etc.

YOU!   The above opening is written in the second person— "you" followed by reader-identification reinforcement: "You've joined the fastest-growing, nonexclusive club in America, the 'bad back' sufferers . . . SEVEN MILLION AMERICANS are treated for chronic back pain and new cases appear at the rate of about 1.5 million per month."

SEE!   (1) Why the increase in back problems? Causes include: (a) we eat more and use our bodies less; (b) we ride in cars instead of walking; (c) we watch television instead of playing tennis or weeding the garden; (d) our work is mechanized, rather than physical; (e) our furniture is built for softness and looks rather than utility. Our lives are comfortable instead of Spartan.

(2) Bad back professions discussed: airline pilots, psychiatrists, secretaries, writers, editors, librarians, desk sergeants, etc.

(3) Physiological explanation of the structure of the spine, "slipped discs," and the tendency of the backache sufferer to rest—and why this is wrong.

(4) Cures. Medical specialists discuss spinal-fusion surgery, body casts, braces, corsets, injections. Dr. D. Keith McElroy disapproves of these, recommending weight reduction and exercises.

(5) Exercise—even while sitting or in the hospital—is the advice of several doctors, who explain in detail.

(6) "Psychosomatic backaches" are common. They stem from both physical and mental factors. Doctors treat emotions. Several case histories of the vicious circle in which somatic and psychic reactions to conflict cause pain.

SO! (1) No one should have back surgery without thorough consultations.

(2) Preventive treatment (weight reduction; hard mattresses; consistent activity not long rests with "spurts").

(3) Avoid braces, girdles, supports. Instead, exercise.

YOU! Exercise on a hard mattress, and telephone your psychiatrist when necessary.

The ABCs of Articles

A second method you can use to outline your idea for an article is the ABCs of Articles. As you can see in the diagram below, you will develop your article from point *A*, getting the reader's attention, to point *G*, goading the reader to act. The following outline is an analysis of "The Loving Message in a Touch" by Norman M. Lobsenz.

A   Two contrasting anecdotes: (1) A wife who doesn't want her husband to touch her. (2) A rebellious teenage son hostile to his father until the latter suddenly embraces him. The boy responds, hugs, cries, and says, "It's the first time you've held me since I was a child."

B   Most of us are painfully inhibited about touching and being touched because our Puritan heritage considered touching "sensual."

C   Touch is a crucial aspect of all human relationships; it can heal wounds of quarreling and comfort us in sorrow and stress.

D   Many expressions indicate the power of touch to convey deep feelings when we speak of a "touching" experience, of "being touched" or "keeping in touch." Dramatic incident of Helen Keller's dog responding ecstatically to her touch, proving "paradise is attained by touch."

E   Infants and children who experience the most touch have higher I.Q.s. Animals prefer affectionate touch to food.

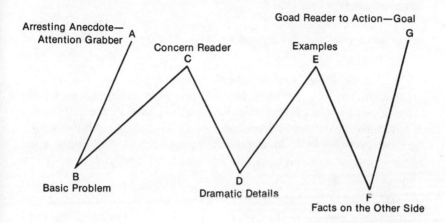

Arresting Anecdote—
Attention Grabber A

Concern Reader
C

Goad Reader to Action—Goal
G

Examples
E

B
Basic Problem

D
Dramatic Details

F
Facts on the Other Side

F   Many Americans avoid physical contact, and we often hear and see the warning "Don't Touch!" Parents refrain from affectionate touching in front of their children, increasing their aversion and inhibitions.

G   Specifically named psychologists give helpful advice:

1   Discuss the idea with your family first. "Don't just suddenly become a 'toucher.' Nothing is more upsetting than an unexpected and unexplained change in another person's behavior." (Dr. Alexander Lowen, psychiatrist)

2   Begin with simple gestures like kissing good night or good morning, hugging when saying "hello" or "good-bye." Learn to discern moods and to know when touching is welcome or will be irritating. (Kids often have no-touch stages.)

4   "Be emotionally honest when you do touch." (Dr. Nicholas Dellis). Do not express affection you do not sincerely feel.

5   "Touch should never be a vehicle for clinging to or possessing another person . . . Try to make . . . touch a source of comfort and reassurance, not a veiled demand."

6   Realize that touching does not always have a sexual meaning. Different kinds of touching mean different things.

Premise: Touch can dissolve barriers between people and break down emotional walls we build within ourselves. Dr. Herbert A. Otto says: "Touch is always an exchange, if not a sharing. Through touch we grow and we enable others to grow."

Summation: Dos and Don'ts

(1) *Never take a break from idea hunting.* Ionesco said, "A writer never has a vacation, for a good writer's life consists of either writing or thinking about writing."

(2) *Take a pen and notebook wherever you go.* The writing profession has two primary advantages over every other: its interrelationship with all phases of life and the convenience of its tools. A machinist or data processor can't carry his heavy equipment with him or even apply it to everyday living as you can apply your tools—your imagination, notebook and pen, and communication skills.

(3) *Don't hoard good ideas,* rather be a spendthrift. The bore who buttonholes you with, "For years I've had this marvelous idea, but I never wrote it," never will—and probably won't get any more good ideas. As Goethe wrote: "Nature abhors a vacuum, and when you correctly spend good ideas, better ones rush in to take their place." Marjorie Holmes says, "Holding back is damming back . . . . Unused ideas are plugs in the channels of creative thinking." She compares the prolific expenditure of ideas to milking the cow so she won't run dry.

(4) *Don't squander ideas* without slanting your manuscript toward the right reader and developing a strong outline before writing.

(5) *Don't expect ideas to come in "instant," complete form* ready for immediate use like a prefab toy or house. Your best ones will probably be the fragments that Henry James called "windblown particles." You must capture them, then evaluate, research, and organize.

(6) *Try to strike a balance between subjectivity and objectivity—* between being too personal with your own thoughts, emotions, and "it-really-happened" experiences and too limited to what other people have written, said, or done. Your own imagineered angle should draw original conclusions after you have summed up and ingested a rich variety of material from various sources. Editors don't like impersonal articles they could get from a government pamphlet,

travel brochure, newspaper, or encyclopedia. They want your unique, professional development of the data you have researched.

(7) *Don't seek absolutely new ideas and don't give up on a good one if you find that it's been done.* Look for a fresh angle—even a reversal or mood change (humor, for example, if it's been handled seriously). The best subjects have been, are, and will be written about, but each time with a slightly different approach: marriage, health, success, diet, longevity, popularity, beauty, to name only a few perennial subjects.

You can always find some variation of a familiar topic. Suppose your field of interest is Indian lore and you're fascinated by Custer and the Little Big Horn tragedy. There has been a plethora of articles, books, and movies on this subject, but Jack Walsh came up with a new approach. He interviewed Lame Deer, a Sioux psychic and descendant of the victors, and came up with evidence that Custer was accidentally killed by his own men who thought he was an Indian in the brush. No Indian ever claimed to have killed him; in fact they kept silent so that he and his men could "save face." Much has been written about Geronimo and Cochise, but what about their mentor, the six-foot-seven organizer of the Apaches, the fierce Mangus Colorado?

(8) *Be businesslike* about your writing career.

A doctor friend told me, "A doctor who considers medicine a business has no business being in medicine."

But have you ever known a competent doctor who always worked for absolutely nothing? Of course not. It's no disgrace in our society for valuable services to bring remuneration.

Why should writers—of all workers—not be paid well for their work? Yet there are scribblers who "slave over a hot typewriter" to write publicity, columns, poems, articles, and other works that they give away just to "see them in print." In most cases they could be reaching much wider readership and earning pride-boosting checks and prestige if they'd learn and apply the latest techniques revealed in these pages.

Contrary to the words of the doctor (who spoke them while we were driving in his Cadillac to his yacht at his private boat club), I'd like to say: "An author who does *not* consider writing a business has no business being an author."

As a writer you are in an age-old, honorable profession—one that may well become your major source of income *and* tax deductions. Of course you must be businesslike about keeping records. You probably have your own methods, but I recommend that expenses for these items be entered in an accurate, and up-to-date Record of Expenses log:

RECORD OF EXPENSES

Materials: _____

    Paper and letterheads _____

    Typewriter (new or repairs & depreciation) _____

    Steel Files _____

    Postage _____

Books and magazine subscriptions _____

Writers' conferences _____

Research _____

Travels _____

Photography _____

Entertaining editors, interviewees, etc. _____

    Such writing-related expenses can be kept in a ledger, in a notebook, or on index cards; cards are preferable for keeping track of manuscripts. Prepare a separate Record of Individual Scripts card for each article:

RECORD OF INDIVIDUAL SCRIPTS

Title _____ Date Started _____ Date Completed _____

Date Sent	Publication, Editor and Address	Date Returned	Comments	Date Sold

To let the editor know you are professional and to keep your records straight, be sure to accompany every script with a self-addressed card or letter that says something like this:

We, the editors of _____ have received the article "_____" by _____, on _____ (date).

Check one:

☐ We are holding it for consideration.

☐ We are purchasing it and will send check forthwith.

☐ We are presently overstocked and out of the market for freelance material. Please resubmit on _____.

☐ We are returning it because _____ .

Signed, _____ (Editor).

Faulkner said, "First you have to know the subject and then you have to know how to write." The following pages will show you how to write today's most-wanted types of nonfiction.

2

Why Nonfiction Now?

"Facts are to the mind what food is to the body—on the due digestion of the former depend the strength and wisdom of the one, just as vigor and health depend on the other."—(Edmund Burke)

"He is not a writer who is unread," said Epictetus two millennia ago, previewing the IRS attitude today that you are not entitled to the many tax deductions available to authors unless you earn money writing.

In today's literary marketplace the best way to be read and to earn remuneration is to write nonfiction. Publishers and editors are constantly looking for articles and books that have the three R's:

Research
Reader Identification
Relevance

Most magazine editors want to buy features that can be expanded into books—especially best-sellers like Jessica Mitford's article "The Undertaker's Racket," which became the book *The American Way of Death.* Nonfiction articles from *The New Yorker* that became famous books include Charles Reich's "The Greening of America," Truman Capote's "In Cold Blood," and Pauline Kael's "Going Steady." *Playboy* article "acorns' that burgeoned into "mighty oaks" of books include Dan Greenburg's shorticle, "How to Be a Jewish Mother," Alvin Toffler's "Future Shock," Alan Harrington's "The Immortalist," and Robert Sherrill's "Justice, Military Style," which became the book *Military Justice.*

The following pages are an attempt to examine some of the major reasons for entering the nonfiction market.

Nonfiction Has Longevity

Longevity is one of many reasons you should learn the newest nonfiction techniques.

A cleverly written article has a greater future than the average short story, which is "here today, gone tomorrow," and many well-researched, reader-identifiable, relevant fact pieces attract contracts and royalty checks from book publishers.

Nonfiction Enjoys a Large Market

Nonfiction is ubiquitous and easier to sell.

Most of the major magazines publish more articles than fiction. It is not unusual for an issue of *Harper's, Esquire, McCall's,* or *Vogue* to feature all nonfiction, with occasional fiction by big name writers or perhaps a book excerpt. Today's readers seem to seek fiction thrills in television, in motion pictures, in exciting newspaper stories of suspenseful skyjackings, jailbreaks, heists, riots, and other headline dramas. Hundreds of famous novelists, including Norman Mailer, Daphne Du Maurier, Kay Boyle, Truman Capote, John Updike, John Hersey, Vance Bourjaily, Herbert Gold, and Jean Stafford, write nonfiction in *lieu* of or in addition to their novels in deference to the current interest in reality writing and truth telling. But they use such fiction techniques as suspense, characterization, conflict, and dialogue to dramatize facts, as you will see in the following pages.

Today's readers are insatiably hungry for facts, and for the facts behind the facts. We are living in a literary boomerang cycle. Yesterday's writers used their infinite imaginative powers to fabricate fantastic miracles that science converted into reality. Air travel and space travel were anticipated by Lukian, Plutarch, Cyrano de Bergerac, Jules Verne, H. G. Wells, Tennyson, and science fiction authors like Otto Willi Gail. His novel *The Shot into Infinity* (1927) described a moon vehicle and a hydrogen-powered rocket with a winged final capsule in which astronauts made a controlled landing. Before that, in 1912, Hugo Gernsbach's *Ralph 124C 41+* invented radar and predicted fluorescent lighting, plastics, sky writing, tape recorders, microfilm, stainless steel, loud speakers, and flying saucers.

The late Aldous Huxley was amazed at the speed with which his *Brave New World* predictions materialized sixty years ahead of schedule, and Oscar Wilde said: "Literature always anticipates life. It does not copy it, but moulds it to its purpose. The nineteenth century, as we know it, is largely an invention of Balzac."

Fiction was king as long as it trailblazed into the future and kept ahead of life. Now that science is catching up and enacting all the fantastics that fiction once imagined, readers want factual writing about contemporary problems instead of make-believe that lags behind.

There is simply more demand for nonfiction today.

Our culture and our thinking seem to be dominated by nonfiction writing to the extent that almost any gimmick, gadget, fad, diet, theory, medical or scientific advice or device becomes popular if recommended by an article or fact book. In the chapter on exposé writing you will see how much consumer-protective legislation was spurred by the writings of the Ralph Naders of various fields, just as our awareness of ecological, technological, and biological dangers and concern over overpopulation were stimulated by such books as Gordon Rattray Taylor's *The Biological Time Bomb*, Alvin Toffler's *Future Shock* and Dr. Paul Ehrlich's *The Population Bomb* and *Population, Resources, Environment*.

Nonfiction Performs a Social Service

Nonfiction writing can be your opportunity to improve society as you fulfill the vital functions of informing, instructing, and inspiring.

Many ideas and opinions that are simmering within you may be on the fiction taboo list. In the case of social evils, injustices, and rackets you would like to expose, nonfiction is the only presentation the reader will take seriously. This is in line with the age-old and continuing tendency to regard nonfiction as "true" and fiction as "make-believe." If you wrote about such polemic subjects as corruption in politics, medicine, law, penal institutions, and education in fictional terms, they would sound like remote problems of imaginary characters instead of vital problems that concern the reader. They would not arouse his total involvement and desire to do something about a crucial situation.

Nonfiction Requires Structure and Logic

Nonfiction will train you to be more specific and businesslike (two necessary qualities for an author).

The new, hard-hitting, dramatized nonfiction style will make all your writing more professional. Fiction writing may tend to rely on unreliable inspiration and wander away from a specific plot line. By its very nature, fact writing is more concrete and to the point; it requires both something definite to say and a structure in which to say it without elaborate embellishment. As Einstein said, "If you are out to describe the truth, leave elegance to the tailor."

Your best way to work is to block out your feature by asking yourself the following questions *before* starting the actual writing:

What is my subject?
What is my individual angle, viewpoint, or approach to it?
What has been published on it and related topics? Where? When? Check *Reader's Guide to Periodical Literature, Cumulative Book Index* and *Books in Print* in your public library.
For what market shall I slant my material?
What will be the focal point and major premise?
What can the reader learn or do as a result of my article? How will it help him improve his relations with others and/or his self-understanding?
Will it inform, instruct, inspire, and/or entertain him? Does it offer new insight into the subject? Does it contain well-researched, fresh, stimulating ideas?
Is it relevant? Is it too controversial, trite, taboo, or contrary to the policy of the magazine I'd like to write it for?
Have I collected enough anecdotes, case histories, statistics, and quotes to prove my point?
Does the market I want to write this feature for use pictures? If so, can I supply appropriate ones?

Nonfiction Hones Your Research Ability

Nonfiction writing will send you out into the world for research material that may inspire future masterpieces.

Spinning fiction stories, novels, and television plays from your own imagination and experience can be ivory-tower-lonesome as you *hermet*ically seal yourself off from life's hectic activity and interfering humanity. Irving Wallace deplores the "anti-life" of being an author, and Truman Capote's self-imposed isolation while writing a novel explodes in wild parties that seem like a boil breaking after long, painful festering.

Yeats called writing a "solitary, sedentary trade," and Hemingway warned, "The further you go into writing, the more alone you are." His great works all resulted from his rushing out to meet life. Talking with an old fisherman on the Havana waterfront inspired *The Old Man and the Sea.* "I am a journalist," Hemingway always insisted. "I report what goes on. I have always been a journalist and always will be. So was Goya. Goya above all. Look at his war drawings and his bullfight drawings."

Reality gleaned from research is the essence of great art, and hunting for facts satisfies the basic hunting instincts in all people— writers as well as readers. Hemingway believed that "Hunting keeps your brains in your head and your heart where it belongs. That goes for all writing. Know your work and material. Hunt it down. Above all—live with it!"

The items you find while research hunting may inspire a great play or novel, just as a historical footnote about a medieval monastery inspired Aldous Huxley's *The Devils of Loudun*, which became John Whiting's play and Ken Russell's movie *The Devils.*

Robert Crichton's researching a rumor that a tiny Sicilian town hid one million bottles of wine from the Nazis developed into his best-seller and movie *The Secret of Santa Vittoria;* as Thomas Costain's research hobby yielded *The Tontine;* as Truman Capote's thorough research for *In Cold Blood* enabled him to write *The Glass House;* and as Paul Wellman's reading the story of an Indian who jumped from a reservation-bound train led to his novel and movie *Apache.*

When Herman Wouk went to the weather bureau to research the typhoon scene in *The Caine Mutiny*, an old man working there gave him the idea for *Slattery's Hurricane*, which sold to a national magazine and Hollywood for enough cash to enable Wouk to quit his nine-to-five job and become a full-time writer.

Although a great writer must be a private person while writing, too much isolation can be a double tourniquet. As it cuts you off from people and life, it also cuts vitality from your writing. Nonfiction work will return you to circulation and to interesting interviews, libraries, and whatever sources you must use to get and reinforce material for your articles.

Today's nonfiction must be built on concrete facts, avoiding generalities or abstract guessing. You must never make statements that you do not prove. Don't merely say that the Secret Witness system in Detroit solves crimes and rewards informers while protecting them. Give proof in accurately researched case histories and statistics. In one month there were three articles on this subject in three different magazines, *Coronet, Rotarian,* and *Reader's Digest,* citing various crimes solved by this same system. When you have a good subject that has been done, don't give up. Dig deep to find fresh, unpublished material. Anecdotes and statistics make the difference between a reject and a sale—and the difference between a $50 and a $1,000 acceptance check.

Specifics make the difference. For instance, in *McCall's* article "How to Stay Younger Longer," Gilbert Cant doesn't make a flat, dull statement to the effect that many people have sought methods to hold back old age. He names names, starting with Ponce de Leon looking for the Fountain of Youth and including the contemporary Rumanian Dr. Ana Aslan, who developed the wonder drug of the stars, Gerovital. Then he writes:

> Before Dr. Aslan, there was Dr. Paul Neihans, with his lamb fetus cells. And back in the 1920s there was a Kansas physician named John Romulus Brinkley whose rejuvenation treatments involving the implantation of goat glands earned him $12,000,000 and made him so famous that he was almost elected governor of the state.

See how much more informative that is than vague generalities? This device always intrigues readers, even in a newspaper feature like Michael Pousner's "Overweight? Big Can Be Beautiful," which begins:

> Author-chef-gourmet James Beard doesn't worry about it till faced with the Hobson's choice of dieting or buying all new clothes.
> Rep. Angelo Roncallo . . . contends it would be worse to be bald. . . .
> Actor William Cannon calls it "beautiful."
> Jimmy Breslin believes it's not really all that important in the great scheme of things.
> And Actor James Coco finds it eminently preferable to grapefruit and cottage cheese.
> It's fat, that's what it is. . . .

Your examples don't have to be drawn from the famous but can be about real, identifiable people from the news who prove your point. *Redbook*'s "Innocent Victims, Innocent Killers" (by Martin

Cohen) avoids the banality of a dull statement like "Emotions such as impatience or ill-temper can cause fatal accidents" with an opening full of specifics:

> *The striking car.* At 10:00 A.M., August 9, 1972, John Tyson, 21, a machine-parts salesman, was driving alone on Interstate Highway 94, 30 miles west of Detroit. For the past hour Tyson had been moving fast, maintaining 70 miles per hour. In a few minutes he would find himself abruptly slowed down in a congested construction zone. Tyson would become impatient. His impatience would flare into irrational anger and turn his vehicle into a lethal missile.

It then specifies and characterizes Tyson's innocent victims, the previously happy Henderson family.

The concrete examples used to dramatize your ideas and avoid narrative monotony can even be defined by age, profession, location—anything that makes them real to the reader. Study this opening of Daniel A. Sugarman's "What Are You Afraid Of?" (a *Reader's Digest* reprint from *Family Health):*

> Linda, 25, is unable to enter elevators without feeling panic.
> Robert, 57, worries almost constantly about his approaching retirement.
> Phyllis, 15, awaits the arrival of her date; her knees feel shaky, her stomach is upset.
> At all ages and at all stages of life, fear presents a problem to almost everyone. . . .

Try to increase reader interest and salability by referring to people (famous or unknown, real or hypothetical), and use dialogue to express their opinions, which give weight to your own ideas and to the premises of your piece. Notice how this technique enlivens the opening of Lonnelle Aikman's "Nature's Gifts to Medicine" (*National Geographic):*

> "I use an old Indian remedy for poison ivy," said a friend. "You boil sycamore bark in water and sop it on. It works like magic."
> "My wife has a 90-year-old pal who claims he keeps away arthritis with a daily cup of alfalfa tea," an editor . . . said.
> "We have an aloe plant in our kitchen," a photographer told me. "It exudes a living lotion, and if I burn my hand, I pull off a leaf . . . squeeze out a kind of jelly, and it stops the pain."

Train yourself to be specific and authoritative. People like numbers. Keep a statistics file. Even if you have no immediate use for them at the time you read the figures, you may someday. Nuggets like the following may inspire you to write new articles:

> All 3.5 billion humans alive today are "helionauts" aboard an almost spherical, massive spaceship whizzing along at a speed of 18.5 miles per second in orbit around the sun. (Irving S. Bengelsdorf, Ph.D.).

> 79 million Americans go to work everyday.

> From 1960 through 1970, 158 magazines went out of business. But 763 new ones came into being . . . In 1961 there were 79 magazines qualified to be called "national general magazines". . . . By 1970 there were 89. (Wade Nichols)

> Military PX exchanges sell $3 billion worth of merchandise annually to 7 million customers. This is the nation's third largest merchandiser (after Sears and J.C. Penney Co.).

> 17 million Americans have arthritis that requires medical care.

> The cost of direct crime-fighting increased 143% from $3.5 billion in 1960 to $7.3 billion in 1971.

> Nader Raider Dr. Sidney Wolfe says that at least 10,000 Americans die annually as a result of 2 million unnecessary surgical operations.

> 46,000,000 Americans will be arrested at some time during their lives. Of these, 10,000,000 will go to prison.

Arthur C. Clarke says nations have spent a trillion dollars on war in the last ten years, and other statisticians insist we're trying to kill ourselves with sports on a lesser scale. Football has a ratio of 3.9 deaths for each 100,000 players. This pales before other danger sports like motorcycling (278.6), horse racing (133.3), auto racing (120), and powerboat racing (15.7).

We're so bombarded by negative statistics that editor Charles L. Gould of the *San Francisco Examiner* asks, "Isn't it time to accept the positive?" He offers such cheerful statistics as:

> More than 196,000,000 of our people WILL NOT be arrested.

> More than 89,000,000 married persons WILL NOT file for divorce.

> More than 79,000,000 citizens and corporations WILL pay more than $160 billion in income taxes.

More than 75,000,000 students WILL NOT riot, petition, or try to destroy our system.

More than 4,000,000 teachers, preachers, and professors WILL NOT strike or participate in riotous demonstrations.

These uplifting statistics have more *reader identification* than negative ones, which brings us to the next reason you should concentrate on nonfiction:

Nonfiction Develops Reader Rapport

You'll learn to know people and be a better person, for today's salable nonfiction must be packed with reader rapport.

The reader's favorite character is himself, and he'll read your problems and experiences, or those of others, only if he can learn from them. Statistics help; if the reader learns that there are 8 million widows in the U.S. or 7,000 cases of a certain disease, chances are that he'll want to be knowledgeable about other subjects, situations, or persons he may encounter.

The following are other ways to increase reader identification:

Use the Second Person or First Person

A few examples: *You Are There, This Is Your Life,* "It Could Happen to *You,*" "*You* Can Stop Being a Procrastinator," "How to Manage *Your* Money," "Ways to Keep *Your* Income Tax Down," "*Your* Personality May Be Killing *You,*" "Are *You* Good Credit Risk?" "Know *You*rself," "*Your* Mind Can Keep You Well," "What Jealousy Tells You About *Your*self," "What's *Your* Food I.Q.?" "Control *Your* Weight," "Why *You* See Geometric Illusions," "Do You Know What *Your* Dreams Mean?" Warren James's article "Saturday Night: Diary of Los Angeles Cabbie" *(Los Angeles)* is entirely written in the second person so that *you* experience all the threats and frustrations and *care* that last year 333 L.A. cabbies were held up, three murdered!

The first person also increases intimacy and identification, as you can see in confession writing, *True* articles, and first person stories in *Reader's Digest, Redbook,* and *Good Housekeeping.*

Choose Subject Matter of General Interest

Use such universal basics as survival, identity, alienation, depression, freedom, involvement, love, birth, death, health, nutrition, recreation and sports, loneliness, rejection, success, and popularity. You can write about everything that concerns lots of people, even such formerly dull or taboo subjects as garbage. Alan J. Weberman bagged $900 for his brief *Esquire* article "The Art of Garbage Analysis," and much, much more for his book *You Are What You Throw Away.*

Be Timely as well as Timeless

The successful nonfiction writer has reverence for relevance. Scour newspapers, news weeklies, and magazines to know what people are currently interested in. Subjects like inflation, pollution, ecology, vandalism, genetic counseling, hydroponics, various types of group therapy, methadone and other drug treatments, high rise cemeteries, busing, bumper stickers, voluntary sterilization, bubble cities, cities under the sea, skylabs, aqualabs, the youth takeover are a few of the many trends you should keep up with.

Yesterday's readers wanted to identify with winners and loved Horatio Alger's *Work and Win, Strive and Succeed, Do and Dare, Try and Trust, Sink or Swim,* and *Struggling Upward.* Today there's a reverse tendency to identify with losers. Charles Shultz attributes the multimillion dollar success of his *Peanuts* books and strips to reader identification. He says: "*Peanuts* chronicles defeat . . . Most of us know what it's like to lose some kind of contest and we can identify with the loser."

Nonfiction Draws on Your Experience

You have something to say—some knowledge or experiences to share. Nonfiction is your chance.

"Everyone is ignorant, only on different subjects," said Will Rogers. It is also true that everybody is *smart* on some subject(s). If you work at a specific job, if you have traveled, served on a jury, or been in an accident or in trouble, or if you've ever solved one or more problems with children, parents, in-laws, neighbors, friends, enemies, or pets, you probably have tips to build into a helpful article. You don't have to be a renowned authority or big name writer, as you should be to sell fiction to top-paying magazines. It's the *content* of your feature that counts.

A white mother wrote such an interesting letter to an editor explaining why she preferred an integrated neighborhood that he asked her to expand it into an article. She enhanced it by researching other mixed areas in which she found children growing up with a tensionless sense of brotherhood. Other parents have sold articles about their children's problems with drugs, bad company, cheating, shyness, handicaps, and all the many challenges that are bitter to experience but can be salable and helpful in nonfiction that contains the three R's. One father wrote a heart-rending article about his child's fatal fall into the boiling geyser pools at Yellowstone. Publication in *Redbook* led to safety devices to protect children throughout our national parks.

Start your own files for the following:

Jobs, places, and people you know well.
Sports, hobbies, and games you are familiar with.
Subjects you would like to know more about and research.
Beliefs and philosophies you cherish.
People of the present and past you admire, as well as those you think zany, absurd, and ridiculous enough to satirize.
Pet peeves that irritate you and what you think should be done about them.

Keep referring to these categories and adding to them as you read on and learn the techniques of different article types.

Nonfiction Can Be Pre-Sold

The eighth reason for writing nonfiction is as great as the eighth wonder of the world: You can often pre-sell your material! See Chapter 3 for a complete discussion of this wonder.

3

Query First

"Successful salesmanship is 90 percent preparation and 10 percent presentation."—Bertrand R. Canfield

One of the greatest advantages of article writing is that you can often practically *sell* your piece before you write it. With fiction you might have several ideas and wish you knew which would be the most salable, but the only way you can get an editorial verdict is to write and submit the completed story (often after many, many rewrites).

You don't have to do all this with nonfiction to test its salability. Why is this?

Since there's no such thing as a new plot, a story's success depends upon its complete development. But the most important thing about the article is its basic idea. What is your subject? How will you tackle it? How will you outline and enliven your presentation? How is it related to the readers of a particular market? What illustrations and anecdotes can you provide? How long will the article be?

These are the main things the editor wants to know. You can tell him in a query letter, which is a dramatized synopsis of your article.

Query writing not only saves the writer valuable time, energy, research work, and wounded pride, but the average editor prefers—often demands—a query before considering a complete article. There are several reasons for this:

(1) Time is precious. A one-page outline and/or summation tells him what he wants to know: your idea and its relevance to his readers, why you're qualified to write it, and how you will handle it.

(2) He likes the idea of your wanting his opinions and guidance before you go ahead.

(3) If your topic repeats or conflicts with something he has "on tap," he can suggest other treatments or perhaps the elaboration of one point in your outline into an article.

(4) He can give you suggestions in many ways. Your idea may be local, and he can tell you how to give it national significance (if this is what he wants). On the other hand, you may offer too general a concept, which he wants narrowed down. He may even offer you additional information, research, photographs, etc., if you query impresses him.

(5) Often (as has frequently been my experience) the editor cannot use your article at the time you suggest it, but he'll keep your query idea, name, and address in his files and send you an order later. Meanwhile you're free to market it elsewhere, and if you've sold it when he contacts you, perhaps he'll ask you to do another angle or a different subject.

(6) Editors are impressed with an author who can condense an article idea into a well-organized query letter. They tend to think of you as a professional instead of an amateur, since established authors don't waste time and talent on a subject no one is likely to want.

The Art of the Query Letter

How can you write a letter of inquiry that will attract an editorial order?

First of all you must realize what a query letter is *not* as well as what it is. It is not a chatty letter-to-the-editor discussing your idea. If it reads this way, he will regard it as just that—a letter telling or offering him your thoughts and ideas. The law says that anything that comes through the mail unsolicited or unordered is a gift. Therefore a friendly message that is not clearly defined as a query letter with a S.A.S.E. (self-addressed-stamped-envelope) could wind up:

(1) in the letters-to-the-editor column.
(2) in the wastebasket (since magazines cannot print all the letters received).

(3) inspiring an assignment to a staff member or some other professional writer.

To avoid misinterpretation, be sure to indicate in your letter that you are offering your subject, title, angle, and outline for the editor's approval and that you want the go-ahead to write the complete article for him on speculation.

You may open with something like: " 'Such and Such' is the tentative title of an article I'd like to write for *Your Magazine* [name it] to help your readers to . . .

If you prefer to open with a dazzling anecdote followed by a tight outline and cannot gracefully work in the fact that you want the order to write the piece, type across the top of your letter: "QUERY. RE: 'Your Title.' "

There is no magic formula guaranteed to get yourself an order, nor is there only one type of format for a query. Writers, being individuals, use different methods and may even vary the presentation for different subjects. Here are some guidelines that have brought success to many of my students and to me.

First, there should be a firm, fresh angle on a relevant subject that is slanted to a particular magazine or group of publications. You must research what has been done, as well as where, when, and how, by looking up your idea and all related ones in *Readers' Guide to Periodical Literature,* going back about seven years.

Your letter should not be amorphous, that is, without developed structural organization. It should not be overwritten, giving too much away, or too sketchily underwritten.

As you plan your query, remember that one of its primary functions is to convince the editor that you know how to attract and sustain reader interest in a worthwhile subject. Your letter of inquiry is a sample of what you have to sell— your writing ability—and you should work as hard at constructing and revising it as you would on the final article.

Some authors consider queries oil wells working for them while they are writing other projects (you may have several out at once— but not the same letter to different publications).

One writer calls a good query letter a "literary firecracker." If the editor sees possibilities in it, he will ignite the fuse by offering you encouragement to go ahead and develop the story. This, of course, is a form of insurance, although it is not legally binding. You may compare a query letter to a bouillon cube, to a concentrated vitamin capsule, or to those miniature Japanese flowers that expand in water. Whatever imagery you prefer, it is true that a query that is well written *is* open-ended and promise-filled.

If you have good writing credits and/or experience in this specific subject or field, say so unobtrusively. You must *never* talk more about yourself than the idea or the magazine you are addressing. If you lack impressive credits, don't admit to being an amateur. Write brilliantly so that your ability will speak for itself!

Although your article proposal should be brief enough to fit on one page single-spaced, it should cover your main points, premise, angle, and title.

An effective device is to pose questions that will intrigue the editor's curiosity and make him eager to learn the answers in your finished article. If you do this well enough, the principle of Gestalt psychology works here. You have begun a circle of interest that the editor may be impelled to complete by asking you to write the piece.

First Impressions Are Strongest

Always address your query letter to a specific editor whose name you will find on the editorial page or in a market list. Be assured that it will be read and considered by a very busy person who can't afford to pass up a crackerjack idea that is professionally presented. Try to catch his interest immediately with an irresistible opening that lures him away from other scripts on his desk, just as he wants his magazine to wrest readers' attention away from its competitors.

Write a lead that is so good that you'll want to use it to start your article. The old rule applies here: "If you don't strike oil in two minutes, stop boring."

Here are some different categories of leads that you should study and look for in magazines. Select the best type for each of the many different kinds of articles you will be writing. (You will probably return to this section often.)

Statement Opening

The old term "narrative hook" is Dodo-dead. If you start with narrative, be sure that it has punch, drama, or shock-power. It must never be a dull warm-up or "Listen-my-children-and-you-shall-hear" narrative that the reader may be inclined to pass up for the more exciting types of leads to follow.

Here are some professional statement openings:

From *True:*

> If you took most of the sport, sun, and prescription eyeglasses Americans wear and got rid of them, you'd be performing a service to mankind.
>
> Of the 100 million spectacles in use in this country, about 75% are a threat to the wearer's health, ranging from simple eyestrain and headaches to blindness . . . .
>
> ("The Scandal in Eyeglasses" by Martin A. Cohen)

> If you look hard enough, you can still find good, usable land in the United States for $300 an acre and less.
>
> ("Where You Can Still Buy Land Cheap" by Max Gunther)

From *Reader's Digest:*

> Conditions are much better on our college campuses today. The kids are even giving back some of the deans they captured last year. As for me, I've been pretty lucky with colleges—for a sandbox dropout. I've picked up 19 honorary degrees, even though every time they put Doctor in front of my name I can hear Crosby in the background saying "quack."
>
> ("The Importance of Having Fun" by Bob Hope)

From *National Geographic:*

> Beyond the clattering blades of the helicopter, the nearly naked figures emerged from the forest—and stepped out of the Stone Age into the year A.D. 1971. They were members of the Tasaday tribe of Mindanao island's green interior. . . unknown to the world . . . .
>
> ("First Glimpse of a Stone Age Tribe")

This can be tricky, theatrical, even deceptive in a satire as long as you make it entertaining and pertinent enough to be worthwhile. All's fair in love, war, and gaining reader interest. For example, boxed like a classified ad:

> TIRED OF THE RAT RACE?
>
> FED UP WITH YOUR JOB ROUTINE?
>
> Well, then, how would you like a chance to make $8,000, $20,000—as much as $50,000—each year working at home in your spare time? No selling! No commuting! No time clocks to punch!
>
> BE YOUR OWN BOSS!!!
>
> Yes, as Assured Lifetime Income can be yours *now,* in an easy, low-pressure, part-time job that will permit you to spend most of each day *as you please!* relaxing, reading, watching TV, playing cards, socializing with friends! All this plus a Lifetime

Security Package that includes *free* medical care, insurance and
all retirement benefits! A free home . . . free food, clothing,
phone and utilities!

NO EXPERIENCE NECESSARY!!

ACT NOW!

There's only one catch to it: No men need apply.

The above suspense-sparked gimmick opening to William
Iversen's *Playboy* article "Love, Death and the Hubby Image" is the
kind of lead that makes the editor sit up and take notice because he
knows it will attract his readers. Needless to say, the piece satirizes
the American housewife's role, which the hard-working bread-
winning male considers a snap—yes, a racket!

Anecdote Opening

A miniature story with an intriguing situation, interesting
characters, and suspenseful drama is the "grabber" that launches the
article into orbit. It always has a cliff-hanger, promising more to
come.

From *Reader's Digest* (reprinted from *Rotarian):*

Shortly after 9:00 A.M. on August 18, 1967, Don Damon
double-parked his mail truck in front of the Tasty Sandwich
Shop in Marshall, Michigan, and unwittingly became a messeng-
er of murder. Walking into the restaurant, he handed a brown-
paper-wrapped parcel to the owner, Paul Puyear. It was
addressed to Puyear's wife, Nola, who was frying eggs and
bacon for a customer. Wiping her hands on her apron, Nola
opened the package—and was killed immediately when it blew
up in her face.

(" 'Secret Witness'—New Weapon Against Crime" by
James Stewart Gordon)

From *Success Unlimited:*

The father of a 17-year-old high school senior had promised to
buy his son a car when he graduated, but changed his mind after
talking to his insurance agent.

("How to Cut the High Cost of Teenage Auto Insurance" by
Joan Gleichman)

Quote Opening

A dialogue lead is often an eye-opener, especially when the
words are those of a person known to the readers of the specific
publication. Usually it's a wise saying.

From *Harper's:*

"Former men," observed Emerson in the dramatic days of the new geological science, "believed in magic, by which temples, cities and men were swallowed up, and all trace of them gone. We are coming on the secret of a magic which sweeps out of men's minds all vestige of theism and beliefs which they and their fathers held . . . Nature is a mutable cloud."
("The Scientist As Prophet" by Loren Eiseley)

From *Cosmopolitan:*

"Power," says Henry A. Kissinger, . . . is the great aphrodisiac." Perhaps that is why every year thousands of single women come to work and live in Washington D.C.
("Washington's Most-Eligible Bachelors" by Marlene Cimons)

From *Playboy:*

There walk among us men and women who are in but not of our world," wrote psychiatrist Robert Lindner. "Often the sign by which they betray themselves is crime, crime of an explosive, impulsive, reckless type. Sometimes the sign is ruthlessness in dealing with others socially even commercially." . . . they are identified as psychopaths.
("The Psychopath" by Alan Harrington)

From *Science of Mind:*

Ernest Holmes wrote that time is a "Sequence of events within a Unitary Whole." It is "a measure of experience in eternity."
("River of Life" by Norma Hammond)
"The New Year is no different from the old unless you make it so." These were the words of my wise grandfather.
("Pulse of Time" by Frances E. Leslie)

Premise or Philosophical Opening

Sometimes a familiar quote is switched appropriately with a fresh, timely twist, as in this lead from *Holiday:*

That old shingle about the kingdom being lost for want of a nail has acquired new meaning in business-conscious Japan: "For want of a hook shot on the eighth fairway, the business merger proposed on the sixth tee was wiped out."
("For Want of a Teeshot, Golfer-San" by Sandra Servaas)

From *Esquire:*

Snatching defeat from the jaws of victory is never a pleasant experience, especially on Capitol Hill.
("Women's Lib in Congress" by Senator Jacob K. Javits)

From *Coast:*

> Some wit once remarked that the best thing about San Francisco is that it has no place to go.
> ("Underground Gourmet in San Francisco" by Morton Grosser)

From *Redbook:*

> If we want to be loved, we must disclose ourselves. If we want to love someone, he must permit us to know him.
> ("The Fear that Cheats Us of Love" by Sidney M. Jourard, Ph.D. with Ardis Whitman)

Question Opening

Curiosity is one of man's most impelling instincts, and a question may be the best way to pull the reader into some articles. Study published ones and how they are answered. Most magazines will have at least one question-lead in an issue: Study the questions *and* the answers given.

From *Redbook:*

> Why are so many daughters angry at and critical of their mothers? Why are mothers too often possessive and "controlling"? Does the relationship between mother and daughter ever evolve into one of harmony and understanding?
> (" Why So Many Women Can't Stand Their Own Mothers" Symposium directed by Sabert Basescu, Ph.D.)

From *Smithsonian:*

> What is the universe made of?
> ("The Greeks' Four Universal Elements—and Then Some" by Isaac Asimov)

From *Harvest Years:*

> Would you believe an all-volunteer emergency squad in a retirement community? Our squad started with 24 people to serve when the doctor left at sundown, and has grown to a 90-member organization on 24-hour duty for nearly 3,000 residents.
> ("Rescue Squad" by Ruth G. King)

From *Science Digest:*

> How can you eliminate 50 tons of destructive insects in one

day? First, find 200,000 Ibis, give them a happy, watery home, then let them go to work.

From the *Los Angeles Herald:*

> Is there a future assassin in your neighborhood?
> In America, where all people are supposed to be "equal," Dr. Gunther Koch describes society's inequality by defining three basic groups of young people: leaders, followers, and future assassins.
> ("Extortion Takes Its Toll in the Public Schools" by Wanda Sue Parrott)

From *Modern Maturity:*

> How old do you think color photography is? 20, 30, 40 years? Charming color pictures were being made almost a century ago by two Frenchmen, Charles Cros and Louis Ducos du Hauron. Working independently, each produced the same color process. Despite antagonism generated when both claimed credit for the invention, they later became friends.
> ("The First Color Photography")

Whether answers to the opening question(s) come immediately or are delayed for suspense purposes, informative, satisfactory replies to stated or implied questions must be given. It is impossible to overemphasize the proper use of the curiosity-pricking question technique in attracting attention. Although editors balance the contents of each magazine with a variety of devices to avoid monotony, question-titles frequently appear on covers and tables of contents.

See how many you can find in addition to: "Can This Marriage Be Saved?", "Where Are They Now?"; "What's in Stock for Wall Street?"; "What Do You Do with a Drunken Giraffe?"; "What Are Tomorrow's Lawyers Thinking Today?"; "Must Marriage Cheat Today's Young Women?"; "How Many Children Are We Entitled to Have?"; "Are You Feeding Your Baby Too Much?"; "Are There Too Many Sights and Sounds in Your Baby's World?"; "Which Diet Trick Pays Off?"; "Are Dirty Movies on the Way Out?"; "Must Our Churches Finance Revolution?"; "How Will the World End?"; "What Do We Do When Everything's Used Up?"; "Biological Superiority: Male or Female?"; "How Breakable Are Your Bones?"; "Can Vitamins Harm You?"; "What's Your Love Style?"; "Did Civilization Arise in Northern Europe Rather Than the Mediterranean?"; "Merger Ahead in Pro Basketball?"; "Who

Would Want to Be a Cop? Or a Firefighter?''; "Why Are You Overpaying for Prescriptions?''

The Secret Ingredient That Works Wonders

As you read the rest of this book and learn to write today's most-wanted types of articles, keep in mind that you must always arouse curiosity and then satisfy it. One sure way to impress the editor with your ability to do this is to ask intriguing questions in your query letter. If the questions are presented with a tight sense of continuity, they can form the basic structure of your completed article.

A good example of this is Ralph Kinney Bennett's *Reader's Digest* feature "The Terrorists among Us,'' in which each section of the body part or "See'' is introduced by a question: Does guerrilla warfare exist in the U.S.? Who are the violence-prone groups? What are the tactics of the revolutionaries? What role do demonstrations play in guerrilla violence? Are the Communists involved? How dangerous are the revolutionaries? What can be done to counter the tide of violence?

Also in *Reader's Digest,* Frank Robinson's article "Don't Be a Crime Target'' answers questions everyone wants solved today: Do you have to live in constant terror? Should you open the door when the bell rings? Must you leave all windows closed? What about owning a handgun? How can you protect your car from thieves when you park? Is it safe to walk at night? What should you do if worse comes to worst and you're assaulted? How can you protect your valuables? What can we all do to fight crime?

Such questions would surely have attracted editorial interest if they had been asked in a query. Perhaps they were.

Instead of the complete outline query with an opening, some authors merely suggest the idea (especially if their work is known to the editor). Even in this case, present it in caption form to capture the publisher's interest. Study those different magazines to see how concise, interest-hooking, and specifically slanted they are:

Question Captions

> Are you chronically tired?
> Do you feel increasingly unattractive?
> Are the children driving you wild?
> Do routine chores seem insuperable?

Are you anxious, irritable, depressed?
Do you want to crawl into a hole?
> ("The Over-Medicated Woman" by Roland H. Berg in *McCall's)*

How could I keep loving a man who expected me to be mistress, wife, *and* breadwinner?
> ("I Married a Lily of the Field" by Margaret Hopkins in *Cosmopolitan)*

Which one of these people walking up your driveway will return to pick your locks and steal everything not nailed down?
> ("Conversation with a Pickman" by William J. Slattery in *True)*

Have you ever said "Why didn't I think of that?"
> ("Look a Little Harder" by Paul Brock in *Success Unlimited)*

What makes an abusive parent?
> ("The Battered Child" by Serapio R. Zalba in *Science Digest)*

Something has happened or is about to happen, but what?
> ("The Scientist as Prophet" by Loren Eiseley in *Harper's)*

Statement Captions

It was the biggest offshore oil fire ever—and licking it took 136 days, $29 million, and endless ingenuity.
> ("Holocaust on Platform B" by Joseph P. Blank in *Reader's Digest)*

The turf of the federal parole board is a landscape of illogic.
> ("No Exit" by Willard Gaylin in *Harper's)*

In this wild corner of an island world you can hear wingflaps of the flying fox and the call of barking deer.
> ("Java . . . Bali: The Exotic Isles" by Martin Litton in *Holiday)*

A Chinese system that emphasizes graceful motion rather than force is said to equal heavy exercise in its health benefits.
> ("Exercise Need Not Be Strenuous" in *Prevention)*

Despite the exotic claims for many farewell-to-fat devices, they are almost certain to reduce just one thing: your pocketbook.
> ("Beware Those 'Quick-Reducing Gadgets' " by Jean Carper in *Reader's Digest)*

The prospects for multiplying our years of youthful vigor are bright and imminent.

("To Be Continued" by Alex Comfort in *Playboy*)

Quotation Captions

Goethe once wrote that "the destiny of any nation, at any given time, depends on the opinions of its youth under five-and-twenty . . . "

("Staying Hip" by Sherman B. Chickering in *Esquire*)

"I am frankly pro-baby," says an outspoken pediatrician, "and I don't like what the drugs given to women in labor do to their babies."

("What Childbirth Drugs Can Do to Your Child" by T. Berry Brazelton, M.D., in *Redbook*)

"Any man more right than his neighbors constitutes a majority of one," said Thoreau. Sussman knows his Thoreau and his health foods and the two combine hilariously.

("Confessions of a Food Freak" by Vic Stephan Sussman in *Prevention*)

"Whether we master life or are mastered by it often depends on how well we learn the way of acceptance." These words in a *Guideposts* article stimulated the following exchange between a bereaved mother and a prominent writer.

("Why Must My Son Die?" in *Guideposts*)

"The proper function of man is to live, not to exist." Jack London

("Enthusiasm Makes the Difference" by Norman Vincent Peale in *Reader's Digest*)

"The era of Psychotechnology cannot now be avoided." Dr. Kenneth Clark

("An Immense Proposal" in *American Psychologist*)

The Detailed Query

Although a selling writer can often get an order on the basis of a brief letter or caption, it doesn't always work. If you think your subject is good for a magazine that isn't impressed by the idea alone, don't give up. Develop a more detailed query letter that may bring out more possibilities than the editor suspected from the mere statement of the subject and angle.

EXAMPLE: I was once bugged by society's discriminating against divorced persons, but I knew my angle would be a taboo in the women's and general slicks at that time. I submitted the idea titled "Why Is Divorce a Dirty Word?" to a men's magazine to which I had previously sold many articles and stories. The editor rejected my "Pity the Divorced Man" slant.

"Forget it," he replied. "Send us other ideas. *Anything* but that!" He proceeded to try to convince me that the divorced man had it made: his choice of chicks, lots of dates and dinner invitations, no nagging, no lawns to mow, no household chores to do, etc.

But I wanted to write a feature that had not yet been done. I researched, interviewed several authorities, and stubbornly resubmitted the rejected idea in the following query letter, which showed the editor new possibilities and changed his mind so much that he built an entire issue around it. Incredibly, he also broke down my too-long article into three separate features for which I received three bylines and three checks! And I'm sure that you can write a better query letter than this:

Dear _____ (Specific Editor):

"Is there any way to avoid alimony?" a man asked a lawyer.
"Yes, there are two ways," was the reply. "Stay single or stay married."

Alimony isn't the only or the worst "splitting headache" that accompanies the break-up of a marriage, and my article, "Why Is Divorce a Dirty Word?" will explore the hypocritical American attitude that seems to prefer infidelity, separation, wife-swapping, desertion, and in extreme cases, bigamy and murder to a clean divorce break.

There will be many documented examples of men suffering from divorce discrimination in many ways:

1. Politically
2. Financially
3. Socially

Why is it that the divorce-stigma doesn't decrease no matter how much divorces increase? During the past fifteen years, one-fourth to one-half of the marriages in U.S. have ended in divorce.

Why is divorce a dirty word in the nation whose slogan for everything else seems to be: "If at first you don't succeed, try, try again"? Why are Americans who are liberal and modern about everything else so medieval about divorce? Why has it become a lucrative racket? Who's to blame? What can we do about it?

The article will answer these questions in a breezy, pithy style atomized with facts, statistics, humorous and tragic anecdotes and quotes from leading doctors, psychiatrists, philosophers, and marriage counselors.

Your readers will be able to contrast our divorce-discrimination with much more lenient attitudes throughout history, for divorce was actually recommended in certain cases in the Old and New Testament, even by the Roman Catholic Church until Charlemagne. Also by the Puritans, Anglo-Saxons, Romans, Greeks, Chinese, ancient Irish, and all races and creeds. Their sincerity and simplicity of customs show much room for improvement in ours.

Our divorce dilemma can be solved, not by outmoded divorce-discrimination but by intelligent divorce-prevention, which will be discussed to the benefit of your readers.

I am willing to write this article on speculation.

Sincerely,

F. A. Rockwell

You can perfect your query-writing ability by working *backward* from a published article you wish you had written. Pretend that you are the author and frame a hypothetical letter of inquiry that he or she might have sent the editor. Here is an example based on a feature by Catharine W. Menninger:

Mr. Specific Editor
Reader's Digest
Pleasantville, New York 10570

Dear Mr. _____:

"What Wives Can Do to Solve the Communication Problem" is the tentative title of an article I would like to write for *Reader's Digest* to help husbands and wives find greater happiness in marriage.

As the widow of psychiatrist Dr. William C. Menninger, I would like to share the story of how Dr. Will and I worked at smoothing out the bumps to build a strong, storm-proof communication line between us.

My story will offer no magic formula for quick success. It does give suggestions—specific steps to try—in cultivating the art of communication and will answer such questions as:

How many ways are there to communicate?
How can you use non-verbal communication to speak for you?

How can you make conversation fun?
How can you find a meeting ground?
How can sensitivity help?
Why are shared thoughts worth more than sleep?
Why should you think before you say anything?
Why should you give him time to "shift gears"?
How and what can you learn by listening?
How can you earn his confidence?
How can you show appreciation?
What words should you remember to say?

I'll be glad to write it on speculation. Would you like 2,000 words? 2,500 words? More or less?

Sincerely

Query Don'ts

(1) Don't forget to address your query to the appropriate editor, and don't make it sound like "a letter to the editor."

(2) Don't try to write for a magazine you are unfamiliar with. Be sure to study recent issues and also check your subject matter in *Readers' Guide to Periodical Literature.*

(3) Don't omit your suggested title, angle, and a S.A.S.E.

(4) Don't write more about yourself than your subject. Your qualifications should be integrated with the material.

(5) Don't send the same query simultaneously to more than one editor at a time, although you may query a magazine on different ideas or different approaches to the same subject.

(6) Don't make your query letter too skimpy or too long, giving away too much information.

(7) Don't tell the editor what's wrong with his publication or that he needs your work to improve it. Of course "letters from our readers" columns often print gripes and brickbats, but these letter writers are customers of the magazine. You want it to become your customer!

(8) On the other hand, don't go too far buttering up the editor and his publication. Sincere compliments of a specific nature are welcomed by the staff, who work hard and enjoy appreciation. But an editor will be spurred to buy your article not by flattery but by a

professionally-written query letter in which you may, of course, refer pertinently to features he has published.

(9) Don't query for fillers, short articles under 1,000 words, or humor (which should be brief for greatest effect).

(10) Don't forget to write in your best, most tantalizing style. Make your query letter a cliff-hanger!

(11) Don't forget to include:

Q = Qualifications of yours for writing this piece; questions that will intrigue and be fully answered

U = Urgency and universality of the subject and treatment

E = Emotional angle and attitude; economical concentration into less than 300 words

R = Research evidence, with perhaps statistics or anecdotes; review of the main points that will be covered

Y = "You and your readers" appeals that will be stressed

(12) The following "Don't" should end every chapter: Don't give up too easily. Keep rewriting, reslanting, improving, and resubmitting a worthwhile idea until it is written as well as you can write it. Never throw away your sincerely well-written efforts. Instead keep them in a separate file marked "Not Sold *Yet*" or "Retired" or "Rejected . . . so far."

Trends change, editorial staffs change, even the minds of the same editors change, and *you* can often *change* your query, angle, title, premise, or script for the better. Acceptance of an article idea depends a good deal on timing and timeliness. Being behind the times is a deterrent except in nostalgic or historical material, which must in some way be today-oriented. It's also possible to be too far ahead of the times. If this is the case with you, the times will probably catch up with you. Keep your advanced ideas on tap while you keep working at others. No use beating a dead horse, but no use retiring a premature bet that, properly nourished, may win races in the future!

4

Interviewing—
Capturing Personality on Paper

"You must look into people as well as at them."—Lord Chesterfield

"Everyone has three characters: that which he exhibits, that which he has, and that which he thinks he has."—Anonymous

When the defunct, once-five-cent-a-copy *Saturday Evening Post* made a comeback at one dollar a copy, it featured more interview articles than any other kind. Most high-paying publications in the U.S. and abroad also buy more articles about people than about other subjects. Why?

Today's readers are so fascinated by other human beings that all writers should adopt the commercial slogan of a successful corporation: "People are our most important business."

The ability to interview will help humanize all your writing and is mandatory if you wish to sell personality pieces to a wide range of markets. Interviews can be sold in various forms: the question-answer interviews featured by publications like *Playboy*, *Penthouse*, *Oui*, *Playgirl*, and *Viva* panels or discussions involving celebrities such as those that appear in *Redbook* (naturally a behind-the-scenes writer has done the research, planned the questions, and directed all that brilliant repartee!); or straight character sketches or personality profiles like those *Reader's Digest* and *New Yorker* buy for upwards of $3,000. Thousands of lesser-paying magazines and newspapers also want people articles from writers who learn and practice interviewing techniques.

Titular Radiance

William Cooper points out that "three kinds of person—the medical man, the realistic novelist, and the personal interviewer—have something in common. Each is trying to sum someone up, truly and completely. . . . He is summing him up in such a way as to get the biggest total."

He calls this quest for the sum total of the personality "the synoptic approach", and he distinguishes its reliability from the unreliability of the spur-of-the-moment impression of someone as a dullard, a brain, or a bore. Such prejudicial snap judgments can be made by anyone, usually are, and are almost always wrong. It is the job of the interviewer to use the proper techniques to bring out the true personality, to add up all the pertinent psychological, philosophical, and unconscious factors to get a correct evaluation of a person—his true *character essence.*

As you learn and practice the following tips on pre-interview preparation, interviewing, and writing the article, try to sum up your subject's character essence in a catch phrase or nickname. (This word comes from the Middle English *nekename,* or *ekename,* which means "additional name") may be an important addition in originality to your material. It is called "titular radiance," that ability of a generalized summary phrase to provide a specific title, angle, and focal point for your finished script.

Here are some published examples of titular radiance: Paul Revere Waking the Country to Environmental Dangers" (Barry Commoner); "American Falstaff" (Bob Hope);"Blythe Spirit of the Right" (William Buckley); "Mexican Mirthquake" (Cantinflas); "Queen of Haute Cuisine" (Julia Child); "The Guru of the Boobtube," "Metaphysician of Media," and "High Priest of Popcult" (Marshall McLuhan); "Conscience of a Nation" (Alexander Solzhenitsyn); "The Cranky Humorist" (S. J. Perelman); "Toastmaster General of the U.S." (George Jessel); "Inventor of the Impossible" (Bill Lear); and "Waterfront Wit" (Eric Hoffer).

In sports a few pinpointing nicknames are: "Clown Prince of Golf" or "SuperMex" (Lee Trevino); "Fastest Man on Wheels" (Gary Gabelich); "Most Daring Young Man on the Flying Trapeze"

(Tito Gaona); "Broadway Joe" (Namath); "Smokin' Joe" (Frazier); "Mad Stork" (Ted Henrick, because he's skinny for a football player, but, like a stork, he can deliver!); "Wilt the Stilt" (Chamberlin) in contrast to "The Stump" (basketball player Gail Goodrich who looks like a Lilliputian next to the NBA giants); and "Hot Rod" (Rod Hundley whose quick, flashy plays make him a menace to traffic on the basketball court). Yesterday's sports stars had even more nicknames than today's. For example, "Babe" Ruth, "The Manassa Mauler" (Jack Dempsey, who was born in Manassa, Colorado), and "Dizzy" Dean (Jay Hanna Dean, whose coach said that his great pitches made the rest of the team look dizzy).

Titular radiance should pinpoint the angle you will stress, and it may give you a great title!

Whom Should You Interview?

The possibilities are unlimited. Start to keep "people files" of the following categories (your local newspapers offer examples of interesting people, many of whom you can meet to add more information to the published feature for an appropriate magazine).

(1) A celebrity—someone who has achieved success by doing something outstanding. Your readers agree with Emerson who said, "I love people who do things." Try to capsulize his achievements in one tight paragraph like this:

> James H. Doolittle is the story and glory of American aviation packed into one man. Back in 1922, five long years before Lindbergh's name was known to the world, a dauntless little bantam-weight boxer who had earned a degree in aeronautical engineering at M.I.T. climbed into a flimsy World War I airplane and became the first man to cross our country by air in less than 24 hours. He is a scientist, a student of aerodynamics, a speed record setter, and a World War II hero who led the first successful bombing raid on Tokyo. As head of the Twelfth Air Force he battled Rommel. He has lived 100 lives, all of them dedicated to his country and to flight.
>
> (from *Woman into Space* by Jerrie Cobb and Jane Rieker)

Develop the habit of summing up a person's contributions that succinctly—even if he isn't famous but fits one of the other groups listed below.

(2) A person with an interesting job, or someone who is in any way associated with a fascinating or timely project.

(3) An unknown in a modest job who has an inspiring philosophy, or a plain, ordinary person who is helping drug addicts, parolees, juvenile delinquents, etc.

(4) An infamous person, perhaps a criminal, hijacker, skyjacker, defecter, or traitor. Such subjects are for exposé publications or tabloids and must not be made heroic in any way.

(5) Someone who was marked for failure but who overcame a handicap to achieve success.

(6) A person who relinquished an established success or one particular goal for another (usually an unselfish one). In these days of longer life and earlier retirement, there are many examples—there are even courses in adjusting to new roles and work.

(7) Anyone you know well enough to make appealing to your readers: perhaps your child, parent, pet, or neighbor. Amelia Lobsenz sold a profile of her four-year-old son, entitled "My Teacher is Three Feet High," and Joan Mills has bagged several *Reader's Digest* checks for clever, informative articles about her offspring. Interviewing your family also bridges the generation gap!

Pre-interview Preparation

Before you conduct a serious interview for publication, gather all the material you can about your subject from all possible sources: from friends, enemies, co-workers, teachers, rivals, scrapbooks, press clippings, and, in some cases, public relations offices or publicity departments. Know everything that's been said or written by and about him. Look for contradictions and little-known angles.

If you have enough data to build an intriguing query letter, send it out and try to get an editorial order first. But you may have to have the interview beforehand.

Before you go into an interview situation, you should bear in mind the paradoxes of interviewing techniques listed below.

Be Subjectively Objective

Be *subjective* enough to identify with the interviewee, so that you understand what makes him tick, and *objective* enough to interpret him accurately to the readers of a specific magazine in an appropriate style.

Playboy's interviews, aptly called "candid conversations," are just that: masterpieces of frank personality probing, often as thorough and strenuous as that of a psychiatrist.

The necessary subjective-objective analysis should apply not only to your subject but also to your own reaction to him and the interview itself. After interviewing the dynamic, exasperating genius-director Roman Polanski about everything from his work and philosophy to the grisly murder of his beloved wife, Sharon Tate, and their friends, *Playboy* interviewer Larry Du Bois broke down his technique of interviewing into four stages that may help you understand the emotional phases you might go through with a difficult subject:

> Stage one: You enjoy him as a gloriously colorful figure with a keen sense of humor who takes great pleasure in entertaining whoever happens to be around him with anecdotes. . . . But his ego is as unbending as a natural law and he has a fierce suspicion of anyone, especially a journalist whose goal is to penetrate the wall of emotional invulnerability he has constructed around himself. So you soon begin to feel this interview is going to be difficult.

> Stage two: Endlessly following him around as he works, you begin to perceive his large talent and his tenacious determination to have any project he is concerned with done *his* way. . . . [Interviewer's sympathy for the director's workers, technicians and himself.]

> Stage three: Traveling with him is exhausting as they zoom through cafes, discotheques, yachts, dinner parties, etc. Polanski is more than a talented eccentric, he is an impossible-to-keep-up-with dynamo who hates "schedules, deadlines and questions he can't get excited about."

> Stage four: Unbelievably, you finish. And the sense of accomplishment and relief can only be described as pure joy. . . .

Who said that interviewing is easy?
Who said that it isn't fulfilling?

Seek the Bad as well as the Good

Another paradox of interviewing is that you must seek bad as well as good traits in the person you are interviewing. Even if he or she is a much admired celebrity, you must "look under the halo for the dandruff," as a sage expressed it. Of course you're not out to do a hatchet job, unless you're on assignment for a sensational tabloid, but the average editor will not buy an all-good whitewash because the average reader cannot identify with a flawless paragon. Even popular movie stars like Steve McQueen and Rock Hudson readily admit to having served prison terms without tarnishing their images. On the contrary, when you interview a negative character, dig for some "plus" traits to make him human, as Gay Talese did with his Mafia figures in *Honor Thy Father.*

Don't Push but Do Probe

You must be a good listener, but you must also be a firm talker and director of the conversation. Manifest that wonderful Greek word *agape* ("to have concern for") and still be the boss.

You should not be too pushy or offensive, but you must get salient facts and basic truths even though the subject may object and want to write things his way.

Do Your Homework

You must do enough research to have a firm knowledge of your interviewee and his work, but you must adopt the questioning stance of your least-informed reader. Bill Rivers says: "The interviewer must simultaneously display knowledge of a subject and complete ignorance of it [in order to learn more]. While he gains confidence by demonstrating that he's no cipher, he must act as a sponge, sitting at the feet of the oracle."

Guard against Bias

Try to blend a marbled mixture of sagacity and spice, depending, of course, on your interviewee. Editors and readers distrust an interview that is either too saccharine or too vitriolic.

Use both of the two extremes that were the opposite purposes throughout the 2,500-year-old history of interviewing. In 500 B.C. Confucius' *Tung Yu* or Philosophical Dialogues crystallized the religious philosophy that Orientals were to follow for centuries. We can learn much from the ancient questioner who knew how to dredge up pithy answers. Examples:

> Q. What one word would best govern the conduct of all?
> A. Reciprocity. What you do not want done to yourself do not do to others.
> Q. What do you think of Lao-tze's moral precept of returning good for evil?

A. What, then, will you return for good? Recompense injury
with justice and return good for good.

The dialogues of Plato continued this tradition of recording the
wisdom of the sages for the ages. But 2,000 years later the pendulum
swung from sagacity to sensationalism, and American "yellow
journalists" invented the term "interview" to describe scandalous
probings that were published for the express purpose of selling
papers by shocking readers.

A few famous examples: the *Boston Newsletter's* questioning
sailors about the death of Blackbeard the Pirate (March 2, 1719): *New
York Herald* editor James Gordon Bennett's interviews with
everyone connected with the murder of a prostitute (April, 1836); and
Horace Greeley's ultra-personal consultation with Brigham Young,
which appeared in his *New York Tribune* on August 20, 1859.

The above emphasis on invasion of privacy and sensationalism
were so offensive that *The Nation* called the interview "the joint
product of some humbug of a hack politician and another humbug of a
reporter." Such diatribes led to continuing improvements and insights that have helped the interview article evolve into the most
popular feature in the majority of American and foreign publications,
as well as television and radio networks.

Be forewarned of the preceding paradoxes and, if feasible, try to
synthesize the sagacious with the sensational as you search for the
character essence of your subject.

How to Interview

(1) Ahead of time, make an appointment with your interviewee
or his secretary by letter, using the techniques in the preceding
chapter. Specify the time you will need, writing something like "May
I have an hour of your valuable time?" or "I would appreciate the
opportunity to interview you for 40 minutes on _____." If the
interviewee wishes to extend your time, fine, but be business-like,
brief, and respect his valuable time.

(2) If you have a choice of the meeting place, try to make it in
surroundings that will add most to your article: a scientist in his lab, a
golfer on the course or at the clubhouse, an artist or entertainer in his
studio—a place where you can see him in action and/or in relation

with those who work with him. If you're writing for the women's magazines it might be better to go to his or her home and meet the family and pets and see the decor, architecture, and landscaping.

You may not have a choice, so be adaptable. Many interviewers like to question a subject during mealtime, finding the informality conducive to a more friendly interview. Some will tell you, "People always talk better when they eat," and of course you can get marvelous free meals this way. I, personally, do not like to be obligated, nor do I like the distractions, which may include hovering waiters, too many cocktails, clattering dishes, clinking glasses, and unclear copy if you're tape- or cassette-recording the words of a salad-cruncher or a soup-slurper.

(3) Plan and memorize from twenty to twenty-five tentative questions, making each a quest for intriguing information your readers want to know. Avoid questions that can be answered with one word, with no or yes. Such answers are dead ends, and you want to spur the interviewee to continue with philosophical or anecdotal nuggets.

For example, *Playboy's* first question to the biologist Dr. Paul Ehrlich, "prophet of environmental apocalypse," inspired a pithy response that expressed the essence of his beliefs:

> *Playboy:* Why do you say the death of the world is imminent?
> *Ehrlich:* Because the human population of the planet is about five times too large and we're managing to support all these people — at today's level of misery — only by spending our capital, burning our fossil fuels, dispersing our mineral resources and turning our fresh water into salt water. We have not only overpopulated but overstretched our environment. We are poisoning the ecological systems of our earth— systems upon which we are ultimately dependent for all of our food, for all of our oxygen and for all of our waste disposal. . . .

After questioning Leon Uris about his books, the interviewer for Bantam Books asked a question that hit a jackpot of an anecdote: "What has given you the most satisfaction in your career?"

The answer surprisingly, had nothing to do with a novel, instead, he told about a libel suit. A Polish doctor who had committed atrocities at Auschwitz concentration camp but who had escaped all punishment sued Uris for mentioning him in *Exodus*. The author fought it, taking two years to collect witnesses and evidence. He says:

I had to. I think the issue in this case—how far a man can go in his behavior toward his fellow men and still claim membership in the human race—I think this is extremely important. The case does so many things to explain why a holocaust could take place in a civilized country just two decades ago. . . .

The court ruled in favor of him but the great victory to me was that he was awarded only one halfpenny for damage to his character . . . and was ordered to pay the court costs of both sides, which amounted to approximately $80,000.

My fighting of this case against enormous odds with a band of very dedicated people from all nationalities working together to make a stand on a great moral issue—I think this was the most important thing I've ever done.

The interviewer's questions evoked interesting material as well as deep insight into his interviewee, not to mention the best-selling novel *QB VII*.

(4) In addition to your preplanned questions, outline a tentative plan of your article with your specific angle and premise. You may want to change them during or after the interview because your information is probably based on what is already known; you want to learn something new. Welcome valuable detours if they lead to a better, fresher treatment.

(5) If you can get permission to use a recorder, bring a good one and plenty of cassettes or tapes. Not only is this a professional method, but it also frees you to listen attentively to your interviewee—certainly this will inspire his confidence much more than watching you sit hunched over a notebook scribbling as he talks.

(6) Arrive on time, neatly dressed and businesslike. It's wise to eliminate awkward self-introductions by presenting your card, which may or may not list your important credits. It should, however, state your name, address, and occupation—"free-lance writer."

(7) Make the most of the first few minutes, which will form your subject's impression of you. Try to mention something fresh, clever, and interesting about his work or field, then steer the conversation along the route of your angle and your preplanned outline.

It's important to evaluate the individuality of your interviewee and chameleonize your style accordingly. An egotist will respond to praise, whereas an introvert may clam up after flattery and not give you good copy until you find the right key that makes him thaw— perhaps some gimmick about his work, hobby, pets, children, or hometown. A joke may break the ice with one person but antagonize another. You should have studied your subject well enough to use your own judgment, but don't waste time!

(8) Maintain enthusiastic interest throughout the interview, politely doing your best to keep the dialogue on the tracks.

(9) If possible, get an "exclusive"—preferably for three months—during which time the interviewee promises not to give his story to another writer or magazine while you are doing your best to sell the article to a first-class magazine. Your editor will appreciate an "exclusive" since it will protect him from being scooped. If the subject refuses to give you this protection, write your very best and try to get to the right market with the best piece.

(10) Before leaving, make another appointment for the interviewee to read and okay your final draft. Arrange for him to sign a "cover sheet" letter that indicates he has seen your article and agrees with your presentation of his facts and quotes. It reads something like this:

> Dear Editor:
>
> I have read the article, "_____" [your title] by _____ [your name]. The information and quotes are correct and as I gave them.
>
> Sincerely,
>
> _____ [signed by interviewee]

(11) Always end the interview with polite thanks, letting your subject know you enjoy him as a person, not just as a possible paycheck.

(12) It is courteous to send a brief thank-you note to the interviewee and to the person(s) who helped you in any way, by gathering material or pictures or arranging the meeting.

Tips on Writing the Interview

The important thing is *not* to put it off. Conversing with a celebrity can be so stimulating that you are hypnotized by his or her charisma and feel sure you have something great. But you can't know how readable and slantable the material is until you play back the tapes or cassettes or transcribe your notes and pin down what you have in article form.

Keep your reader in mind while writing your profile, answering questions he would ask and giving him information and ideas that will inspire, instruct, inform, and entertain him in a warts-and-all, frank style. Be as lively as interviewer Oriana Fallaci, whose motto is: "I make scenes and I yell and scream. I do almost anything to get a story." Her profiles are so fascinating that they appear in magazines all over the world and are collected in best-selling books like *The Egotists* and *If the Sun Dies.* (The latter includes interviews with American astronauts and space bigwigs.)

Besides representing your reader in the questions you ask, try to give him something that will make his own life happier and more meaningful. A good way to do this is to dig for and discuss the interviewee's philosophy.

Barry Farrell's first question to R. Buckminster Fuller was:

> *Playboy:* Is there a single statement . . . that would express the spirit of your philosophy?
>
> *Fuller:* . . . If we do more with less, our resources are adequate to take care of everybody. All political systems are founded on the premise that the opposite is true. We've been assuming all along that failure was certain, that our universe was running down and it was strictly you or me, kill or be killed, as long as it lasted. But now . . . we've discovered that man can be a success on his planet . . . this is the great change that has come over our thinking.

Try to elicit the person's basic philosophy that jibes with the titular radiance, angle, and character essence you will emphasize. You may have to revise your pre-interview concepts, or perhaps they will be reinforced.

Here are a few examples of boiled-down philosophy. B. F. Skinner is more pessimistic than Fuller:

> Man has not evolved as an ethical or moral animal. He has evolved to the point at which he has constructed an ethical or moral culture. . . . Science does not dehumanize man, it de-homunculizes him, and it must do so if it is to prevent the abolition of the human species.

Heavyweight boxing champ Joe Frazier:

> Life is wonderful, man! There's just *nothin'* better than livin'. The thing about it is, you got to do your own roadwork. Nobody can do it for you. Everybody's got some kind of roadwork, preparation, whether you're settin' out to be a secretary, lawyer, nurse, salesman. If you don't have that roadwork done, nobody

can help you. If you *do* have it done, everybody can help you.

Knute Rockne

When the going gets tough, the tough get going!

Eric Hoffer:

People who bite the hand that feeds them usually lick the boot that kicks them.

Congressman Julian Bond:

I rest best when my mind and body are busy.

Harold Nicholson:

The ideal holiday is not rest but change.

Chess champ Bobby Fischer:

Americans like a winner. If you lose, you're nothing. . . . I'm going to win, though. . . . I want to get some money together. Like take professional football. All those athletes making hundreds of thousands of dollars. Contracts, endorsements. If there's room for all of them there ought to be room for one of me. I mean, after all, I'm a great goodwill ambassador of the U.S.

Ann Landers:

Know and care about what is happening in the world around you. A person whose conversation is current and interesting is ageless.

Nelson Rockefeller:

There is no problem on God's earth that cannot be solved by man so long as he works at it hard enough and long enough.

Author Marjorie Holmes:

A writer has a moral responsibility, because writing is communicating ideas; and good ideas can improve the world. But wrong ideas, evil ideas, life-debasing material can do great harm and great damage. A talent for writing is a gift, and our gifts should be well used.

> (from an interview with Jane McNeil Jablonski that appeared in *Writer's Digest)*

When You Are Interviewed

Let's look ahead into your future writing success. Perhaps you have a best-seller, a moderate seller, ubiquitous articles in print, and, as an achiever, you'll be written up in your local or trade papers and maybe even be on one of the talk shows!

Irving Wallace says:

> Whenever I am interviewed [about my novels] it seems that I am asked the wrong questions. Therefore I give the wrong answers, which do not represent my true feelings or natural wit. I do best ten hours after an interview when, tossing in bed, I finally think of the answers I should have made to questions that should have been asked. In those night hours, I sometimes fantasize the perfect interview: me with me.

To avoid frustrations, misunderstandings, and a dull or disappointing interview you should do your pre-planning, pump priming, and self-analyzing before the meeting.

Here are some guidelines to help you make a success of it:

(1) When the interviewer first asks for an appointment, ask what aspect(s) of your life and work he is most interested in.

(2) Try to find out what market or readers he will represent.

(3) Review what has been written and said about you and sort out what you liked, what you didn't like, and what you'd like corrected or completed. Be reasonable and agreeable if you can't manufacture the "image" you'd prefer to have.

(4) Try to anticipate his questions by interviewing yourself ahead of time, objectively pinpointing your faults, failures, philosophy, and attitudes toward vital issues, problems, and people in your favorite fields. Try to formulate these cleverly, even if you supplement your original thoughts with clever quotes from other people. Use those you disagree with as well as those that jibe with your ideas.

Except for the preceding pre-interview preparation and observing punctuality, being interviewed is the reverse of interviewing someone else. Instead of guiding the conversation, you must let the interviewer sit in the driver's seat. After each question, think through your answer and visualize it in print before speaking aloud. Don't talk too much and be sure that what you say is pertinent, vivid, and clear. If you think there might be any misunderstanding write out your opinion (for a published interview, not on television of course).

If the interviewer doesn't offer to let you see his article before he submits it for publication, politely ask to do so, assuring him that this will be to his advantage and that you'll have some improvements after thinking things over.

Don't ask when the piece will appear. He probably doesn't know and you'll embarass him. It is permissable, however, to request a copy of the publication in which the interview appears. Do *not* accept or pay money for the interview or be hampered from telling the truth as you see it.

Finally, don't thank the interviewer. He should thank you, even though you may have benefited from being interviewed, which Norman Mailer calls a therapeutic "psychic housecleaning."

Most people agree with actress Nichelle Nichols, who says: "Being interviewed is like coming out of a steambath. It's exhausting because you are forced to think deeply about yourself. It's worse than a psychiatrist's couch."

Anything you can do to ease tensions and make interviews enjoyable for both parties (no matter which end you're on) is a good idea. Other helpful tips are included in the following acronym:

I = Intriguing questions prepared in advance and organized in a clever sequence following your tentative article outline.

N = New angle on your subject.

T = Titular radiance, truths, and timely projects of the person.

E = Essence of interviewee's character.

R = Reader identification, relevance, and research (done ahead).

V = Viewpoint (his opinions about facts, as well as yours); visualization of description of person and surroundings.

I = Interesting jobs, travels, failures, and successes of his or her past, present, and future.

E = Entertaining style that fits the subject and magazine for which you plan to write your article.

W = Whos, whys, wheres, whens, and what fors in his relationship. Most markets are pushovers for appropriate namedropping!

5

Wanted: Good Biography, "The Literature of Superiority"

"Biography is the most universally pleasant and profitable of all reading. . . . A well-written life is almost as rare as a well-spent one."—Thomas Carlyle

"The best teachers of humanity are the lives of the great."— Orson Squire Fowler

Regardless of contemporary trends, biographies are perennially popular because of life's limitations. Each of us can live only one life in time and space. But delving into well-written, thoroughly researched biographies enables us to live other lives in other circumstances. As philosopher Count Hermann Keyserling said, by absorbing the essence of other lives we can become many persons instead of just one.

By experiencing other people's problems, conflicts, actions, failures, and triumphs, we learn lessons that enrich our own existence. We realize that "the greats" suffered weaknesses and failures, that ignoble villains had moments of nobility, and that a few were able to rise from among mediocre millions to achieve fame or infamy.

Emerson wrote: "In every man there is something wherein I may learn of him and in that I am his pupil." Even though strong fictional characters may also be parables to truths, we are more inclined to believe the verities of real people in their biographies. Their very real achievements disprove such misconceptions as "everything's been done and you can't do or create anything new" and today's dangerous "something-for-nothing" attitude. The ideal success story proves that everything has a price that can and must be earned.

But the genre of biography is versatile and includes less inspiring, sometimes sensational life studies. Many of the exposé types seem to satisfy the reader's gossip or voyeur instincts as they bare intimate truths.

All biographies—whether lofty or lustful—offer their readers rare opportunities. Normally we can only view ourselves from within and other people from without. But a biography gives us a chance to understand characters from within and without simultaneously, thus imparting to mortals a godlike omniscience. Perhaps that's why Thomas Carlyle called biography "the only true History." He said: "There is no heroic poem in the world but is at bottom a biography . . . also there is no life faithfully recorded but is a heroic poem of its sort, rhymed or unrhymed."

A well-written biography attempts to offer a complete whole (Gestalt) of a person's life and its meaning. This compensates for reality's frustrating habit of thrusting us into contact with a fascinating character or new figure about whom we learn relatively little.

In the play, A Woman of No Importance by Oscar Wilde, Lord Illingworth says, "The Book of Life begins with a man and a woman in a garden." To which Mrs. Allonby adds, "It ends with Revelations." All of the interesting incidents and actions in between make readable, salable biography.

These are some of the requirements you should keep in mind when selecting and planning the life story you will write. Other literary fashions—Gothics, historical novels, pornography—may come and go, but biographies will stay with us forever. Several of those published long ago continue to be reprinted and used as required reading in educational fields as well as in libraries, for they may be the most accurate records of their historical periods available.

Over a century ago when novels were "the thing," Emerson anticipated our current appetite for true-life stories when he wrote: "These novels will give way by and by, to diaries or autobiographies—captivating books, if only a man knew how to choose among what he calls his experience and how to record truth truly."

Benvenuto Cellini insisted that it was the duty of anyone who has performed anything praiseworthy to record the events of his life. A surprising number of eminent persons have done just that. Queen Victoria wrote detailed daily accounts of her activities and thoughts that were invaluable aids to her biographers decades after her death. Many others, like John Bunyan, set down their inner emotional struggles. Chateaubriand titled his self-revelations *Memoirs from Beyond the Grave.* Dr. Albert Schweitzer immortalized his philosophical and physical activities in his *Out of My Life and Thought,* and De Gaulle's angle was *Memoirs of Hope: Renewal and Endeavor.* Of course they are not all that serious. Many are humorous, like Ben Franklin's, or satirical, like Mark Twain's. You must choose your own mood, style, and pace.

Study the style and techniques in best-selling autobiographies such as: *Go East, Young Man* by Supreme Court Justice William O. Douglas; *Weed: Adventures of a Dope Smuggler* by Jerry Kamstra; *Billie Jean* by Billie Jean King with Kim Chapin; *My Life in the Mafia* by Vincent Teresa with Thomas C. Renner; *One Life* by Dr. Christian Barnard and Curtis Bill Pepper; *My Several Lives: Memoirs of a Social Inventor* by James B. Conant; Alexander Solzhenitzyn's *The Gulag Archipelago* (and his previous autobiographical best-sellers, *First Circle* and *Cancer Ward);* Louis Nizer's *My Life in Court* and *The Jury Returns;* F. Lee Bailey's, *The Defense Never Rests;* Julius Horwitz's *Diary of A.N.: Welfare Cinderella; Navy Diver* by Joseph Sidney Karneke as told to Victor Boesen; George Plimpton's sports autobiographies—*Mad Ducks and Bears, Paper Lion, The Bogey Man, One for the Record,* and *Out of My League;* Rose Kennedy's *Times to Remember; Warden's Wife* by Gladys Duffy with Blaise Whitehead Lane; *Journey Out of Nowhere* by Nancy Smith; *Confessions of a Stockbroker: A Wall St. Diary* by Brutus; Xaviera Hollander's *Happy Hooker;* Lynn Caine's *Widow;* Stewart Alsop's *Stay of Execution* (about the author's dying of leukemia); John Berryman's *Recovery* (in which the author describes his attempted suicide and comeback); *The Double Helix* by microbiologist-geneticist James D. Watson (which dramatizes how he and his partner, Francis Cricks, discovered the nature of DNA, the substance that carries instructions for all living cells); and Nathan Shapell's *Witness to the Truth.*

Don't count yourself out if your own life and accomplishments are less intriguing than the examples listed above. Most autobiographies of notable or notorious persons are published under shared bylines or are ghost-written. When you are proficient at this popular genre, you can attract remunerative assignments writing the autobiographies of celebrities or criminals.

Meanwhile, keep journals and jottings about your own thoughts and activities, using a title like "My Life—and What I Am Doing with It." You'll derive a better understanding of yourself and find that it's really great fun! Madame de Staël wrote in her *Memoirs:* "If I write the record of my life, it is not because it deserves attention; but in order to amuse myself by my recollections."

When and if you become a famous author, the public will want to read your autobiography. Among the fine ones by and about writers are Lillian Hellman's *An Unfinished Woman* and *Pentimento*—a symbolic title that is an art term describing what sometimes happens as an oil painting ages and becomes transparent, showing what the artist first put on canvas, then painted over—Christy Brown's *Down All the Days,* Graham Greene's *A Sort of Life,* Edmund Wilson's *Upstate,* Eudora Welty's *Losing Battles,* Dr. A. L. Rowse's *A Cornish Childhood,* Hemingway's *A Moveable Feast,* William Saroyan's *Not Dying,* Sean O'Faolain's *Vive Moi!,* Henry Miller's *Tropic of Cancer,* Norman Mailer's *Advertisements for Myself,* and Anne Morrow Lindbergh's *Bring Me a Unicorn, Hour of Gold, Hour of Lead,* and *Locked Rooms and Open Doors.*

Films have also been based on autobiographies, among them: James Joyce's *Portrait of an Artist as a Young Man;* Faulkner's *The Reivers;* Barbara Graham's *I Want to Live!;* Roy Campanella's *It's Good to be Alive!;* Lillian Roth's *I'll Cry Tomorrow;* and Henri Charrière's *Papillon.*

Whether you ghost write the autobiography of another or write your own, strive for balance and objectivity. For instance, in describing early years, avoid the two unrealistic extremes that have been called "the diaper rash" school and the "trailing clouds of glory" school. The former stresses a miserable childhood, dwelling on scatological details along the lines of Freud's anal-sadistic period of infantile development (apparent in the memoirs of such writers as James Baldwin, Brendan Behan, and George Orwell). The latter extreme paints all aspects of childhood as the never-to-be-recaptured "good old days," the euphoric, sacrosanct Paradise Lost described by Wordsworth:

> There was a time when meadow, grove and stream
> The earth and every common sight to me did seem
> Apparelled in celestial light—the glory and freshness of a
>   dream.

Always remember Emerson's advice "to record truth truly." Nothing is all good or all bad, and you must write with dimension and fairness—as stated in the premise of Sean O'Faolain's autobiography: "The truth of it is that they were both wonderful times and nightmare times."

You should strive for such *objectivity* when you write biography, although you must blend it with *subjectivity* as you tune into your subject so much that you assume his identity, sharing his innermost thoughts, feelings, hopes, defeats, and triumphs. John Mason Brown described this "must" when he began his biography of dramatist Robert E. Sherwood:

> You cease living your own life when you start writing someone else's. . . . Without your being aware of it, you are no longer alone within yourself. Your heart and mind have a new tenant.

Likewise, the great biographer André Maurois wrote of the harmonious synthesis of historical facts with the personalities of the writer and his subject, whom the author chooses in order to respond to a secret need of his own nature. He wrote *Ariel: The Life of Shelley*, he said,

> . . . because it was an expression of one of my conflicts. Shelley had come from a family from which he wanted to escape, and so did I. The problem of Shelley was also my problem. My personality was also expressed in *Disraeli*. He was Jewish. I was Jewish myself. He was for me an example of how to get on with a Christian society. Proust, Chateaubriand and Balzac I did because I admired them as writers. The choices were guided by my inner feelings. . . . I couldn't spend three years of my life with someone I didn't like.

The Ten Commandments of Biography

The following ten commandments are offered as a guide to writing the best possible biography. Hopefully, by following them, a publisher will find your work among the chosen.

Choose an Intriguing Subject

By being intrigued by your subject, you will work tirelessly to intrigue others. Certainly this was true for the writers described below.

Ever since childhood, Lady Antonia Fraser was so fascinated by Mary, Queen of Scots, that she read everything she could find about her, acted her tragic role in school plays, took up the Queen's sports, and designed her wedding dress after Mary's (she's saving it to be buried in). Empathy was so strong that her biography, *Mary, Queen of Scots,* is unforgettable.

Writing of Oliver Wendell Holmes, Catherine Drinker Bowen said: "I found myself possessed by a witches' frenzy to ungrave this man, to stand him upright, see him walk, jump, dance, tell jokes, make love, display his vanity or his courage as the case may be."

Check what has been written about your subject in your public library's card catalogues and in *Reader's Guide to Periodical Literature.* Read everything you can find, whether written for children or adults. What is the angle of each? How will yours differ? What fresh material do you have access to (journals, diaries, letters, speeches, interviews, etc.)? Has he or she been written about too much? Arnold M. Auerbach described an overdone subject this way:

> I have a shameful truth to herald:
> I'm getting tired of Scott Fitzgerald.
> Must every single soul who knew him
> Pay biographic homage to him?

Tune in to Current Trends

Study the most popular subjects and backgrounds according to reliable publications like *Printers' Ink.* You'll find first of all that readers are more interested in adventurers, athletes, scientists, inventors, doctors, artists, musicians, psychics, politicians, lovers, princes, criminal lawyers, rebels, and rogues than in average businessmen, teachers, clerks, and others in pedestrian jobs.

Men and women of ethnic minority groups make salable subjects for juvenile as well as adult biographies: Blacks, Indians, Chicanos, and hyphenate Americans. Women, another minority group, are coming into their own, and any woman of accomplishment may make an excellent biographical subject—from a contemporary women's liberationist all the way back to *Gloriana: The Years of Elizabeth I* (by Mary M. Luke) and *Jennie: The Life of Lady Randolph Churchill* (by Ralph G. Martin, who also wrote *The Woman He Loved* about Wallis Simpson, Duchess of Windsor). (Several biographies of Queen Victoria have been written, by Cecil Woodham-Smith, Elizabeth Longford and Arthur Benson and Viscount Esher.)

Double-feature biographies are popular now, including Elliott

Roosevelt's *An Untold Story: The Roosevelts of Hyde Park*, Joseph P. Lash's *Eleanor and Franklin*, Joan Haslip's *The Crown of Mexico: Maximilian and His Empress Carlota*, Judith Campbell's *Elizabeth and Philip*, Garson Kanin's *Tracy and Hepburn*, Christopher Isherwood's *Kathleen and Frank*, Richard Hough's *Captain Bligh and Mr. Christian: The Men and the Mutiny*, Warren G. Harris's *Gable and Lombard*, Lillian Gish's *Dorothy and Lillian Gish*, Gordon N. Ray's *H. G. Wells and Rebecca West*, and John Leggett's *Ross and Tom* (about two successful authors who committed suicide, Ross Lockridge and Tom Heggen).

As if people want more for their money, there are even triple features like Mary M. Luke's *A Crown for Elizabeth*, which chronicles the lives of the children of King Henry VIII: Mary, Edward, and Elizabeth. Even more popular are composite biographies: Stephen Birmingham's *Our Crowd*, *The Grandees* (about prominent Jewish-American families) and *Real Lace* about America's Irish rich; Christopher Elias's *The Dollar Barons;* J. B. Priestley's *The English;* Diane Johnson's *Lesser Lives;* Andre Manners's *Poor Cousins* (about Russian Jews who came to America to escape persecution); Richard Griffith's *The Movie Stars;* William S. White's *The Responsibles: How Five American Leaders Coped with Crises* (Truman, Eisenhower, Robert Taft, J.F.K., and L.B.J.); Jan de Hartog's *The Peaceable Kingdom* (about Quaker leaders); Virginia Cowles's *The Rothschilds* and *The Romanovs;* and Irving Wallace's *The Nymphos and Other Maniacs.* You can probably think of many other titles that promise a cluster of biographies instead of just one like *The Borgias* (by Clemente Fuscros), *The Medicis, The Overreachers, The Aristocrats, The Donner Party, The Israelis* (by Amos Elon), and *The Men Who Made the Movies* (by Richard Schickel).

Noting that they are sprinkled through recent best-seller lists, group biographies would seem to be a now, new trend. But are they? Hardly. The world's first great biographer, Plutarch, grouped forty-six lives in pairs—a Greek and a Roman according to the similarity of their work or circumstances. Centuries later, multiple biographies became the specialty of the father of modern biography, Lytton Strachey, whose works include *Eminent Victorians* (Florence Nightingale, General Charles Gordon, Cardinal Manning, Thomas Arnold, etc.) and *Books and Characters,* which covered a literary spectrum from Sir Thomas Browne to Stendhal and from Voltaire to William Blake.

The never-ending popularity of the composite biographical work may give you an idea for your own grouping.

Amass All Possible Material

Painstaking research is the backbone of a good biography. If your chosen biographical subject is living or recently deceased, interview everyone you can who knew him or her. Take copious notes or record dozens of tapes or cassettes. Seek informational tidbits everywhere; scour encyclopedias, biographical dictionaries, and Library of Congress index files. If your subject is or was a doctor, spend time in medical libraries; if an attorney, haunt law libraries. Reviewers praise A. L. Rowse's books because they say he

> has an archivist's nose. He scents the truffle under dusty papers, the precious fact buried where previous scholars have passed unheeding. The British Museum, the Folger, the Bodlein, the muniment rooms of aristocratic houses are his El Dorado.

Catherine Drinker Bowen says there are two distinct phases of research: (1) gathering all the facts regarding the life and times of a subject, and (2) verifying those facts as absolutely accurate either through additional reading and research or by visiting the places where the subject lived and worked. She herself went all the way to Russia in quest of facts and authentic atmosphere for her book about the Rubinstein brothers and to England to research the life of Sir Edward Coke.

Irving Stone moved his whole family to Italy and actually worked in the Carrara marble quarries before writing *The Agony and the Ecstasy*. He went to Holland, France, and Belgium to gather and authenticate details for his Van Gogh study, *Lust for Life*, to New England to research *Those Who Love*, and to Austria—wherever Freud studied and worked—for *Passions of the Mind*.

You can *deduct* your travel expenses from your income tax while you *induct* flavor and verisimilitude into your book. And you'll surely get your best information, incidents, and inspiration where your biographical subject did.

After you have accumulated multitudinous anecdotes and facts, construct a tentative outline for a forward-moving, dramatic, suspenseful story.

Be Selective in Your Choice of Material

Choose what fits best into your outline and what is necessary in personalizing your biographical subject and his important peers.

Hemingway insisted that any accurate biographical portrait would have to cover twenty-four hours a day for over fifty years, which would be not only impossible but boring. Delete whatever clutters or detracts from the preplanned story line and whatever diffuses the character focus you will stress. Every published biography or autobiography is the rich distillation of from five to fifty times as much researched material, and the successful biographer is a careful tightrope walker on the fine line between too much and too little.

One way to distill a wealth of information is to relate a characterizing anecdote. If you're writing about dynamic Teddy Roosevelt campaigning for "the strenuous life," you could explain that he wouldn't let photographers snap their shutters when he had his hands in his pockets. Instead, he showed his vitality by gesturing with them as busily as a prizefighter.

Incidentally, most subjects should be dramatized as busily doing things. Even the brave quadraplegic, Jill Kinmont, who was crippled while skiing, is usually pictured teaching and helping children. You will find that it's better to choose active, doing-something subjects if you want your biography to sell to a visual market like movies or television. However, action doesn't have to be frenetically physical. It can be psychologically moving, just so long as definite scenes are presented, preferably fraught with emotion and/or characters in interesting juxtaposition.

Be sure to characterize each person not by labeling but by dramatizing his trait in an incident or anecdote. In *Buckminster Fuller: At Home in the Universe,* Alden Hatch shows Fuller's humor and humanity in interesting ways. For example, Hatch tells us that, at a World Series game, Fuller put on a New York policeman's uniform, went into the non-smoking section and made smokers put out their cigarettes. He also tells us that Fuller dances a softshoe while frying breakfast steak.

In both Garson Kanin's *Tracy and Hepburn* and in Charles Higham's *Kate and Spencer,* we read that when Kate first met her unimposing leading man, she scoffed, "I'm afraid I'm a little tall for you, Mr. Tracy." To which he replied, "Don't worry, honey, I'll cut you down to my size."

Elizabeth Langhorne's *Nancy Astor and Her Friends* is rich with the amazing activities of the beautiful, ill-educated American who was the first woman ever elected to the British Parliament. We see her sharp confrontations with male chauvinist Winston Churchill, who said that whenever he saw her in the House of Commons he felt "as though some woman had entered my bath and I had nothing to protect myself with except my sponge."

If you were writing a biography of Muhammed, you might show his gentleness and love for his cat by recounting the time he found it sleeping on the skirt of his sacerdotal garment when he heard the signal for prayer. Since it was his duty to perform the ceremony, he cut off the skirt of his garment so that he wouldn't awaken the sleeping cat!

Highlight Paradox and Dramatic Contrast

Concentrate one dramatic contrast both within your biographical subject and between him and other persons or ideologies, the way biographer Robert Lee Scott, Jr. sets brave-stubborn Flying Tiger Claire Chennault against his opponents, General Marshall and "Vinegar Joe" Stilwell.

In Tom E. Gaddis's *Birdman of Alcatraz,* Robert Stroud's antipodal traits include homicidal temper versus tender patience with a drenched sparrow, hatred of mankind versus love of birds. Although he was a two-time murderer of men, he worked hard to find a cure for septic fever in birds and wrote a valuable book about bird diseases. In addition to these and other contrasts within Stroud, the author adds conflicts with Warden Harvey Shoemaker, who is his nemesis, just as policeman Javert was Jean Valjean's antagonist in *Les Miserables.*

Richard Friedenthal's *Goethe* stresses the writer's Faust-like mixture of earth and spirit, genius and ordinary human foibles, growth and stasis. In fact any good biography of Goethe would focus on contradictions rather than give a one-sided picture seen in individual opinions of him: Emerson thought he was the greatest author who ever lived; Claudel called him a "great, solemn ass"; Jung claimed he was a true "prophet"; Evelyn Waugh scoffed at him as a "wayward dabbler in philosophy"; and Paul Valery said he was "one of the luckiest throws that fate has ever allowed the human race to make."

Paradox is often featured in titles: Norman Fruman's *Coleridge: The Damaged Archangel;* Joyce Cary's *Pessimist in Love with Life,* T. A. B. Cooley's *Democratic Despot: A Life of Napoleon III.*

In reviewing Gore Vidal's *Burr,* Edward Weeks points out the author's emphasis on paradox:

He was a maze of contradictions: priding himself as a gentleman but in money matters irrational and in dalliance as free as a goat; contemptuous of Washington as a general while admitting that he was the only man who could hold the Army and Congress together; boasting that he was "indifferent to slander," yet killing his brilliant rival for a despicable remark. . . .

Fawn M. Brodie's *Thomas Jefferson: An Intimate History* makes our third president more human than his familiar all-hero image. By dramatizing his passions as well as his perfections, his frustrations and failures as well as his triumphs, his inconsistencies as well as his consistencies, and his love affair with his quadroon slave Sally Hemings (whose children he fathered) as well as his affection for his wife, she makes him *real.*

In his book *How the Weather Was*, Roger Kahn calls Babe Ruth "a holy sinner": "He was a man of measureless lust, selfishness and appetites, but he was also a man undyingly faithful, in a manner, to both his public and his game."

Every interesting person has bad as well as good traits. Leo Tolstoy said his brother could never be a great writer for, while he had all the virtues required, he lacked the vices. Look for all shades of characterization. James MacGregor Burns opens his biography of Franklin Delano Roosevelt by calling him a "deeply divided man":

> . . . divided between the man of principle, of ideals, of faith on the one hand and, on the other, the man of *Realpolitik*, protecting his power in a world of shifting moods and capricious fortune. . . . He could be bold or cautious, cruel or kind, intolerant or long-suffering, impetuous or temporizing, Machiavellian or moralistic . . . .

In all his biographies Robert Payne seems to agree with Lord Acton's premise that "all great men are bad men." His life studies of Hitler and Stalin, Gandhi, Marx, Mao, and Malraux, as well as *The Great Man: A Portrait of Winston Churchhill*, treat greatness as a felony that compounds evil with good, inhumanity with humanity, pride with egomania, and ends with means. He says:

> . . . Churchill had more in common with Hitler than one would like to believe. . . . That he was "great" in his own terms seems undeniable; for a while he strode the world like a colossus. But it would be more true to say of him that he was a tragic figure, blinded by ambition until at last ambition consumed him in its fires and he was left powerless while in power during his second premiership.

He quotes Churchill's own writings to fortify this opinion:

> All great movements, every impulse that a community may feel, becomes perverted and distorted as time passes, and the atmosphere of the earth seems fatal to the noble aspirations of its people. A wide humanitarian sympathy in a nation easily degenerates into hysteria. A military spirit tends toward brutality. Liberty tends to license, restraint to tyranny. The pride of race is distended to blistering arrogance. The fear of God produces bigotry and superstition.

Payne stresses similar paradox in *Marx,* whose "mind was predatory, capricious and obsessed with violence," yet he had a nobility of spirit and was chiefly concerned with the defense of human freedom. He would probably oppose the excesses and brutality of Communism today and would be one of its victims, Payne argues.

Draw Your Subject into a Unique Focus

No matter how many personality angles you bring out, they must reach a focal point that represents your personal attitude toward the subject. In this way, you will distinguish your work from others about the same person.

In his biography *Edison,* Matthew Josephson stresses the inventor's good nature. After losing a fortune with his ore-milling process he said, "Well, it's all gone, but we had a hell of a good time spending it." He advised a minister to install lightning rods because "Providence is likely to be absent-minded." Jay Gould, who was the prototype of Teddy Roosevelt's "malefactors of great wealth," swindled Edison of promised wages. This humorless, ambitious man was generally hated, and telegraph workers striking against him sang, "We'll hang Jay Gould to a sour-apple tree!" But Edison held no grudge against him "because he was so able in his line."

Degna Marconi's *My Father, Marconi* delineates this inventor's eccentricity, forgetfulness, irascibility, tenacity, devotion to duty, harshness, and gentleness. She also discusses the fact that, as a teenager, he flunked his courses at school while working independently on experiments based on Hertz's electromagnetic-wave theories, that led to his wireless telegraphy. Here, the biographer presents a broad spectrum of character traits, but spotlights one throughout—his tenacious nonconformity.

Jean Renoir's *Renoir, My Father* is an intimate, personal portrait of a folksy man, whereas Francois Fosca's *Renoir, the Man and his Work* is a businesslike, factual, objective study of how the artist painted and sold his works.

Many years before Merle Miller's *Plain Speaking* gave us a complimentary view of Harry S. Truman, when the ex-president was still scoffed at as an uncouth, foul-mouthed bumbler, Alfred Steinberg presented the first admiration-filled angle in his biography *The Man from Missouri.* He wrote:

> . . . when the veneer of his tumultuous era in office is stripped away, and his frank language along with his excessive loyalty are forgotten, what remains is a man of strength and patriotism who made great and courageous decisions. Within his lifetime he can already be called the most underrated president in his country's entire history.

A startling statement for its time, this angle turned out to be prophetic of a reversal in public attitude.

Regardless of how controversial the person is, and no matter what opinions history, other writers, or public attitudes are or have been, you must set forth your own clear-cut angle, as Norman Cousins does Albert Schweitzer's saintliness, as biographer Paul Briand does Amelia Earhart's modesty, as Fulton H. Anderson does Francis Bacon's prophetic farsightedness, as Philip Shriver Klein does President Buchanan's realistic competence, and as Robert W. Johannsen does Stephen A. Douglas's ambitious vitality.

Ask yourself, as W. H. Auden did of Van Gogh: "What is the single most important fact about him?" There are always several possible answers. Auden's was "that he painted pictures." Stephen Spender's answer was "that he was religious." Irving Stone's angle was Van Gogh's psychotic torment as a love-hungry man. Another answer might be that he dedicated his whole life to the downtrodden and oppressed, or that he always shared the workers' point of view, or that his emotionality distinguished his work but extinguished his rationality.

If other biographies have been written for adults or juveniles about your subject, study the various angles and plan to stress a viewpoint that is different, with fresh substantiations. Each of the two simultaneous biographies of Ralph Nader has a different approach. Charles McCarry's *Citizen Nader* is negative. He calls the reformer technology's "first saint": ". . . a man whose workoholic nature and vitriolic attacks on business and government are seen as a function of a rather mechanical, compassionless, inhuman being." In contrast, Robert F. Buckhorn's *Nader: The People's Lawyer* is positive, documenting and verifying the subject's various investigative studies and his contributions to consumer protection.

Likewise, Cornelia V. Christenson's *Kinsey: A Biography* covers his childhood, his youth, and his experiences as an accomplished zoologist and as the world's foremost authority on the gall wasp—all prior to his famous sex study in 1938—whereas Wardell B. Pomeroy's *Dr. Kinsey and the Institute for Sex Research* is concerned with post-1938 developments, his marvelous rapport with people, his collecting 18,000 sexual histories, and the impact of his work on society.

Each of the many biographies of Mussolini has an entirely different angle. *Mussolini: An Intimate Biography by His Widow* (Rachele Mussolini as told to Albert Zarca) relates the domestic side of the dictator. His hero-heel complex is stressed in *Mussolini* by Laura Fermi, the Nobel prizewinner's wife who grew up in an Italy permeated with the official myth of *Il Duce,* but who became more objective after she emigrated to the U.S. in 1938. Her book underscores the paradox of the undisputed leader of his country for twenty-five years, whose thwarted, anarchistic nature eventually found fulfillment in bringing destruction to Italy. Christopher Hibbert's biography, published in America as *Il Duce: The Life of Benito Mussolini* and in England as *Benito Mussolini: A Biography,* spotlights Mussolini's histrionic nature. Charles F. Delzell's *Mussolini's Enemies* focuses on the opposition of 100,000 Italian Partisans in the civil war against the leader after 1943.

Before beginning research and work on your own biography, be sure to study carefully the specific angle of each related work. Don't be discouraged if there are many as long as you can come up with a unique approach.

Research All Secondary Characters

Research and fully characterize all the dramatis personnae in your subject's life so that your biography will not be a monotonous one-person show. Matthew Josephson's *Edison* acquaints us with such industrial wizards as George Westinghouse, J. P. Morgan, and Jay Gould. Ralph G. Martin's two books about Churchill's fantastic mother (*Jennie: The Romantic Years* and *Jennie: The Life of Lady*

Randolph Churchill) brilliantly characterize prominent personalities of Edwardian England, showing how most of them fell under Lady Churchill's spell. Margaret Leech probably won a Pulitzer Prize for *In the Days of McKinley* because of her exhaustive research and the dynamic development of all characters, especially the tragic Mrs. McKinley. An excellent delineation of the exotic Lafcadio Hearn appears in the biography *Rudolph Matas* (by Dr. Isidore Cohn and Herman B. Deutsch), although Hearn has only a "walk-on" part.

In Irving Stone's *The Agony and the Ecstasy* we come to know all of Michelangelo's friends and enemies as vividly as we do his patron, Lorenzo de Medici:

> Forty years old. Lorenzo had a rough-hewn face that appeared to have been carved out of mountain rock; a jutting jaw, a turned-up nose, large dark eyes and a mass of dark hair. He was just over medium height, with a sturdy physique which he kept in condition by hard riding and hawking.

J. B. Priestley's autobiography sketches vivid portraits of G. B. Shaw, John Galsworthy, James Barrie, and other writers of his day—just as both of Lillian Hellman's autobiographies give us superb characterizations of such literary luminaries as Dorothy Parker, Ernest Hemingway, F. Scott Fitzgerald, Edmund Wilson, Nathaniel West, Alexander Woollcott, and Dashiell Hammett. An autobiography must share the spotlight to keep from becoming a boring ego trip.

The all-important highlighting of the paradoxes of personality, as discussed earlier in this chapter, must be worked out for other characters in your subject's life, too. Ernie Bradford's *Cleopatra* dramatizes contrasts within all of its principals. Julius Caesar, conqueror of half the world, greatest soldier since Alexander, and brilliant historian and strategist, was also a rake, being utterly unscrupulous in money and sexual matters (his enemies called him "every woman's man and every man's woman"). Marc Antony, another great Roman general, was tall, handsome, and as muscular as a gladiator; he was also a notorious drinker and womanizer who often traveled with his mistress, the actress Cytheris, and a band of whores, actors, actresses, and seedy characters. He was described by Renan as "a colossal child, capable of conquering the world, but incapable of resisting a pleasure." Both, of course, loved and were loved by Queen Cleopatra, who was an astute politician, a brilliant linguist, and a clever manipulator as well as beautiful, charismatic, feminine woman.

Evoke a Sense of the Times

Recreate the times in which your subject lived so authentically that you and your readers will be transported to those surroundings and know exactly how people lived, talked, thought, dressed, worked, and played. Richard M. Ketchum titles his book *Will Rogers: The Man and His Times*. This subtitle should be the invisible subtitle of *every* biography.

Become as familiar with your biographee's world as Paul Wellman was with Theodora's sixth-century Constantinople in his *The Female*, as Kate Caffrey was with the Pilgrim crossing and landing in her *The Mayflower* (she includes not just characterizations of the white leaders and their Indian guide, Squanto, but also authentic letters and documents down to the complete passenger list), John L. Thomas was with pre-Civil War abolitionism in his *The Liberator: William Lloyd Garrison*, and as Charles Ferguson and Robert Bolt were with sixteenth-century England in *Naked to Mine Enemies* and *A Man for All Seasons*.

Biographies are today's most popular means of living history; they help to fulfill man's yearning to exist in other times. For instance, if you want to relive fascinating eras of Scottish history, read John Prebble's *The Lion in the North;* if you want to go back into Russian history, read Ian Grey's *Catherine the Great* or *Peter the Great* or Virginia Cowles's *The Romanovs*, which establishes rich background flavor immediately with:

> Seventeenth century Moscow was the bastard child of East and West: a bizarre mixture of chanting priests and torture chambers, of gilded ikons and oriental seraglios. Although the Russians had been converted to Christianity at the end of the tenth century, the Mongolian invasion 250 years later had turned their piety into superstition, introduced autocracy in its most despotic form, and left behind a society both savage and perverse.

Anyone who wants to go back to the French Revolution can do so vicariously by reading biographies of those who lived during that period, including the many works on Marie Antoinette, Marion Ward's *The DuBarry Inheritance*, Jean Orieux's *Talleyrand: The Art of Survival*, J. F. Bernard's *Talleyrand: A Biography*, and Robert Christophe's *Danton*, to name only a few.

Modern biographies dramatically revive many eras of British history, all the way from Martha Jones Rofheart's *Fortune Made His*

Sword (about the first truly English king, Henry V—his predecessors all spoke French) to Robert Payne's *The Great Man: A Portrait of Winston Churchill* and Judith Campbell's *Elizabeth and Philip*.

A thorough knowledge of a historical era can be profitable as well as professional, and biographers who thoroughly research their subject's times and contemporaries often produce subsequent biographies of the latter. Mary M. Luke became familiar enough with the royalty of sixteenth-century England to write several books, including *Catherine, the Queen* (about Catherine of Aragon), *A Crown for Elizabeth,* and *Gloriana: The Years of Elizabeth I.* Antonia Fraser has given us *Cromwell: The Lord Protector* as well as *Mary Queen of Scots* and *King James VI of Scotland, I of England.* Dr. A. L. Rowse, the foremost authority on the Elizabethan period, wrote excellent biographies of such luminaries as Sir Walter Raleigh, William Shakespeare, and Ben Jonson.

Ralph G. Martin's exhaustive studies of Edwardian high society resulted not only in two best-selling books about Lady Randolph Churchill, but also in *The Woman He Loved,* about the Duke and Duchess of Windsor and their empire-shaking love affair and marriage.

You should research and recreate an era so vividly that your reader will become an eyewitness to bygone events, as Jim Bishop takes us back to *The Day Lincoln Was Shot* and *The Day Kennedy Was Shot,* to Dr. King's fatal trip to Memphis in *The Days of Martin Luther King, Jr.,* and to FDR's 1945 in *FDR: The Last Year.*

It pays to concentrate on one era until you become an authority. Through thorough research and interviews, Bob Thomas has written several biographies about Hollywood's golden past, including *Selznick, King Cohn,* and *Thalberg,* as well as the more recent *Marlon: Portrait of the Rebel as an Artist.*

Research must be just as painstaking for a novel of this type. Taylor Caldwell spent forty-six years researching and writing *Dear and Glorious Physician,* studying more than a thousand books about St. Luke and his times. The exhausting investigative work and travel Irving Stone does for his biographical novels boggles the mind. Gore Vidal obviously was thoroughly familiar with the early history of the United States and our founding fathers when he wrote *Burr.*

What, then, is the difference between these works, which are classed as fiction, and *bona fide* nonfiction biographies? Although there is not a great deal of difference in the preparatory work and craftsmanship, the historical novelist can take more liberties in heightening the dramatic conflicts and imagineering details of the dialogue, emotions, and thoughts of his characters. It is true that every word cannot be documented, but because the author's embellishments are in character, they increase the verisimilitude and humanization, and thus boost the chance of motion picture and television sales. They are also understandably more popular. Hotchner's *Papa* was translated into many more languages than William Carlos William's official biography of Ernest Hemingway.

Whichever category you choose to write, fiction or nonfiction biography, try to increase reader identification by emphasizing parallels to contemporary times while you resuscitate historical ones. What similarities are there in politics, education, material versus spiritual values, war scares, delinquency, nonconformity, labor problems, etc.?

Taylor Caldwell became fascinated by the advanced knowledge of ancient Babylonians, who used hypnotism and psychosomatic medicine as we do today. In fact, Abraham, a resident of Ur in Babylonia, brought psychosomatic medicine to the Jews, who used it through the centuries. We haven't yet rediscovered all their secrets, many of which were destroyed by the Romans, and today's energy crisis and medical problems could benefit from their volumes of knowledge. For instance, they are said to have cured cancer with strange "stones" and to have lighted their temples and ship's sails at night with a "cold fire, more brilliant than the moon."

Current interest in Women's Liberation increases the demand for biographies of women who forged ahead in male-dominated societies. By evoking the times in which such women lived, you will make their achievements much more dramatic and relevant—and your work more salable.

Plan a Significant Main Premise

Biographer Margaret Coit says, "I write because I have something to say." She believes that, unless you give your reader worthwhile insights into life, your book will be worthless. Without such insights, a work is meaningless, regardless of electrifying personalities or interest-holding action.

According to the bedrock beliefs of the biographee and the biographer, the premise may be as negative as that of Samuel Beckett ("The major sin is the sin of being born") or as spiritual as that of Thomas Mann, who wrote:

> A difficult work of art, like battle, peril at sea, or danger to life, brings us close to God in that it fosters a religious mood and makes us raise our eyes reverently in an appeal for blessing, help, grace.

Stewart Alsop's *Stay of Execution* sets forth several premises that may help others share the author's experience of facing imminent death, including:

> 'God tempers the wind to the shorn lamb.'   (Laurence Sterne)

> There is a time to live, but there is also a time to die.

> A man who must die will die more easily if he is left a little spark of hope that he may not die after all. My rule would be: Never tell a victim of terminal cancer the whole truth—tell him that he *may* die, even that he will *probably* die, but do not tell him that he *will* die.

A cheerful affirmation of life permeates *Not Dying,* the autobiography of the long-lived William Saroyan. The title derives from his succinct response to a woman who asked him, "To what, Mr. Saroyan, do you attribute your old age?" He replied, "Not dying." Throughout the book he maintains that the purpose of everything is to ward off death—to postpone its arrival a little longer.

The prologue of Bertrand Russell's great autobiography begins:

> Three passions, simple but overwhelmingly strong, have governed my life: the longing for love, the search for knowledge, and unbearable pity for the sufferings of mankind. These passions, like great winds, have blown me hither and thither, in a wayward course, over a deep ocean of anguish, reaching to the very verge of despair.

The premise should be the soul of a biography, providing the best key to full understanding of the subject as well as giving the reader some philosophy with which to identify. Here is the theme of *Autobiography of a Schizophrenic Girl* by Renee: "Only those who have lost reality and lived for years in the Land of cruel, inhuman Enlightenment can truly taste the joy in living and prize the transcendent significance of being a part of humanity."

Typical of their cultures, the Western writers extol life over death, whereas an honorable death is often preferable to a compromised life in the true stories of such Japanese writers as the Nobel prize winning novelist Mishima, whose hara-kiri with his mistress was a ritual rebellion against Japan's current abandoning of its ancient traditions.

A premise from the Indian viewpoint appears in *No Foreign Land* by Wilfred Pelletier and Ted Poole, the autobiography of a Great Lakes Indian who tried things the white man's way but who couldn't stand it. Pelletier explains that the reason most of his people are reluctant to join the march of civilization is that they think it's going backwards!

While gathering material for your biography and conducting interviews, be aware of possible premises and write down all appropriate philosophical thoughts and interpretations. Do the same when you read life stories. Observe how the biographer may graft on his own opinions of his subject. In his biography *De Gaulle,* Brian Crozier attributes the French leader's failure to this fact: "It was not his fault that he was born in the wrong century for a career of the scope of Richelieu or Napoleon I. But it *was* his fault to have behaved as if he were living in a previous century."

Guglielmo Marconi's hard work philosophy comes through his daughter's biography of him in his own words: "Genius is the gift of work continuously applied. That's all it is, as I have proved for myself." On the contrary, Finis Farr's biography *Frank Lloyd Wright* refutes the fact that hard work is enough. It proclaims that even full-blown genius can be blighted by arrogance and megalomania, that the man who tries to deceive others deceives himself, and that the artist who has contempt for mankind corrupts his work.

Love of humanity is the theme of all biographies of Dr. Albert Schweitzer, whether they expound the credo that his sacrifices at Lambarene equal atonement for the sins of whites against blacks, or whether it's a defensive premise like the one in Gabriel Langfeldt's *Albert Schweitzer: A Study of His Philosophy of Life.* Langfeldt answers clerical condemnations of Schweitzer's "heresy" (because he did not follow orthodox dogma) by proving that the doctor was more truly Christian than they, and that his theory of the reverence for life follows Jesus' word: "He who loseth his life . . . shall find it."

Both Rousseau and Hazlitt were concerned with life's inadequacies and miseries, but each suggested a different remedy; Rousseau suggested a retreat from civilization back to nature, and Hazlitt asked us to work within the framework of society to improve its institutions. Ronald Grimsley's biography *Jean-Jacques Rousseau* embroiders the existentialist's credo: "I aspire to the moment when, freed from the body's shackles, I shall be *myself* without contradiction, without diversion, and shall need only myself to be happy." On the other hand, Herschel Baker's biography *William Hazlitt* maintains that man is the product of society and must improve its machineries, for human misery is rooted not in the laws of nature but in institutions that can and must be changed.

Ferret out the subject's philosophy as the most important thing about him, the mainspring of his life and action. Colette believed "Happiness is a matter of changing troubles," Robert Frost's credo, "Of all the virtues, courage is best," is similar to Isak Dinesen's slogan: "Often in difficulty—never afraid." In *Malraux: Past, Present, Future,* André Malraux predicts that "the next century's task will be to rediscover its gods."

Write with Flair and Style

Write your biography as if you were presenting it for television or the motion picture screen—with high-voltage action, dialogue, and suspenseful scenes. Because your aim is to "record truth truly" does not mean that you shouldn't relate facts and happenings in a dramatic way. A successful biography is a creative work heightened by the author's unique style and psychological intimacy with the persons, times, and events in his book. As John Fuller wrote, "Surely all history is as much an act of the imagination as the novel."

After you have accumulated your research material, decide on the best place to begin and work out an interesting plot arrangement. Even though you are telling the truth, you must never do so in a dull way, nor should you feel obliged to follow a chronological timetable if this will not be the most exciting presentation of a life story.

Luther Alive by Edith Simon opens with Martin Luther's dramatic disappearance in 1521, which he found necessary in order to escape being burned at the stake as a heretic. The papal ban had branded him thus:

> His teaching incites to rebellion, schism, war, murder,
> robbery, arson and the extermination of Christianity. . . . He
> has burnt the canon law. . . . We have labored with him, but he
> recognizes only the authority of Scripture, which he twists to his
> own convenience. We have given him twenty-one days. . . .
> Thereafter Luther is to be regarded as a convicted heretic. . . .
> No one is to harbor him. His followers also are to be outlawed.
> His books are to be expunged from the memory of man.

From then on Luther's disguises and escapes make the book as exciting as a Hollywood chase movie. We see him in action, very much "alive" as the "obscure, mangy friar" who challenges the absolute powers of church and state, as the black-bearded knight "Squire George" who is hidden by his "abductor," as the happy husband of the former nun Katharina von Bora, and in interesting juxtaposition to his friends and enemies. A later biography, *Luther* by Richard Marius, emphasizes the religious rebel's impact on history.

If you were to write the biography of Martin Luther for children, you would work out a different plot line, focusing on his youth.

Mary M. Luke's *A Crown for Elizabeth* begins with the heartaches and humiliations of seventeen-year-old Mary Tudor at the hands of her stepmother, Anne Boleyn, and her father, Henry VIII, because she will not forswear her mother's marriage. After the beheading of Anne, Mary is promoted, and her previously favored little half-sister Elizabeth is demoted. Subsequent vicissitudes befall other women connected with the controversial king throughout this composite biography that leads up to Elizabeth I's accession.

Marie Antoinette, by Philippe Huisman and Marguerite Jallut, starts out in Empress Maria Theresa's lively royal court in Vienna where the heroine, one of the Empress's sixteen children, is reared permissively and gaily. We then see her first years as happy-go-lucky Dauphine of France, her bright life and love affairs as Queen, and her tragic death with her husband Louis XVI.

If you apply these ten commandments to researching, preplanning, and writing your biography, you will probably find your work rewarding and rewarded. And you'll agree with Catherine Drinker Bowen, who says:

> Writing biography is an exciting business. Like courtship, it has its moments of gratification and its days of despair, when history closes her doors and will not show her face. But, if I had to choose, I would live the biographer's life over again. I cannot conceive of time spent more entertainingly, to myself if to no one else.

6

The Survey Article

If you are not yet ready to plunge into a full-length biography or conduct an interview with a bigwig, you may find a shortcut to publication via the survey or roundup article.

The survey, symposium, or roundup article involves querying several persons on attitudes, philosophies, or experiences related to a given subject, then editing and reorganizing their feedback into your own unique feature.

If you do it correctly it should work for you as successfully as the Star System worked in Hollywood and as surely as All-Star games attract big sports crowds!

As you plan your topic, market, and persons to be queried, remember the dictionary definitions of *survey:*

1. To examine for some specific purpose; review in detail
2. To look at or consider in a general or comprehensive way
3. Comprehensive study or examination

Select a relevant subject of interest to a particular readership and then send a set of related questions to appropriate celebrities with stamped, self-addressed envelopes. The feedback will probably enable you to build one of these currently popular features. You might have a piece for a minor market—a fan magazine, tabloid, supplement, or specialty publication—on movie stars' or other celebrities' favorite midnight snacks, foreign foods, jokes, or sports; on their fears or bad habits; on their eeriest ghost, ESP, or hypnotism experiences; or on their secrets for getting a good sleep, getting over stage fright, or bringing up their kids.

One of my students sold one titled "Nine Stars Reveal What They've Learned from Their Children," flower-bouqueted with their replies to his questions.

Survey nonfiction covers a wide spectrum, from easy-to-write shorticles to major works like Barbaralee Diamonstein's *Open Secrets: Ninety-four Women in Touch with Our Time*, Leonard Shroeder's *The Last Exodus* (about the difficult escapes of modern Jews from the U.S.S.R.), Peter and Barbara Wyden's *How the Doctors Diet*, or Studs Terkel's best-seller *Working* (for which the interviews took three years!). Using professional interviewing techniques, this skilled journalist-author queried hundreds of American workers about their jobs and how they felt about them. Then he edited and organized his material and wrote the book in a "drinking buddy" style that penetrates casual conversations to reveal people's need for work, but also for appreciation, prestige, and meaningfulness.

Terkel says, "The reason the Silent Majority is so silent is that they aren't asked the right questions."

You, too, will find that asking the right questions will work wonders with famous people as well as with the silent majority. You should get many ideas from the published titles mentioned in this chapter.

Celebrityitis and You

Millions of television viewers watch Johnny Carson, Dick Cavett, Mike Douglas, David Frost, Merv Griffin, David Susskind, and Dinah Shore because of the prominent guests on their shows, just as your nonfiction article can star famous people—but with you in charge.

Suppose you have strong feelings about a certain subject: women's liberation, men's liberation, inflation, love, happiness, loneliness, open marriage, waterbeds, "no fault" insurance, retirement, popularity, health, diet, ESP, or the occult—anything with reader identification. Mr. and Mrs. Reader aren't likely to be as interested in what you think as they are in the opinions of famous people. Use your own idea as bait and you may come up with a great bouillabaisse that can sell to a wide variety of markets.

How to Reach People

You can contact celebrities at their studios or business addresses, writers through their publishers, actors and actresses through the Screen Actors' Guild or *Variety*. If you have difficulty locating someone, your public librarian may be able to help you by consulting such reference works as the *Who's Who* books and *Celebrity Register.*

Send your carefully worded questions to twice as many celebrities as you plan to use because some may overlap and some may refuse your request for information or ignore it altogether. You'll probably find entertainers cooperative for several reasons: most of them want and need publicity and enjoy the competition and representation with other "Greats". Furthermore, they usually have press agents or publicity staffs to handle their mail, answer legitimate questions, and provide pictures (which you should be sure to ask for).

If you read about someone in a book or magazine, you can write to him or her in care of that publication, marking your letter "Please Forward to _____. URGENT!"

This letter can vary according to the specific type of article you are writing, depending upon how in-depth your survey will be. Whether you write to request a personal interview or a filled-out sheet of answers to your written questions about a specific subject, be sure to introduce yourself and your purpose. Begin your letter along these lines:

> I am a professional author preparing a survey article for a national magazine. My piece will feature the thoughts and quotes of the foremost persons in various fields [or . . . in your field of _____ , as the case may be].
>   Since I admire your work in _____ [be specific here]. I naturally wish to include you with other renowned personalities.

The above is meant as a very general guide; your own wording always best.

You do not have to mention the magazine you are writing for unless you have a firm order or are one of its "staffers." If you are free-lancing on speculation and the celebrity asks where the article will appear, you can say, or imply, that magazines keep their plans as confidential as auto or clothing manufacturers to prevent being scooped.

Writing Your Feature

After you have gathered various opinions on your subject, your work is by no means over. Now is the time to scrutinize, cut, and balance the material so that there will be variety instead of repetition. Even if everyone basically lines up in favor of or against your chosen topic, the information you give your reader should not overlap or bog down.

For instance, if you're writing a roundup for the United States Bicentennial on "Why I'm Glad I'm an American," you'll quote people who are all affirmative, but you'll highlight differences in their reasons, and you'll do everything you can to sharpen and dramatize your copy.

While you're gathering material and whipping it into shape, you should be thinking of your specific reader and what he wants to know. The survey article, like everything you write, should be slanted for a definite market and feature the subjects and people that that publication's readers are interested in, as *Time* published "The Relentless Ordeal of Political Wives."

The Men's Market

High-paying men's magazines like *Playboy* like masculine-oriented topics discussed by and for men. One of their "Symposium" features, titled "POWER!" was captioned:

> . . . Who has it? What's it like to have some? What can be done to spread it around? Machiavelli was unavailable, so we asked four other guys.

The four persons interviewed were: Robert Evans, Ralph Nader, Robert Townsend, and Murray Kempton.

Movie mogul Robert Evans built his phenomenal success on his goal of survival "in a business where many expected me to fail." His philosophy of power boils down to:

> Power works in a self-perpetuating way: The more you have, the more you want, like a snowball rolling down a hill, gaining momentum and losing control. But that's not me at all; I'm not concerned with increasing or perpetuating my power, and I'll tell you why. It's the position that gives you the power, not the man. All the people who play up to you, who work with you obediently, who extend themselves in every way, do it for your position, not for you. . . . I'm still just a cog in a corporation. . . .

Crusader Ralph Nader built his own popularity and power by attacking big business power. He discusses the evils and dangers of corporations, unions, and government's power "to limit people's options and opportunitites, and even their expectations; to change their behavior; to impose penalties on them; and to withhold benefits and rights that should be theirs." He writes:

> In a complex society, most people fail to grasp how power is being used against them, much less do anything about it. . . . Our American Revolution was based on the cry "No Taxation Without Representation." A more appropriate cry for today would be "No Victimization Without Representation." People walking down the street breathe contaminated air that causes respiratory diseases. Industry produces that pollution, so industry is, in effect, governing these people, determining what kind of air they shall breathe. . . .

Nader stresses the importance of forcing those who make the decisions to experience the conditions the victims experience.

Robert Townsend (Madison Avenue braintrust and author of *Up the Organization*) offers an entirely different angle. He blames *people* for being powerless:

> The trouble with power is that so few people really want it. 99 employees out of 100 in large organizations are actually after, or will happily settle for, merely the trappings of power—the big office, lots of secretarial help to add to their problems, the limousine, the private parking place, the country-club membership. If you've ever had these trappings, you know they don't provide much real satisfaction. . . . *Real* power you get by becoming a servant of the people in your organization—not their master, insulated from them by as many hierarchical layers as possible. . . .

Journalist Murray Kempton stresses the reversal of the power of the powerless over the powerful in a different way. He cites many examples and arguments that prove that the more power a bigwig has, the more he can be victimized by less important people: "The more awesome anyone makes himself to the innocent, the more abounding a resource he is to the larcenous." Nameless crooks steal $50,000,000 from Howard Hughes . . . a man-in-the-street can chop down a president . . . a troublemaker like Abbie Hoffman can overpower whole city Police Departments . . . an ordinary citizen on a jury can influence the Chief Justice of the Supreme Court.

Although this was a longer, more involved article than many survey articles, it does prove a point. One of the chief values of the survey is to demonstrate the complexity of an issue by showing how differently individual authorities in contrasting fields approach an assigned subject that interests specific readers.

Another *Playboy* article presents writers discussing their contrasting attitudes toward fame—a perfect choice of subject for the men's market. "The High Cost of Fame" finds Mario Puzo (*The Godfather)* insisting that fame is a destructive force to an author. It destroys creativity and privacy; one is exposed to the shock of meeting the world and having it waste one's time; it corrupts the emotional processes and causes impatience with aspects of ordinary life; and it turns one's attention to material acquisitions. James Dickey (*Deliverance, Buckdancer's Choice)* agrees that anticipation is better than realization, and says he'd like to start all over again. He compares fame to riding a tiger and being afraid to dismount. Kurt Vonnegut, Jr. also deplores the disadvantages of being invaded and invited, as well as the money worries of being rich, but he considers these a small price for the pleasure of fame. Studs Terkel (*Hard Times* and *Working)* writes: "As she looks now, the bitch-goddess is none other than the weary B-girl at the nearby tavern. The one I've always known." Gay Talese *(Honor Thy Father, The Kingdom and the Power)* insists that losing has always fascinated him more than winning.

It's interesting to note that the majority of these successful writers put down fame. Although only Dan Wakefield (*Going All the Way)* says it's a great Superman thing, Joe McGinniss (*The Selling of the President)* does admit that, "Success has relieved many more pressures that it has presented." Perhaps Michael Crichton offers the best-balanced view of all:

> . . . you can get wrecked by . . . success. It opens up all kinds of corrupting power. But I don't think it has to be that way. The adjustments you must make don't necessarily have to destroy you. . . . I spend a lot of time monitoring myself.
> I sound like this experience is a curse. I don't think it's a curse. I think it's great. It's worth it. I *think.*

The Women's Market
The traditional women's markets are particularly interested in appearance, health, beauty, and romantic and domestic subjects. *Cosmopolitan* likes surveys along the lines of "Daredevil Women,"

"How I Lost My Virginity," and "Everything You Can Do in Your 20s to Stay Young and Beautiful in Your 40s and 50s." In this last-named feature by Mallen De Santis, valuable advice is given by top experts in their fields: Dr. Robert Atkins, specialist in carbohydrate metabolism and obesity control; Charles Revson, cosmetics tycoon; Vidal Sassoon, hair stylist; Nicholas Kounovsky, physical-fitness authority; Georgette Klinger, skin-care expert; Dr. Allan Fromme, psychologist; Romana De Vries, facial-exercises teacher; Dr. Frederic D. Zeman, internist; Gladys Lindberg, nutritionist; Dr. Norman Orentreich, dermatologist; Marjorie Craig, author of *Miss Craig's 21-Day Shape-Up Program;* Dr. Ivan Popov, European youth doctor; Dr. Alfred Speirs, plastic surgeon, and Swami Satchidananda, Yoga teacher. All those, plus the secrets of Cary Grant, Arlene Dahl, Gloria Vanderbilt, and Merle Oberon (who, through right exercise, diet, and thinking, proves her philosophy: "Middle-age is moving up to 60!").

Always keep up with new magazines that appear on the publication scene. If you send them a professionally-written survey on a relevant subject, you will find that they are easier to crack than the major standbys because they haven't yet developed a large backlog or big stable of favorite writers.

Viva and *Playgirl* are bolder than *Cosmo* but like subject matter pertaining to sex and all areas of self-improvement. You might question several women (celebrities or not) about what they want in a man and how to find Mr. Right; age, race, or religious differences between spouses or lovers; how "liberated" they'd like to be; their view on living together, new-type vs. old-fashioned marriages, homosexuality, plus many other ideas you'll get from reading the text and advertisements in recent issues of the magazine.

For *Ms,* you could survey different women on such subjects as sexist discrimination in literature, children's education, employment, politics, or the movies. This publication is more serious and less "sexy" than the others. Be sure to analyze several issues of each magazine thoroughly to study the specific policies, angles, and attitudes of each. You could even sell them a man's angle on a vital subject—one that could promote better understanding between the sexes!

Redbook has featured roundup articles about aging, inflation, women's liberation, "Forty-Four Women Who Could Save America," and "Innocent Victims of Watergate: Four Women Tell Their

Stories." Recurrent and uniquitous are the roundup articles on dieting. One *Cosmo* survey is titled "My Favorite Crash Diet," which quotes the weight-loss methods of people in all fields: politics, acting, writing, business, etc. Variety is the keynote here, not just in the persons quoted but in their tricks, which range from drastic fasting and expensive spas to mild limitations and exercises—from Jack La Lanne's strenuous calisthentics to jogging, swimming, bicycling, walking—and including Danny Thomas's advice to "push yourself away from the table three times a day." A more limited diet angle is featured in the *Ladies Home Journal's* "How First Ladies Diet," by Frances Spatz Leighton. This survey examines the slimness secrets of former first ladies and gives their favorite menus for breakfast, lunch, and dinner, along with recipes. Tabloids feature such diet surveys as "Women VIPs Tell How They Keep Slim on Washington Banquet Circuit" and "How Stars Lose Weight." *McCall's* has published several surveys, including "The Fear of Growing Older," in which Claudia Dreifus arranged and taped a "rap session" between seven women who discussed their specific views of aging. It was captioned:

> Many women dread the thought of no longer being young. Here seven of them—ages 27 to 45—talk frankly about their feelings and the special joys some of them have found in middle age.

Also in *McCall's* are seasonal surveys like "Christmas Is Time for Loving: Four Tidings of Comfort and Joy from Katherine Anne Porter, Jean Stafford, Gwendolyn Brooks and M. F. K. Fisher" and "Famous Classmates: Their First Time in Print." The latter article shows how high school annuals predicted the futures of such celebrities as Gloria Steinem, Betty Friedan, Pat Nixon, Johnny Carson, Ronald Reagan, Mary Tyler Moore, Abigail Van Buren (Dear Abby), and Ann Landers.

The Tabloid and Other Markets

A marvelous market for survey features is provided by tabloids, of which there are many, including *National Enquirer, Modern People, Tattler, Midnight, National Insider, The Star, National Examiner,* and *National News.* (There may be more or less by the time you read this.) Most of the ones I studied favored screen stars of both sexes, but occasionally there's a more erudite symposium like *National Enquirer's* "Loneliness—the Most Dangerous Sickness in

America Today." Here narrator-moderator Jacqueline Himmelstein questions three psychiatrists about the dangers of our current epidemic of loneliness, which produces drug addiction, alcoholism, alienation, physical diseases, and suicide. Although they offer a variety of opinions and examples, they all agree that if "loneliness continues to spread, it will destroy the U.S. as a nation."

Try to set up differences of opinion for reader interest, but also tie the various strands into a consistent premise no matter which market you write for. The voracious tabloids like crisp, brief articles with not-too-deep premises. Here are a few recently published titles to show you what they go for: "10 of Hollywood's Leading Male Stars Reveal What They Look for in a Woman" by Brian Dodds (it also goes into disagreeable traits that turn specific men off); "5 Famous Women Tell How They Relax" by Claire Safran; "Instant Beauty Secrets from Some of the World's Most Glamorous Women" by John B. McLain; "Shyness Almost Kept These Stars from Fame" by Duane Valentry; "America's Top Stars Reveal Their Most Terrifying Fears"; "Film Stars Who Rely on Occult Devices"; "Many of Hollywood's Older Stars Simply Refuse to Act Their Age"; "Sisters of Celebrities Share Common Plight (It's Tough Living in a Star's Shadow)"; "Hollywood Stars Share Their Favorite Christmas Jokes."

All of the tabloids seem to buy many roundup articles about movie stars. Here are some published titles that might trigger your own ideas: "The Ghosts that Haunt the Stars"; "The Tragedies that Shaped the Stars"; "How Hypnotism Helps Hollywood"; "Even Top Stars Fight Personal Misfortune"; "Majority of Actors Don't Earn the Big Buck"; "Shame of Stars Who Scorn Marriage"; "How Superstars Behave Backstage"; "6 Glamour Actresses Tell Why Sex Appeal Doesn't Have to End at 40"; "Sensuality Secrets of Hollywood Stars"; "How Advertising Pays Off for Many Actors"; "Favorite Midnight Snacks of the Stars"; "Star-Studded Deadbeats"; "Stars Who . . . Depend on Prayer to Guide Their Lives . . . Have Annoying Habits . . . Boast ESP Powers . . . Sleep in the Nude." In addition to "Stars Who . . ." a favorite title is "Stars Tell How . . . Their Fathers Influenced Their Lives . . . They Suffer When TV Shows are Cancelled."

Readers also seem to love the format of "Stars Reveal . . . Things We Couldn't Live Without . . . The Moment I Realized I Was

No Longer a Child . . . the Grim Reality of Drugs' Effect on Their Children . . . Their Bad Habits.''

Of course all surveys do not concern Hollywood personalities. They can be about well-knowns in any field who share a common denominator, and they should give the reader the feeling of "peeping behind the scenes.'' A few popular titles are: "Famous People Reveal Their Secret Natures by Gestures''; "Famous Women Reveal Secrets for a Happy Marriage''; "Many of Our Self-Made Millionaires Are School Drop-Outs Who Made It the Hard Way''; and "America's Most Wanted Women (from the FBI Priority List).''

Those articles without bylines were probably staff-written; if you had submitted them, they would have been published with your byline!

A tabloid recently featured "How Will Those Retirement Years Affect You?'' by Jean Davison. It rounded up quotes from retirees as well as gerontologists. This popular subject with increasing identification appears frequently in different markets.

One of the best of the features on this subject was published in *National Retired Teachers Association Journal,* it was longer, more intellectual, and more in-depth than the newspaper article. In "Today's Retirees—The New Revolutionaries,'' Leonard Davis elaborates the premise: "We will destroy those stereotypes of aging that imprison people.'' His goal of inspiring readers to meaningful retirement is enhanced by the roundup technique that uses big names to add lustre and authenticity. For instance, cellist Gregor Piatigorsky discussed "Creativity in Aging''; Dr. James Birren gave a medical view in "Coping with Life's Stresses''; Dr. Nathan W. Shock went into "The Biologist's View of Aging''; and Buckminster Fuller wrote inspiringly of "The Miracles of Our Lifetime.''

The Sunday supplements also buy many surveys, as in *Family Weekly's* regular feature, "A Celebrity Symposium.'' Lately they've published such articles as "The Beauty Secrets I Treasure Most,'' "My Favorite Breakfast,'' and comedian Joey Adam's "How I Roast 'Em,'' which gives the secrets of the fine art of insulting people and tells how different celebrities react. Also, they often survey sports stars on a subject.

The survey or roundup article is not only easy to sell but also easy to write. In some cases the authors don't even bother with personal interviews; instead, they pluck information from news items and other articles and build a feature on something famous people have in common. Examples: "Top Reporter Lists 10 Women Who Squander Most Money on Clothes and Other Fripperies" by Fred Sparks; "Dozens of Brilliant Men Were Dummies in School" by Susan Forano; "The Presidency: A Rich Man's Game—Though a Few Paupers Made It to the White House"; "Many of the Richest Stars Are Downright Stingy" by Marie Miller; and "The High Cost of Hollywood Divorces Forced Some Stars into Bankruptcy."

Getting Ideas for Your Article

Now that you know what is selling, get to work on your own survey or roundup article(s)!

You can get ideas for survey articles everywhere. Study calendars and almanacs, looking about six months ahead to centennials, birthdays, and holidays that are meaningful to everyone, collecting opinions from down-to-earth people as well as VIPs. Perhaps something like "What was your most memorable Christmas . . . Thanksgiving . . . Easter?"

In May, roundup articles appeared in which celebrities evaluated their mothers. *Family Weekly* featured "Famous Women Look Back and 'Remember Mama,' " compiled by Alan Ebert, which stressed the inspiration, confidence, companionship, and wisdom that all mothers should give their daughters. At about the same time a tabloid, *Modern People,* came out with "Top Stars Remember Mom" by Duane Valentry. It was on the same subject but with entirely different celebrities. It presented a broader scope since it cited the great influence mothers had on men (Van Cliburn, Andy Williams, Lawrence Welk, Monty Hall, Glen Campbell, and Dean Martin) as well as women (Doris Day, Hayley Mills, Gracie Fields, and Loretta Young).

You, too, can write about a subject that already has been done if you use a different angle and different quotes for a different market. You might even come up with a better article for another publication with your own unique touches.

Get in a "collecting" mood, selecting relevant ideas, people, topics, and places with a common denominator—subjects that are of interest to many people or at least to a special segment of readership.

You can glean ideas from living, talking to people, and reading *everything* that's timely—even items that are seemingly dull! For instance, according to Environmental Protection Agency statistics, the dirtiest cities in the U.S. are New York, Gary, Indiana, and Los

Angeles. The cleanest are Seattle, San Francisco, Dallas, San Antonio, Boston, Memphis, Houston, Kansas City, Missouri, and Toledo and Columbus, Ohio.

There you have an idea worth developing for a survey: several places with something in common. Choose your approach, market, and targets for questioning, perhaps city mayors, environmentalists, or celebrities who travel a lot or are ecologically active, or foreign visitors.

Next, plan questions that will dredge up informative and varied answers. Something on the order of "Why is ____ the cleanest?" "What do you recommend to keep it that way?" "What threats are there to this idyllic situation?" "Who are the bad guys?" "What can people of other cities do to keep theirs clean?" Plus whatever other questions will interest your readers.

In the case of the dirtiest cities, questions may be along the line of "Why is this true?" "How do the people feel about this reputation?" "What are the statistics on respiratory diseases?" "How and when has the situation changed in contrast to the past?" "What is being done to clean up your city?" "What are you personally trying to do?" "What should the citizens do?" "What shouldn't they do?"

When you ask the right questions of interesting and famous people and edit their answers, your article will practically write itself.

7

The Exposé Explosion

"It is a newspaper's duty to print the news and raise hell!"
—Wilbur Storey

Although this was written a century ago, it is truer of all publications today than it was then. Exposés are wanted by editors and readers for a variety of reasons, all summed up by the popularity of the man called "Consumer Advocate," "Public Interest Lawyer," "Crusader," and "World's Champion Whistle-Blower"—Ralph Nader. Because of his exposé writings and actions we have safer cars, X-ray machinery, meat, coal mining, and gas pipelines, and more carefully examined and exposed lawmakers—not to mention more exposé articles and books.

The following is an attempt to explain why today is the age of the exposé explosion.

Our technological advancement has produced more sophisticated means of perpetrating wrongs and crimes and exploiting innocent victims.

Most people have more money, which makes them the targets of the gyp artists. For example, oldsters who receive social security and/or pension checks (perhaps also welfare money and food stamps) are often naive, weak, lonely, and susceptible to the friendly con artists who offer them companionship and/or a chance to make a killing via the "pigeon-drop" game—in which they offer to put up a sum of money "in good faith" in order to get the oldster's savings. Another trick is the cruel Medicare Refund Game, in which "officers" bring Mr. or Mrs. Senior Citizen a refund in the form of a fifty dollar bill that requires change. When the victim goes to his hiding place to get the money, the rest is easy for the crook.

Of course oldsters aren't the only people exploited. All of us have been deceived by false advertising, overcharged for auto, television, or home appliance repairs, or prescription drugs; squeezed by inflation, endangered by racketeers, thieves, con men, pollution, flammable clothing, hijacking, radioactive accidents, nuclear wastes, oil spills, and poisons in our food; deafened by jet noises; demoralized by smut-peddling and pornography; and weakened or cheated by government ineptitude and extravagance, by strip mining, and by wanton destruction of our natural environment.

In addition to spiraling wrongs, we have wider and deeper publicizing of them through the largest, quickest, and most effective mass media in history: through television, radio, newspapers, magazines, and communication satellites. The exposé explosion is a spin-off from today's information explosion. We have a more informed, inquisitive, and active populace—one that is tired of being fooled and exploited and that demands to know the truth.

The inherent gossip instinct is a contributing factor, plus another characterisitc of today's typical American—alienation or depersonalization. "The good old days" are often characterized as having been warm with friendliness, neighborliness, and strong family ties, with generations usually living together or at least in close communication. People helped each other and, in return, had someone to depend on. This is not usually true today in our increasingly megalopolis-oriented society, which porduces the alienation defined by Eric and Mary Josephson in their book *Man Alone* as "a feeling or state of dissociation from self, from others and from the world at large." Jacques Ellul, an equally sharp critic of our runaway technology, says, "When the edifice of the technological society is completed, the stains of human passion will be lost amid the chromium gleam."

It should also be noted that today's alienated American is not as self-sufficient as he pretends to be. He needs help and protection from swindlers and other injustices. The writers and editors who fill these needs are the public's knights in shining armor. Readers avidly read exposés of evils and villains, hoping to learn how to protect themselves and avoid trouble.

When you learn to write and sell useful, verified exposés, you can serve society by improving the quality of life for your fellow men—bonuses to editorial checks and bylines!

There have been gratifying results of writers' exposés. Thanks to those in the vein of Rachel Carson's *Silent Spring*, dangerous pesticides have been banned and we have environment-protecting legislation and antipollution activists. Jessica Mitford's and Ruth Harmer's exposés of mortuary abuses led to investigations of the industry, plus the formation of hundreds of new, inexpensive, dignified memorial clubs. Exposés of automakers' irresponsibility led to seat belts and other safety devices and many recalls of cars with faulty parts. Ninety-three percent of all consumer legislation was originally stimulated by written exposés: the truth-in-lending, truth-in-labeling, and conflict-of-interest laws, the banning of cyclamates, DDT, harmful phosphate (in detergents), and other chemicals, as well as new rulings regarding cigarette and drug commercials on television.

We now have an Office of Consumer Affairs in the White House (Washington, D.C. 20506) and consumer offices in every state to which abused Americans can take their gripes. Most communities have police protection meetings and university and adult education courses that alert and inform the confused consumer. They feature such lecture programs as "Human Gullibility," "Making Effective Consumer Decisions," "How Consumers Respond to Advertising," "The Art of Deception for Fun and Profit," "Consumer Protection in _____ [state]," "Medical Quackery," and "Can We Buy Non-Polluted Foods Today?"

If there are such courses in your area, you should enroll, not just for your own protection but to get authenticated facts, statistics, and advice for your exposé writing.

Keep a *gripe file* of newspaper items that report on frauds and wrongdoers, and list things that irritate you personally. When you are duped or are seething with indignation at some injustice or racket, you may have your best ammunition for writing a successful feature. But if you "talk it out" to everyone or spout off editorially without disciplining your emotions, slanting your ideas for the proper market, and researching and organizing the material in the most effective way, you may not even hit the bull, let alone the bull's eye!

Author Marc Brockman calls himself "the world's unluckiest consumer" because he has had so many problems with faulty purchases and inefficient repair work. As a result he wrote the article

"How I Became My Own Consumer Advocate," in which he outlined (and expanded upon) five rules for untying the Gordian knot and solving consumer problems:

1. Never tell your story for the practice.
2. Don't blow your cool.
3. Don't let distance deter you.
4. Don't be shy about speaking out.
5. Never doubt your ability to win.

His article was featured in *Family Circle* along with the addresses of consumer offices all over the U.S. and such useful information as the fact that you can get the names and addresses of the presidents of many American corporations by sending twenty-five cents for the booklet "Information for Consumers" to:

CUNA INTERNATIONAL
P. O. Box 431
Madison, Wisc. 53701

For writers, Brockman should have added to his five rules: learn the techniques for building a publishable exposé article, adding researched data and case histories to your own experience, and giving the other side of the story. (Because one individual or company was unfair doesn't mean that all in the same field are.)

As with all nonfiction articles, before writing the article be sure to structure it in the Hey! You! See! So! You! outline, the ABCs of Articles outline, or this more specific acronym-outline based on the word *exposé:*

E = *EVIDENCE* that the *EVIL EXISTS*
X = *X-PLUS RESEARCH* that enables the reader to *X-RAY* through the surface facts, statistics, and convincing case histories to deeper truths and understanding of the subject
P = *PERSONAL INVOLVEMENT* for the reader; how he is affected
O = *OBJECTIVITY* in gathering all facts for both sides, reinforced by the *OPINIONS* and *OBSERVATIONS of OTHERS*
S = *SEEDS of motivation* and the *SET-UP* that *STIMULATES* the evil and enables it to thrive and be a menace; the *START* of it all—who and what are responsible

É =   *EXAMPLES* of remedies to rectify the situation usually with *EMOTIONAL APPEAL* to the reader to act, feel, and think!

You should include all of these ingredients in any of the many different types of exposés you wish to write, whether it be consumer, medical, political, criminal, sports, economic, or some other field of reader interest.

Evidence That the Evil Exists

In order to be effective, an exposé must present evidence that an evil does exist. Your readers will not go beyond the first paragraph if the sense of the evil does not drive them to read further. The following published articles illustrate this principle.

"Beware Those 'Quick-Reducing' Gadgets" by Jean Carper (published in *Reader's Digest),* is captioned: "Despite the exotic claims for many farewell-to-fat devices, they are almost certain to reduce just one thing: your pocketbook." It begins:

> Via radio, television, and the press, Americans are being flooded with ads for miraculous-sounding "exercise" equipment: inflatable shorts "guaranteed to reduce your waist, hips, and thighs a total of 6 to 9 inches in just 3 days"; magic belts that "melt away excess flab"; body suits that "tone the muscles even while you sleep"; effortless exercisers that "streamline your body and strengthen your heart all in just 2 minutes a day." Whatever their shape, size, or price, they all imply a quick, easy substitute for proper diet and exercise—and Americans are forking out millions of dollars to acquire them.
>
> Yet, in the view of most medical authorities, these gadgets are ineffective and some are even dangerous . . . .

Another *Reader's Digest* exposé feature, "New Drug Menace: Teen-Age Drinking" by James Lincoln Collier, is captioned:

> Alcohol problems among adolescents are suddenly permeating every level of society, bringing misery and ruin to thousands of young lives.

It opens poignantly with direct, confessional quotes from youngsters whose alcoholism is typical of a burgeoning number of their middle-class peers. Immediately these appalling specifics are followed by verified statistics:

> According to the National Institute on Alcohol Abuse and Alcoholism, 1.3 million Americans between 12 and 17 have

serious drinking problems. About one-third of our high-school students get drunk at least once a month. And arrests of teen-agers for drunken driving have tripled since 1960; 60 percent of the people killed in drunken-driving accidents now are in their teens. A recent survey by the National Highway Traffic Safety Administration reveals that one-fourth of those high-school students who drink say they have driven three or more times when drunk.

From the beginning, there is no doubt that this evil *does* exist, affects everyone, and must be faced, studied, and solved.

Similar proof and dramatization of examples appear in every professional exposé. Be sure that yours opens with impact that is quickly documented. Write your own title and caption in a style that fits your planned markets and that competes with already published ones. Use something as strong as Nathan M. Adams's "The Shocking Thievery of Military Weapons," which is captioned:

> Political terrorists and common criminals are now using dead-ly grenades, automatic rifles, and even machine guns looted from U.S. military installations here and abroad.

or as in "Our Shameful Nursing Homes" by Kenneth Y. Tomlinson, which proves that:

> . . . in scores of America's 20,000 nursing homes, one finds irrefutable evidence of deaths due to neglect, dehumanizing physical facilities, food little better than garbage, and patients needlessly drugged so they will be easier to handle.

Gene Lowall's "$27 Million in 'Bogus Bread'" warns the readers of *Argosy* of the "hot cash ripoff," as counterfeiting is known in rackets jargon. Last year more than $27 million in bogus five, ten, and twenty dollar bills were seized. This is "only the tip of the iceberg of fake currency floating around in the $53 billion-odd legit currency circulating daily throughout the nation." Each Christmas season the evil increases as people spend more money more quickly; thus, *Argosy* made the article a December feature.

X-Plus Research That X-Rays through the Surface Facts

As you can see in the above examples, statistics give a solid basis to the premise and proof of the author's research and thoroughness. Other examples:

The cost of direct crime-fighting increased 143% from $3.5 billion in 1960 to $7.3 billion in 1971, with an even greater increase in 1972.

Nader Raider Dr. Sidney Wolfe maintains that more than 10,000 Americans die annually as a result of unnecessary surgical operations.

Arthur C. Clarke says nations have spent a trillion dollars on war in the last ten years, and other statisticians insist that we're trying to kill ourselves with sports on a lesser scale. Football has a ratio of 3.9 deaths for each 100,000 players; motorcycling, 278.6 deaths; horse racing, 133.3 deaths; auto racing, 120; and power boat racing, 15.7. These statistics lend weight to what might otherwise be a superficial statement of opinion.

Personal Involvement for the Reader

There are many ways to assure reader identification, as has been pointed out in Chapter 2. To recapitulate the advice given there, you should: (1) use the first person or the second person; (2) choose subject matter of general interest; and (3) be timely.

While many periodicals struggle for existence, the tabloids are increasing in titles and circulation, mostly because of their usually relevant, documented, identifiable exposés, which are published freely without advertising-pressure. Many are "firsts," later copied and followed through by major publications.

Here are some published titles from this easy-to-crack market:

FIRST PERSON: "The Cancer Threat in Our City Streets"; "Government Giving Away Our Coal Reserves"; "Our $125-a-Day Hospitals—Where Does All That Money Go?"

SECOND PERSON: "Your Job Can Give You Cancer"; "Your Tax $$$ Support Oddball Research Projects"; "Pre-Sweetened Cereals Can Be Dangerous to Your Health"; "You Are Being Poisoned by Pollution"; "Government Is Approving Thousands of Food Additives That Threaten Your Health"; "How Air Force Bureaucratic Bungling Costs You $3 Million"; "How You Lose Money by Being a Woman."

COMPREHENSIVE KEY WORDS AND SUBJECT MATTER: "Entire Populace Is Infected by Cancer-Causing Pesticide" (aldrin or dieldrin); "Drinking Water Can Cause Cancer"; "The Poison So

Powerful It Menaces All Americans"; "Cadmium Peril Feared Worse Than A-Leaks"; "Doctors Dupe Millions by Prescribing Worthless Drugs"; "140,000 Americans Die Each Year from Prescriptions Given by Doctors"; "Fluoride in Water Dangerous; Government Goofed in OKing Use of the Chemical" (Nader); "Insurance Hucksters' New Slogan: Con the Elderly"; "The UN Has Spent $5 Billion of American Taxpayers' Dollars but Won't Tell How"; "How the AMA Bought Off Congress"; "Common Aspirin Linked to Cancer"; "Runaway Inflation is Ruining the Health of Millions of Americans"; "Giant Aircraft Company Pocketed $6 Million of U.S. Taxpayers' Money"; "Deadly Chemical Still Widely Used" (dioxin); "Horrors of Silicone Quackery Force Female Victims to Live a Nightmare"; "Tax-chiseling Doctors Use Guise of 'Seminars' to Write Off POSH Trips."

You can find many more, all timely, shocking, but verified.

The personal scandal in many of these rags may turn you off, but the exposés are usually not in the same sensation-seeking category. In fact they often lead to investigations and reforms. Nor are the writers "hacks." Notice how many are bylined and/or use quotes by revered authorities, often U.S. legislators. For example: Senator Harry F. Byrd wrote a tabloid article titled "Millions of Your Tax Dollars Are Being Wasted on Foolish Research" (with detailed proof); Senator Mark Hatfield penned "U.S. Sent $25 million of Tobacco to Starving Nations Last Year—Under Food Program"; Senator Thomas F. Eagleton claimed that the "U.S. Postal Service Pocketed Millions in 'Air Mail Rip Off'"; William Proxmire claimed "Business Moguls Ruining Our Economy by Raising Their Own Salaries' Charges U.S. Senator"; and Representative George Mahon exposed "Pleasure Jaunts on Warplanes Costing You Countless Millions." There are also valuable exposés by law enforcement officers like Chicago Police Force Detective Jack Muller who proved that "Nine out of Ten Sex Criminals Are Going Free."

Objectivity in Gathering All the Facts

Don't go overboard in condemning the industry or subject you're exposing. If there's anything good to say about it, do so. If you're exposing mail-order fraud perpetrated by unethical operators in the $45-billion-a-year mail-order industry, you must give deserved credit to trustworthy companies like Sears, Montgomery Ward, and Spiegel's. If you're writing about college cheating, give examples of honest students. If you lower the boom on oil companies, lumber outfits, strip-miners, etc., be sure to "give the devil his due" and show improvements, ethical people involved, and services rendered to society, if any.

Seeds of Motivation—The Start and Cause

An exposé should provoke the reader to ask "Why?" Only through exposing causes can you hope to suggest remedies, and no remedy will ring true unless it treats the motivating or causative factors. The following should give you an idea of how this section of an exposé should be developed.

In the previously mentioned article "New Drug Menace: Teen-Age Drinking," several reasons for the situation are given:

(1) Social acceptability . . . "young people see movie and television stars drink, and many ads make liquor appear the normal accompaniment to having fun."

(2) Parents are more permissive, grateful that their kids aren't on drugs. Little do they realize the dangers of alcohol addiction and impending tragedies.

(3) Drugs are harder to get, more expensive, and not as glamorous as they used to be.

(4) The liquor industry is pitching to the youth market with "pop wines" called Strawberry Fling or Orange Fling, which are vodka mixes packaged to look like soda pop.

Another exposé feature alerts the readers to the alarming upswing in birth defects which mar the lives of 1,375,000 children under six. They spend 6,000,000 days a year in hospitals, costing $190,000,000. The four major and direct causes of birth defects are:

1. Drugs, including overdoses of synthetic vitamins.
2. Viruses, such as rubella, which causes German measles.
3. Radiation, such as X-ray treatment.
4. Faulty diet.

The seeds of motivation for youth's pill-popping mania include escapism from the pressures of the modern world, fear of the bomb, the desire for kicks, curiosity about what it's like to "turn on," the desire for self-gratification, rebellion, and the pill-popping example of their elders.

The devastation of strip-mining goes back to the Federal Mining Law of 1872 enacted during the gold fever in the West. Because the land from the Rockies to the Pacific was empty, unwanted, and government-owned, anyone could go digging or sluicing for minerals for five dollars an acre. The law still stands, permitting exploiters to ravish our forests and lands.

Examples of Remedies

This is the most important, and should be the best thought-out, section of your article. It is your chance to be *original* or different, since you will derive your solutions from many opinions. On the subject of oil spills, *Reader's Digest's* solutions include more responsible operational procedures on the part of drillers and transporters of oil, better training that will prevent tanker collisions, and stronger legislation of the type enacted in Maine, Washington, and Massachusetts (which enforces liability for oil spills.) *Science Digest*, on he other hand, elaborates on a new scientific method of freezing or jelling liquid oil when things begin to go wrong.

Ralph Nader's *Ladies Home Journal* feature exposing the two million unnecessary surgeries performed annually in the U.S. (as a result of which thousands die) advises:

1. Choose a surgeon with great care. (He then tells how.)
2. Find out whether the hospital in which the doctor practices is accredited by the American Hospital Association. One-third of all hospitals in America aren't.
3. What is the doctor's reputation?
4. Did he take a complete medical history, welcome your questions, and give you a thorough examination before recommending treatment?
5. If surgery or other radical treatment is prescribed, get other expert opinions.

Conclusion: Reputable doctors won't resent your consulting someone else. And if yours does resent it, this may be reason enough to question his judgment.

Prevention expands this valuable advice in its feature "A Shopper's Guide to Surgery: 14 Rules on How to Avoid Unnecessary Surgery." Condensed, they are:

1. Don't go directly to a surgeon for medical treatment.
2. Make sure the surgeon is Board certified (explained).
3. Make sure the surgeon is a Fellow of the American College of Surgeons.

4. Even if your family doctor and surgeon agree that surgery is necessary . . . get an independent consultation before subjecting yourself to surgery.
5. Make sure any surgery is performed in an accredited hospital.
6. Don't push a doctor to perform surgery on you.
7. Make sure your doctor and surgeon explain both the alternatives to surgery and the possible benefits and complications of surgery.
8. Frankly discuss fees.
9. Check the surgeon out with those who know him or have used him . . . patients and associates.
10. Make sure the surgeon knows and is willing to work with your doctor.
11. Consider a surgeon who is part of a group practice, preferably one that includes internists, surgeons, and other specialists.
12. Select a surgeon who is not too busy to give patients enough time and attention.
13. Be on guard if some of the operations that are most often performed are proposed for you (including those called "remunerectomies" due to the remunerative factor). Dr. Norman S. Miller writes of "hip-pocket hysterectomies" because the "only benefactor is the surgeon's wallet."
14. The patient, not the doctor or surgeon . . . is entitled to make the decision on wehther to have surgery. "This is your life."

Whether your remedies are many or few, they must be beneficial enough to make your exposé the "service" article that editors and readers want more than any other. Solutions to significant problems are so vital that entire articles are often devoted to one or more remedies. A few popular ones are: "New Gadgets to Stop Auto Theft," "TIP is Turning in Pushers," "How to Stop the VD Epidemic," "Suicide, the Preventable Loss," "Secret Witness— Criminal Catcher," "A Time for Toughness in America," and "How to Protect Your Child Against Drug Abuse."

Be sure that your exposé is not an incomplete "what's-wrong" feature, but a full-bodied "what-can-be-done-about-it" help to readers and society.

Outline for Maximum Effectiveness

Practice breaking down published articles of this type in the outline structures we have discussed and organize your material into one of the following frameworks.

The E-X-P-O-S-É Outline

The following is an analysis of "Air Pollution Inside Your Home" by Andy Sugar, published in *Saga*.

> EVIDENCE: The caption states: "According to the National Safety Council . . . 1,600 Americans lost their lives last year from being exposed to poisonous gases and vapors, with 1,100 of them occurring in and around the home . . . 70% of these deaths were due to carbon monoxide fumes from either defective heating equipment or automobiles left standing with their engines running."

> X-PLUS RESEARCH: Examples of families suffering because of chemical poisons in highly advertised household cleaners, carbon monoxide poisoning accelerated by air-conditioning, and other causes. Quotations from experts enhance the case histories and statistics. The Home Ventilating Institute said, "University tests have established that as much as 200 pounds of grease-laden moisture are given off in the average home." The study then goes on to name chlorine, the poison gas of World War I, and other death-causers.

> PERSONAL INVOLVEMENT: The second person is often used, and, of course, the subject does concern all readers. Example: "If having your lungs bombarded with carbon monoxide, poisonous utility gas, dust and grease particles, and asbestos fibers isn't enough to make indoor pollution a problem, there's always the danger from hundreds of household chemicals."

> OBJECTIVITY: The article explains what is being done to improve the situation by the GAO (General Accounting Office). It checks the ARS (Agricultural Research Service) and makes it enforce the Federal Insecticide, Fungicide, and Rodenticide Act, Manufacturers of sprays, powders, liquid cleaners, and other pollutants have been forced to put warnings on the containers.

> SEEDS OF MOTIVATION: The author examines the causes of pollution thoroughly: the highly advertised 60,000 pesticide products sold to the consumer, the dangerous mixtures, faulty appliances, heaters, as well as carelessness, etc.

EXAMPLES OF REMEDIES:

1. Don't use harsh sprays or other potentially dangerous chemicals for cleaning the house or killing pests. Use washing soda, wick dispensers, etc.
2. Keep humidity between 50 and 75 percent.
3. Install plastic instead of asbestos tile, floor, or wall coverings.
4. Do not run a car near a window or air intake vent.
5. Check all heating equipment for defects.
6. If possible, install electric or hot water heating systems in the home.
7. Most important, lend support to the many organizations fighting air pollution.

The HEY! YOU! SEE! SO! YOU! Outline

The following is an analysis of "Faulty Blood Bank Collection" by Ralph Nader, published in *Ladies Home Journal.*

HEY! Anecdote: 55-year-old Joseph W's open heart surgery was successful, but 80 days later he was back in the hospital with serum hepatitis (liver disease), which he'd contracted from contaminated blood during the operation.

YOU! You or your family may well be among 2,500,000 Americans who will receive blood transfusions in the next year. Women are concerned because many from 20 to 50 die as a result of bad blood in transfusions.

SEE! Causes of this evil: No control of donors or their health. A nine-month study by the *Chicago Tribune* turned up grisly accounts of people who are health risks making a "living" by selling their bad blood. Many skid row bums earn booze money this way. 20 percent of the nation's blood donations comes from commercial (profit-making) blood banks that have low or no standards. Many case histories, quotes, statistics such as: seventeen states have no laws on blood banking, and twenty-one have laws that protect blood bank hospitals and doctors from liability when transfused blood adversely affects a patient.

SO!
AND
YOU! This dangerous situation must be corrected and you should:

1. Donate your blood. If you have received, your responsibility is even greater to give.
2. Check hospital policies. Unless it uses only

> volunteer blood you have no assurance that you won't receive high risk blood.

3. Find out how volunteer blood banks operate in your community. On campuses? In skid row?

4. If victim learns that he has been given high risk blood, find out if the donor has been traced and removed from the list of suppliers.

5. Support corrective legislation like the Veysey Bill. Write your congressman! Get involved!

The ABCs of Articles Outline

The following is an analysis of *"Pesticides: Handle With Care"* by Fred Warshefsky, published in *Reader's Digest.*

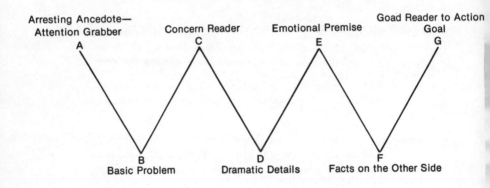

Arresting Ancedote— Attention Grabber
A

Concern Reader
C

Emotional Premise
E

Goad Reader to Action Goal
G

B
Basic Problem

D
Dramatic Details

F
Facts on the Other Side

A   About a 4-year-old girl who fainted and fell down, was rushed to the hospital where her head injuries misled doctors to diagnose and treat brain concussion. She died. "An autopsy showed the real killer—pesticide poisoning."

B   Pesticides designed to kill weeds, rats, and insects, poison and kill many American children and adults, but doctors are not required to report such cases.

C   150 million pounds of pesticides per year are sold in the form of dusts, sprays, jellies, and liquids, causing 50,000 cases of non-fatal pesticide poisonings by mouth alone, plus many more from skin absorption and inhalation, according to U.S. Poison Control Bureau of the U.S. Public Health Service. This affects most readers.

D   This section of the article distinguishes between 2 chemical groups of pesticides: chlorinated hydrocarbons and organic phosphates. The author explains differences and gives case histories, causes of the tragedies (carelessness, accidents, transferring pesticides to different containers, spilling, etc.)

E   We need increased educational warnings and controls through stricter licensing exams for exterminators and other commercial uses of pesticides to protect our population.

F   The U.S. Public Health Service is trying to enlighten the public through articles like this, through federal labeling laws demanding warnings about the dangers, and through forced registration with U.S. Department of Agriculture of the 60,000 different pesticides now on sale.

G   Goad the reader to be careful and follow safety rules set down by the American Medical Association:

1.   Lock up pesticides when not in use.

2.   Destroy or discard empty pesticide containers immediately.

3.   Close windows and keep children and pets inside closed houses during general community spraying, which should be done only in health emergencies.

4.   Doctors must be kept up to date with pesticide poisons and effects, and expert advice should be available to everyone on a twenty-four-hour basis.

5.   All users of these chemicals must be aware of their dangers.

Slant the Exposé for Specific Markets

Keep the E-X-P-O-S-É outline in mind as you slant your ideas for the many markets that publish exposés: men's, women's, special interest periodicals, and the mushrooming tabloids that are printed in imitation of the successful *National Enquirer.*

All of the various markets use these pointers, although the subjects and style vary with the magazine type. The men's magazines like *Playboy, Esquire,* and *Penthouse* reveal scandals and behind-the-scenes information on a higher level, such as corruption in government, the military, business, and medicine.

Well-researched articles in *Playboy* include "Who Runs the Government?" "The Drug Explosion" (which exposes corporate pushers), "Aerospaced Out," "The Public Be Damned!" "Confessions of a Corporate Headhunter," and "The Executive Stiletto."

Penthouse joined *Playboy* in denouncing Dr. David Reuben, author of the successful books *Everything You Always Wanted to Know about Sex . . . But Were Afraid to Ask* and *Any Woman Can.* One of their best exposés, "Licensed to Kill," was about the inequalities in licensing auto drivers and the resultant traffic fatalities. Typical *Esquire* exposés include "The Impotence Boom" and "Dr. Nolen Buys Cheap Aspirin." The latter, like *McCall's* woman-oriented feature, "The Overmedicated Woman," proves that Madison Avenue and the medical-pharmaceutical complex are making us hypochondriacs and drug addicts. Dr. William A. Nolen's feature opens:

> When I walk into a drugstore and see all the medicines on the shelves I wonder, "Who in the hell needs all those things? No one I know, certainly. Most of the patients I see aren't even sick."
> That's right. Somewhere between 50 and 60% of the patients who walk into a doctor's office have no physical ailments. Their backaches, headaches and "gassy" stomachs aren't caused by discs or brain tumors or ulcers; they're emotional in origin. . . .

His angle—that we don't need the heavily advertised medicines we're conned into buying—is reinforced with documentation and quotes from twenty-five doctors who tell what they take for a cold. *Not* the drugs they prescribe! Their favorite remedies range from Scotch or bourbon to "Norman Vincent Peale's Power of Positive Thinking combined with a little Christian Science." (Nolen later wrote the exposé book *Healing: A Doctor in Search of a Miracle.)*

Other *Esquire* exposés, like all well-slanted articles, reflect the interests of their readers and include "Learning to Love Unemployment" and "The Private Eye as Illegal Hero."

Argosy takes its role of grand protector so seriously that its prime monthly feature, "Watchdog for Justice," alerts its readers to the perpetrations of the "bad guys" and praises the "good guys" who help uphold justice.

The men's pulps strike no-holds-barred blows at wrongs in stronger, more sensational language. An example of the style Archer Scanlon uses in his "New Pesticides That Kill," which exposes fatal phosphate poisons (substitutes for banned DDT), opens with a HEY! YOU! shocker:

> How would you like to eat nerve gas, breathe nerve gas, have nerve gas enter your body through the pores of your skin?

You wouldn't?

Well, you are. No matter where you live, the nerve gas that the German scientists developed in the closing days of World War II, the nerve gas that leaked out of an Army storage tank in the West a couple of years ago and slaughtered 7,000 sheep, the nerve gas that can wipe out every creature on earth—*that* nerve gas is being used by farmers, ranchers, homeowners and little old ladies with flower boxes on their windowsills, to kill insects.

And it is killing people. . . . It is destroying other Americans, countless thousands of them, condemning them to insanity, paralysis or a brain-damaged condition that turns them into vegetables. . . .

Powerful throughout, it closes sardonically with:

. . . Why should Big Business poison us, pollute us, give us unsafe tires, killer cars, exploding aerosol cans? Yet Big Business continues to get away with it, despite all attacks on the venality that is killing and injuring thousands of us every year.

Have a good dinner tonight. And if you swallow some of the poison they're shoving down our gullets, relax. It's happening to all of us. Nobody's out to get *you*, man, so don't get paranoid about it. We're all drowning in the same sea of poison.

That's a sample of the hard-hitting style used in the well-structured, thoroughly documented exposés that abound in the men's pulps. Their subjects aren't much different from those that pepper the tabloids, so if you have ideas along this line, you have a wide range of markets. Here are some typical tabloid titles: "Water You Drink May Be Slowly Killing You," "Drinking Milk Is Deadlier Than Cigarettes," "TV Is Ruining Your Child's Future," "Communists Stole 1972 Olympics from Us by Doping Their Athletes with Forbidden Drugs," "Why Love Potions Are All Fakes," "Pollution Causes Cancer . . . Birth Defects," "TV Toy Commercials Brainwash Kids into Blackmailing Parents to Buy Them," "Government Weather-Tampering Is Causing World Floods," "Diesel Fumes, Not Cigarettes Are Responsible for the High Rise in Lung Cancer," "Light Pollution is Newest Threat to Health," and "U.S. Ranks 25th in Male Life Expectancy; 14th in Female: A Shocking Indictment of the American Medical System."

More low-key are the exposés in the traditional women's slicks that warn of dangers threatening the housewife-mother; these articles usually point out what's wrong with our schools, hospitals, politics, or laws. The new women's magazines like *Ms.* attack sex discrimination or race prejudice in such fields as jobs and credit, and contain such features "Stewardesses against Coffee-Tea-Or-Fly-Me." Some titles that have appeared in women's magazines are: "Why Doctors Are Losing Faith in the Pill," "Why Shouldn't Your Husband Take a Pill?" "Runaway Kids," "Gonorrhea: The Truth about a Shocking Epidemic," "Faulty Car Repairs," "X-Ray Hazards and How to Avoid Them," "High-Pressure Land Developers," "Corrupt Charity Rackets," "The Truth About I.Q. Tests," and "The Myth of the Civilized Divorce."

Restrictions in the women's magazines come from the advertisers who help finance the publication; you can't always expose such dangers as food coloratives or preservatives or poisons in cosmetics and household cleaners—or anything that might conflict with reader confidence in the magazine's advertisers.

If your gripe concerns a subject that might be taboo here, slant it for a man's magazine, tabloid, science, or nutrition publication like *Prevention,* which offered exposés that led to the banning of hexachlorophene, cyclamates, and other dangerous chemicals. They like authenticated articles like these: "Aspirin: Too Dangerous to Go Uncontrolled" by Jill Klein; "Food Labeling: A Joke Except for the Victims" by Arthur D. Koch; "FDA Wants to Stop Your Vitamin Supplements"; and "Battling the Medical Establishment."

Special interest magazines always want subjects in their field. Here are some *Science Digest* titles: "The Cancer Rip-Off" by Lee Edson; "Antibiotics that Kill" by Arthur Freese; "Nuclear Terrorism: A Threat of the Future?" by Theodore B. Taylor, Ph. D. with Douglas Colligan. Another article by Colligan, "What Scientists Do to Their Human Guinea Pigs," is captioned: "In the name of 'humanity' scientists experimenting with humans have done some remarkably inhumane things."

Quality markets like *Atlantic* or *Harper's* feature intellectual exposés like "Murder in the Schoolroom" by Charles Silberman, "The High Cost of Cure" by Dr. Michael Crichton, "Psychiatrists and the Poor" by Robert Coles, "Welfare, the Best of Intentions" by Irving Kristol, "Prisons" and "The Undertakers' Racket" by Jessica Mitford, "Soak the Sick: New Boom in Profit-Making Hospitals" by Roger Rapoport, and "The Curious Case of the Indicted Meat Inspectors" by Peter H. Schuck.

General publications like *Reader's Digest* buy material of concern to a large segment of the American public. Here are some of their favorites (in addition to those already mentioned): "Time to Root Out Labor Racketeers," "Closing Costs: A Booby Trap for Unwary Home Buyers," "A Clear Call to Congress—Control Spending Now!" "Danger! Hazardous Materials in Transit," "Accident Fraud Is Highway Robbery," "How Organized Crime Corrupts Our Law Enforcers," "Why Should Lawyers Have Fixed Minimum Fees?" "Tyranny in the IRS," "The Coal-Black Shame of the UMW," and "In Pro Sports, the Dollar Is King."

Exposé Don'ts

(1) Never write this type of article in white-heat anger or revenge, without calmly researching, structuring, and slanting for a specific readership.

(2) Don't try to cover too much territory or expose too many different evils in one article. Choose a narrow view of a broad subject that is relevant and significant.

(3) Don't write anything you cannot prove. Not just *your* opinions or experiences but complete documentation of your claims from reliable sources.

(4) Don't forget to keep a detailed bibliography of your source material. In the case of newspapers, write down the section and page number as well as date and title of paper.

(5) Don't dramatize or publicize wrong actions so explicitly that your article becomes a "How-To." There have been some on counterfeiting and making bombs, for example, that give explicit instructions. This is dangerous and the very reverse of the "service" article the editor and reader want from you.

(6) Don't write solid narrative—set forth your ideas in interesting anecdotes as well as giving statistics and specifics.

(7) Don't write exposés unless you first get a good lawyer!

8

Travel Writing
(Turn Your Recreation into Creation)

03/09/07

> The three great values of travel are educational, recreational and inspirational. Travel educates a person by broadening his outlook on life and his relations with people in a way that cannot be learned from books. . . .
>
> Travel provides a change of climate and scenery, which is often more necessary for certain ailments than medicine. Although travel may be considered the richest of all pleasures, it may also be considered a good investment.
>
> A. B. Zu Tavern

When you write and sell articles or books about your travels, you will reap richer rewards than other tourists because of special tax deductions for research related to writing. These are so great that most high-income authors travel to keep from giving so much of their earnings to the IRS.

In addition to incomparable inspiration, stimulation, and income, you'll soon learn that travel writing is easier to sell now that place dropping has succeeded name dropping in our current epidemic of travelitis.

More people are traveling, wanting to travel, and planning trips than ever before because of higher incomes, increased leisure, earlier retirement, cheaper fares, go-now-pay-later plans, travel clubs, charter flights, easy rentals of MLUs (Mobile Living Units, including

houseboats, motor homes, and trailers), and television's populariza-
tion of interesting places via travelogues and documentaries.

There are also many more markets for travel features. In
addition to travel standbys like *National Geographic, Holiday,* and
Travel and Leisure, every big airline has its own in-flight magazine, so
does every major auto manufacturer and auto club—as well as
insurance companies, like Allstate *(Discovery).* There's a host of new
trailer, bicycle, motorcycle, and MLU publications—all excellent
free-lance markets. Newspapers and their supplements, as well as
women's, men's, religious, juvenile, and career magazines, now
feature travel and travel-related material all year round instead of just
in season.

Study the specific markets because the slants differ, but this
can be to your advantage—you may be able to make several sales
from one vacation. Stress a sports, fishing, or hunting angle for the
male or outdoor market, a scenery-shopping-cultural-and-fun-things-
to-do viewpoint for a woman's magazine, and a historical, informative, or natural history emphasis for a youth publication.

Your writing will be more vivid and exciting as your joy in
escaping from humdrum routine into a colorful new environment
enlivens your descriptions. Before you go away (or on the way),
you'll read glowing, factual brochures and books about the place(s)
that will ignite your own enthusiasm and spark your writing style.

It's almost impossible to write dully about a trip you've
dreamed of taking, then worked long and hard to make materialize!

Pre-trip preparation, including reading and inquiring, will
enable you to get more out of your traveling so that it can be a thrilling
earn-while-you-learn, be-paid-as-you-go, fun-work experience. A
travel writer is like a fountain that works while it plays and plays
while it works—giving refreshment to others. One sage described
travel as "the frivolous part of serious lives and the serious part of
frivolous ones."

While jet-setters and randomly wandering tourists enact the
spirit of *dolce far niente* (it's sweet to do nothing), your own
productive pleasure in writing about your trip will make you realize
that it's sweeter and less guilt-inspiring to do something. You'll enjoy
sharing your travel experiences with an increasingly travel-hungry
public, helping others get more out of their trips, warning them of
pitfalls, and perhaps developing another hobby into cash—
photography.

"One of the good things about travel," says Alistair Cooke, "is the way it rouses some senses that tend to lie dormant, in a permanent snooze, in the country you live in." And after you're an established travel writer, you'll probably have expense accounts, pre-trip orders, and a travel column! And you'll be much more popular and important in our place-dropping society than if you just bore friends with home movies.

Today, there is a universal need for different people to know, understand, and respect each other. We cannot hate what we understand, we cannot war unless we hate, and we cannot be annihilated unless we war. You can contribute to world harmony by traveling in the friendly spirit the Greeks called *philoxenia*—"love of the foreigner." This is a greater asset than cash or knowledge of a language and will enable you to write travel material that may usher in a stimulating new lifestyle and perhaps lead to a book series like *Fodor's* (Travel Guides to) *Hawaii . . . Europe . . . Mexico,* etc.; Fielding's many guides to almost everywhere (four books on Europe alone—*Fielding's Guide to Europe, Conversation Guide to Europe, Fielding's Selective Shopping Guide to Europe,* and *Low Cost Europe);* Sydney Clark's *"All the Best"* books *(All the Best in South America . . . Scandinavia . . . Europe . . . Belgium . . . Caribbean . . . England . . . France . . . Italy . . . Mexico . . . The Orient);* Arthur Frommer's (known as "the guy who got rich giving others the travel itch") never-ending "_____ *on $5 a Day"* series; John Gunther's *"Inside"* books *(Inside Asia . . . Europe . . . Africa . . . Latin America);* Willard Price's *Incredible Africa* and *The Amazing Amazon;* Kate Simon's *New York, Places and Pleasures* and *Mexico, Places and Pleasures.*

The T-R-A-V-E-L Outline

The following are some specific tips to help you professionalize your "Where-To" writing, based on the word *travel.*

T = Timeliness *and* titular radiance
R = Reader rapport *and* research
A = Angle *and* anecdotes
V = Visualization *and* verisimilitude
E = Emotional enthusiasm *and* expenses (exchange)
L = Lead *and* location

T = Timeliness

Be sure to write about a place you have been to recently so that your facts are authentic and up-to-date. If you were there long ago, check with current tourist bureaus, consuls, and travelers, or make a return trip. Your reader wants accurate information, prices, and conditions as they will exist when he goes there.

T = Titular Radiance

Use your imagination and word wizardry to give a place an intriguing label or nickname. This trick, which so enhances today's travel features, dates back to 985 when Norwegian explorer Eric the Red named a country that was under 10,000 feet of ice "Greenland" to lure chilly Scandinavians there.

Think up glittering titles that peg the *essence* of the place and study published examples of titular radiance like these:

"Belize, the Awakening Land," "Chelsea: London's Haven of Individualists," "Silvery Taxco: Mexico's Sterling City," "Hydra—Isle of Joy for All Escapists," "Vancouver, City of Charm and Chairlifts," "Paris the Pickpocket" (also called "City of Light"), "Caloric Copenhagen," "Alaska— America's Jolly White Giant," "Columbia—Gem of the Continent," "Corsica—Scented Isle," "Kenya: A Swinging Preserve," "Zurich— Enchanting Toy City," "Glamorous Morocco: Part Bible, Part Hollywood" (General Patton's term), "Iceland: Land of Steaming Hot Waters," "Freeport, Grand Bahamas: Klondike in the Tropics" (also called "Monte Carlo in the Gulf Stream"), "Romantic Rio: City of 1000 Delights," "Sintra: Eden of Portugal," "Saalbach: Austria's Hidden Ski Jewel," "Côte d'Azur. The Artists' Workshop," "Cripple Creek: A Ghost Town with Spirit," "Liège: City at the Crossroads," "Teheran—A Magic Carpet to the Land of 1,001 Sights," "Gibraltar: England with Sun," "Rarotonga Island—A Paradise Found," "Civita— A Doomed City Returning to the Dust," "Phoenix— Playland for Sports Devotees and Sunday Cyclists," "Sri Lanka: Undiscovered Gem," "Calcutta: India's Maligned Metropolis," "Amiable Amsterdam," "Bangkok—City of Angels," and "Martinique—Pearl of the Antilles."

Jerry Hulse refers to the nickname "Wrinkle City" for Victoria, British Columbia, because:

> The title alludes to retired military officers who sun themselves on the city's benches and stroll its grassy lanes. Some claim there is more action during a blizzard in Twin Falls than one will encounter in Victoria the entire year.

Even in a composite travel article like Lowell Thomas's "Nature's Seven Greatest Wonders" he uses descriptive titular radiance for each: "Grand Canyon: Greatest Cleft on Earth . . . Victoria Falls: The Smoke That Thunders . . . Glacier Bay: Alaska's Frozen Dreamland . . . Mammoth Cave: Kentucky's Ancient Honeycomb . . . Mt. Everest: Earth's Pinnacle . . . Baikal: Siberia's Giant Lake . . . Yellowstone National Park: A World Apart."

R = Reader Rapport

You must take your reader to your chosen destination and make him or her (not you or someone else) the hero of the adventure. There are two opposite ways to involve the reader: the bargain-paradise approach, which implies that he can't afford *not* to go there, and the snob pitch, which points out how *in* this place is to "important people"— therefore it's not to be missed. Relating the exotic to the familiar is also an effective technique:

> . . . Few foreign influences have so great an impact on the American cultural scene as the art of Japanese gardening. Thousands of Americans come to Kyoto each year primarily to see the great gardens here. Some come simply to enjoy them. Others come to glean some bit of artistry that might be incorporated in a garden back home.
> (Louise Dibble)

Using the second person puts your reader in the scene but is monotonous if it's overdone:

> Did you ever think you'd like to own an island? A small, peaceful place in a warm climate, surrounded by fish-filled waters, with a comfortable, Somerset Maugham sort of house in which you could play king of the mountain? . . . Marina Cay is a 6-acre polka dot in the Virgin Islands. . ."
> (Judith M. Farris)

or:

> Maybe you'll travel to the moon someday and maybe you won't. But in the meantime there's a reasonable facsimile of it as near to you as southeastern Idaho.
> (Rafe Gibbs)

or:

> You can do most anything—even skiing—on a tight budget.
> I stumbled onto ways to shuss down some of Europe's most glamorous slopes for a song.
> (Dori Lundy)

R = Research

You will be a more proficient travel writer—and thus a more salable one— if you follow the advice of Sam Johnson, who wrote: "He who would bring home the wealth of the Indies, must carry the wealth of the Indies with him. So it is with traveling: A man must carry knowledge with him if he would bring home knowledge." Before you go away, bone up on everything you can find on the region(s) you will visit, all the way from ancient legends and history to the newest roads, revolutions, politics, and personalities. Read enough to get different opinions so that you can write from a fresh angle and so that you are acquainted with a complete bibliography of the subject.

Give your reader accurate facts and statistics. He depends on you to be an authority who obtained information from reliable sources. Look at this opening:

> The world has never seen anything like it before or since—700 rooms; a 1,200-seat theatre; 180 miles of aqueducts and canals to supply water for 1,400 fountains; a greenhouse for 3,000 orange and pomegranate trees. It took 36,000 men to build it, 5,000 servants to run it. Operating costs were staggering.
>
> We speak, of course, of the fabled Castle of Versailles. Versailles was built mostly by Louis XIV in the late 1600's. But its early age of opulence ended abruptly with the French Revolution and was followed by an era of dismal neglect. . . .
> ("Versailles Reborn" by J. D. Ratcliff, published in *Reader's Digest*)

You may know nothing of Bhutan, located north of India in the Eastern Himalayas, but John Scofield's research for his *National Geographic* feature "Bhutan Crowns a New Dragon King" tells you of its new king, 18-year-old Jigme Singye Wangchuck, "the youngest of the world's 29 reigning monarchs," and of its capital Thimphu, "hulking amid rice fields," then and now:

> A decade ago 8,500-foot-high Thimphu lay at the end of a seven-to-ten-day trek through leech-infested jungles and up steep river gorges. Now an asphalt road coils 112 miles northward from the Indian border to span the 45-mile crow's-flight distance, reducing the journey to six hours by jeep.

His richly researched article yields facts about its Buddhism:

> Giant prayer wheels stand at the entrances to most Bhutanese temples. The huge drums are tightly packed with strips of paper

on which a four-word prayer, *"Om mani padme hum"* is repeated, often millions of times.

Then Scofield explains the natives' belief that endless repetition of this prayer ("The jewel in the lotus") will enable them to enter paradise without the cycle of death and rebirth.

A = Angle

One of the main differences between an unsalable, amateurish article and a professional success is that the former slapdashes kaleidoscopic impressions haphazardly or narrates his own itinerary, whereas the latter uses a single approach that puts the place in clear focus for the reader. An often-written-about locale can be freshly described and sold if a new angle is presented. In an *Esquire* feature, Ray Bradbury presents a *reverse* rebuttal to all anti-Los Angeles articles, his angle is clear in the title "Los Angeles is the Best Place in America." It opens:

> This will not be an article describing the acne, carbuncles, dandruff, sexual gymnastics, racial difficulties, political ineptitudes, hairy freak-outs or the non-rapid transits of L.A. Others have already spat on us, bit, pummeled, stoned, kicked and despised us over the years. . . As yet unborn, our enemies mound us with flowers and spade our burial ground.
> I come then, not without some irony, to praise. . . .

Encapsulated, his favorable angle is reinforced shortly thereafter:

> . . . our madness is light, free, frivolous, witty; we self-start, we self-propel toward creativity.
> Energy attracts energy.
> Freedom attracts freedom.
> Openness of the few can become openness of the many.
> That is why, by this century's end, L.A. will be the one and only most important city in the entire U.S.A.
> Tomorrow the World.
> Why?
> Because for centuries mankind has prated and declaimed about the importance of the individual.
> Rarely until now has a city quite like L.A. arrived as seedbed to not force-grow but encourage the single man, the single woman, with the single idea which can change a town, blush a state to a new color, and finally renovate an entire nation.
> L.A., the flood tide of that vast middle class we pretend to be afraid of, will be the salvation of the Ideas of our Time. . .
> How come?

> Because we paraphrase Oscar Wilde thusly:
> Life will die if held too tightly
> Life will fly if held too lightly,
> Lightly, tightly, how do we know
> Whether we're holding or letting life go.
> The Angeleno knows exactly how not to hold. How to shape
> without shaping. How to know without knowing. The old Zen
> archer would recognize his familiar silhouette treading the
> coastline horizon at dawn. . . .

Harrison E. Salisbury's angle on Russia (in *Travel & Leisure*) reiterates Churchill's statement: "Russia is a riddle wrapped in a mystery inside an enigma."

Noel F. Busch's angle in his article "Dizzying, Dazzling Houston," is put over in a dizzying, dazzling style. For instance:

> . . . Big, bustling, booming. It can dazzle a newcomer. Gleam-
> ing fifty-story skyscrapers just up. High-speed expressways
> twist and spin off in every direction. Tree-and-grass-covered
> pedestrian malls on built-up concrete platforms span streets and
> highways. It's the city of tomorrow. . . .

After zooming the reader all around the miracle metropolis that rises from the prairie, and introducing fabulous people and places, the author ends up trying to figure out what makes it tick:

> But I found out that Houston does not tick, it spins, and that
> trying to get a clear picture of everything going on produced a
> kaleidoscopic blur. Houston is, as a visiting Scotsman once
> commented, "a place where the traveler can no longer
> rationalize or explain what he sees."

Study all the ways others have written about your subject so that you can stress a different approach.

Avoid straight narrative by dramatizing your material with anecdotes—little scenes spiked with human interest. Even the straight-laced *National Geographic* often opens its articles with an anecdote, perhaps a humorous one like:

> One wintry morning an indignant lady telephoned
> Washington's most popular weather forecaster with this fiery
> blast:
> "I wish you'd come out here and scoop this 6 inches of 'partly
> cloudy' off my driveway!"
> (Walter Orr Roberts, "We're Doing Something About the
> Weather")

Here's another humorous anecdote that opens a *National Geographic* article by characterizing "Finland, Plucky Neighbor of Soviet Russia" (by William Graves):

> A Finnish lumberjack, so the story goes, was chased by a large and hungry bear. Coming to a river, the lumberjack jumped in and swam halfway across, when he noticed a second bear waiting for him on the other bank. Then, say the Finns, the lumberjack began to laugh—because he had heard that laughing prolongs a man's life.   Finland has much in common with the lumberjack; it is a country often caught between bears. Through centuries of precarious history, the Finns have been threatened, fought over, invaded and exchanged among powerful neighbors. With Russia alone, they have fought dozens of wars—and lost nearly all of them.
>
> Like the lumberjack, Finns are proverbial for their *sisu* —a word that means, among many things, hardiness. Like the lumberjack, too, the Finns have a gift for laughter. In 1939 when the Soviet Army invaded Finland, outnumbering the defenders by astronomical proportions, the Finns joked grimly among themselves: "So many Russians! Where will we bury them all?"

More serious is the following anecdote that opens a more frightening article in the *Geographic*:

> A score of naked warriors stared at us, granite-faced. Some of them spoke urgently in the gutteral language of West Irian's Asmat people, but I could not understand.
>
> As I helped my wife out of our canoe onto the steep bank below Sagopo village, I looked in vain for the chattering women and children who usually come to the landing place to welcome strangers. A single female face, daubed with ocher as for some special occasion, appeared at the doorway of a thatched stilt house. The woman handed a bow and arrows to the warrior leader and then vanished.
>
> The atmosphere disturbed me. The men were tense and uneasy, and the village was unnaturally silent.
>
> "There's something wrong, isn't there?" I asked . . . our linguistic companion.
>
> "Yes, and we'd better get out of here," Bert answered tersely. "I'll explain why later."
>
> We shoved off into the shallow, swift Undir River. I started the outboard motor. Quickly it pushed us around a bend out of sight of the village.
>
> "It sounds unbelievable," said Bert, "but Andreas and Ndep here"—he indicated our nervous guides—"say we walked right into a headhunting raid."
>
> (Malcolm Kirk's "Headhunters in Today's World")

Pertinent anecdotes should be used to relieve the monotony of narrative description. They can be about anything of interest in the present, future, or even legends about the past. In "Greece's Immortal Isles," Christopher Lucas tells us:

> After God created planet Earth . . . He had a handful of rocks left over; so He tossed them over his shoulder and they became the Isles of Greece. This divine windfall totals some 1,500 islands (only 166 are inhabited) tucked away in the Aegean Sea.

Appropriate anecdotes that strengthen the mood and angle can appear anywhere—beginning, middle, or end, like the following conclusion of John Kings' *Reader's Digest* Armchair Travelogue, "Wyoming: The Land Beyond the Plains," the angle of which is the anti-progress individuality of the plainspeople:

> "Why," boasted one Easterner, "in New York we could put all of you out here into *one* of our skyscrapers."
> "Mebbe so," replied one oldtimer. "But we ain't gonna like it!"

V= Visualization and Verisimilitude

Use graphic writing, similes, metaphors, and a plethora of details to create word snapshots that make the place come to life. Coyote country in Arizona is the land of "tall saguaro cactus and desert pink sunsets. It's winter vacation country. Sunny days and 10-gallon hats. A mesquite fire at night and a coyote yip-yipping to a skyful of a million diamond stars."

Macao is "the Portuguese eyelash hanging on the mainland of China"; Puget Sound is "a collection of islands that on the map looks as if it had been put together by a jigsaw puzzle-maker with a mean streak"; New Mexico is "where that which is ancient, atomic, arid, and astonishing all blend together into an unbelievable mosaic as colorful as any ever designed by a Navajo blanket craftsman."

Athletic imagery appears in *Sports Illustrated*:

> Like a gambler trying to kick the habit, the Colorado River rushes westward toward Las Vegas, then makes a sharp left turn at the city limits and runs straight down the map to the Gulf of California.

Use vivid writing alive with sensory stimuli like:

> (Quebec's) air is singing with the ringing of church bells, the lonesome plaint of steamboat whistles and the beeping of horn-happy motorists. Everywhere the sky is pierced by towers,

cross-topped spires, statuary, and steep copper roofs designed to shed snow. Many of the buildings have a dreamy, slightly lopsided look, reminiscent of a medieval French town.

Not just sights and sounds, but smells, too! One article points out that Greeks love sweet-smelling basil and grow it everywhere— in windowboxes, in gardens, and around doorsteps. They may even greet you with a sprig of basil or wear it behind their ears. "Most Aegean isles smell of thyme, sage, oregano and of jasmine when the night is still and warm. But Samos blends with these the scent of pine woods," (Melville Bell Grosvenor in *National Geographic*).

Sprinkle your description with flavorful words that are typical of the place. If you write about Greece, you might shudder in the breath of the *meltemi* (winds); drink *ouzo* or *retsina* or *barbounia* wines; feast on *souvlaki* (shish kebab); play *tavli* (backgammon), or shy away from dark caves in which there may be *kalikantzaroi* (gremlins). For "good morning," people say *kalamari*, which sounds like *kali mera*, the word for squid—a situation that has great potential for an anecdote.

E = Emotional Enthusiasm

Since the travel article is a where-to-go piece, it should sparkle with excitement that makes the reader want to go there. Be enthusiastic about the place and its special events, whether you describe hiking up holy Mt. Athos in Greece, skiing on a volcano in northern New Zealand, do-it-yourself pearl diving on Venezuela's Margarita Island, or enjoying a luau in Hawaii, a tamaaraa in Tahiti, the native Wayangs shows in Singapore, a Noh play in Tokyo, or any particular feast, festival, or fiesta.

Try to submit seasonal material six months ahead of the date on which the event occurs: submit in February a piece featuring Danish Days (late August or early September) in Solvang, California; April for Aloha Month in Hawaii (October) and six months ahead of Morocco's annual Marrakech Fantasia, when all the tribes gather to perform on lightning-quick Arabian steeds.

Capture the anticipation of future happenings rather than reiterating familiar facts of the past or present — for instance, the proposed future replacement for the ancient Colossus at Rhodes by sculptor Felix de Weldon, who built the Iwo Jima War Memorial in Washington.

Don't be afraid to be emotionally enthusiastic about the *mood* of the place (which jibes with the angle). Contrast the following:

[Cuernavaca, Mexico, is] the only place in the world where the citizens suffer from year-round spring fever. Even the jumping beans don't jump.

versus:

Vehemence, gustiness and a tendency to roughhouse have always been characteristic of Venezuela. A visitor today encounters a somewhat rowdy, even trigger-happy atmosphere.

On the first night of Carnival in February, I went to a flamboyant dance in a leading hotel in Caracas. . . . Two tough cops with submachine guns searched every man who entered— mostly opulent citizens of the upper class.

Enthusiasm should electrify your nonfiction as much as your fiction, as Bradbury's does in the aforementioned *Esquire* article. In building his pro-Los Angeles angle and mood, he uses enthusiastic imagery to put down the cities that usually put down L.A.:

San Francisco is the Taj Mahal, a beautiful corpse laid out, wondrous to see, but as procreative as a hermaphrodite.

Chicago is Lenin's Tomb. People line up to go in and look at the soot and the rabbits. They come out smiling. Death makes them happy.

Detroit is ten thousand miles up the wrong end of the rhino.

And then there is that larger mugger's mausoleum on the East Coast, that ninety billion dollar funeral on its way to oblivion, anxious for mortality so that it can one day be reborn . . . New York . . . it is Doomed.

No matter what you say, be enthusiastic. Remember, readers read to keep from being bored!

E = Expenses (Exchange if foreign)

Inform your reader of the current situation in currency and expenses. Foreign exchange broker Nicholas L. Deak says:

The majority of travelers still carry only dollars because they are so utterly unfamiliar with the currencies of foreign countries. But since the dollar has grown weaker, Americans traveling abroad are finding it more desirable to carry some currency of the countries they're going to.

In my own experience, hotel rates in Paris and London doubled in less than three years. Make sure your information regarding expenses is as up-to-the-minute as possible, and advise travelers of the best places to exchange U.S. money or traveler's checks.

L = Lead

Your opening must attract immediately, often giving the location as well as combining other facets of the T-R-A-V-E-L outline. It must fit the subject and the magazine. Virile, gutsy leads for *True* begin with a bang:

> The Landrover roared hell for leather across the plain, jouncing, twisting and skidding as John Taylor fought to get within noosing range of the big gnu.

Another:

> When men decided to throw a fence across the Colorado River, one of America's wildest rivers, things began to happen. Cities were populated, railroads were built and a sportsman's paradise was created.

Other snappy leads:

> There's a real revolution that the silent majority should be aware of: The revolution in off-season travel in Europe.
> (Arthur Frommer, "Europe, We Love You but the Season's Over," *Holiday*)

> "If the world had any ends," wrote Aldous Huxley four decades ago, "British Honduras would certainly be one of them."
> This statement is still widely quoted but I disagree...
> (Louis de la Haba, "Belize, the Awakening Land."
> *National Geographic*)

> It's obvious that the composer of "Moonlight on the Ganges" never came anywhere near the Ganges.
> You remember he pictured it as one of the world's truly romantic rivers? Well, had he seen it he'd probably have given his song a title something like "Here's Mud in Your Eye."

> Salem, Mass.—This town may be bewitched, but its citizens aren't the least bit bothered or bewildered.
> Awed perhaps—by the endless procession of tourists who keep the cash registers ringing like burglar alarms.
> (Jerry Hulse)

A quotation lead is a good way to avoid the all-narrative trap. The quotes may be old sayings, proverbs, or lines spoken or written by named or unnamed persons. It's worth your while to do enough research to find pertinent quotes to include in your article whether in the body or at the beginning.

Here are a few quotation article openings:

"Poor Sitka: So close to heaven, so far from the Czar."
This saying dates from 1799, when east-thrusting Russian traders chopped out a city facing Siberia in the forbidden islands off Alaska's southeastern peninsula.
("A Touch of Russia in U.S." by Stuart Nixon)

"Peru is a difficult, sometimes uncomfortable, and in places, cold country—I was thrilled every minute," said a North American woman traveling in Peru.
("Peru in the Process of Change" by Despina Messinesi)

"If you want to see the most beautiful country in the world," Renoir once wrote of the Côte d'Azur, "here it is."
Although it was Cézanne who, in 1893, first discovered the intense sunlight, the sparkling Mediterranean, and the silent groves of cypress, olive and eucalyptus, there is perhaps no artist of the first century more closely identified with the French Riviera than Renoir.
. . . he was followed there by Matisse, Dufy, Bonnard, Cocteau, Léger, and Modigliani. After World War II, Picasso and Chagall arrived.
("Côte d'Azur: The Artists' Workshop" by Ivan Fuldauer)

Note the principle of name dropping and how appropriate it is here.

"Shrimp among whales," a proverb calls Korea, long a battleground for Asian power struggle.
("Rare Look at North Korea" by H. Edward Kim)

L = Location

Your reader wants to be place-oriented, the sooner the better. Alec Blasco-Ibanez opens with the location of Iceland:

. . . this Kentucky-sized North Atlantic isle sitting placidly at some 64 degrees north—just south of the Arctic circle—or about the same latitude as Fairbanks, Alaska, southern Greenland, Siberia and the middle of Norway, Sweden, Finland, is really the land of 10,000 smokes or geysers, set upon a lukewarm isle warmed by some big volcanoes and the Gulf Stream.

Then he proves that *Greenland* should be called *Iceland*, as we pointed out in the beginning of this chapter!

He begins a piece about San Lucas, Baja California, also by locating it: "It's the southernmost tip of California, and it extends dramatically out into the heaving swelling Tropic of Cancer waters where the Pacific meets the Sea of Cortez."

Try to plan to include most, if not all, of the T-R-A-V-E-L techniques in your article and look for them in published ones. Take Alan Linn's Armchair Travelogue in *Reader's Digest*:

TITULAR RADIANCE—"Wild, Lovable Crete" (the title, mood and trait)

RESEARCH—Specific figures as to size, population of 75,000, streets named for Cretan and Greek revolutions, historical data (ancient and recent), specific dress, food, drink, customs, etc.

ANGLE—Previewed in the title, the wild-lovable trait is dramatized in the opening ANECDOTE:

> Yorgo puffed thoughtfully on his gurgling water pipe. The bells on his sheep jingled musically in the Mediterranean twilight. Almost every evening since I'd come to the island of Crete, Yorgo and I had shared a cup of thick Greek coffee beneath a scented lemon tree and engaged in the No. 1 Cretan pastime —arguing.
> "That movie, *Zorba the Greek*, was unfair to us," Yorgo asserted. "It implied that Cretans are wild and impetuous. We were so insulted that we tore up the theatre."
> "That shows how emotional you are," I said. "Nikos Kazantzakis, who wrote the story, was a Cretan. He knew you best. Wild, tender, crazy, maddening—Zorba epitomized the Cretan character."
> "Po, po, po, po!" Yorgo clucked. Then he was whistling "Zorba's Song," snapping his fingers and prancing over the cobblestones. I had lost another argument. On Crete, dancing always beats logic.

This opening anecdote (as well as the rest of the article) is alive with *all* the techniques: READER RAPPORT through characterization, VISUALIZATION and VERISIMILITUDE, EMOTIONAL ENTHUSIASM—all accomplished in an attractive LEAD. Then he *locates* Crete and gives *researched* facts about its present, past, and ancient past.

Add Human Interest

Human interest is so vitally important to travel writing that without it even a feature that has superb research and brilliant descriptions of places can be lifeless and unsalable. People are always primarily interested in people. This does not mean you and/or your traveling companion(s), but colorful personalities who typify the area and the culture you are writing about and who give the reader an idea of the kind of persons and attitudes he is liable to meet there.

The following suggestions should show you how you can inject human interest into your travel writing.

(1) Tell how the denizens of this area differ from other people. Honor Tracy's article "With Pride as Their Armour" is captioned: "Whatever may have been felt about Spaniards . . . no one has ever found them dull," and it opens:

> Noble, haughty, passionate, stoical, lazy, devout, generous, frugal, brave, cruel, proud—such tags have been freely bestowed on the Spanish race throughout its history. . . Whatever may have been felt about Spaniards it was not indifference.

But generalizations can never be as effective as individualized portraits like the one in the preceding Crete example. In Patricia Raymer's *National Geographic* article "Wisconsin's Menominees: Indians on a Seesaw," we meet:

> Sanome Sanapaw. . . stout and barrel-chested [who] set the pace as he lumbered through the ancient unaxed forest. Like his father before him, the 59-year-old Menominee had taught his sons all they needed to know about setting bear traps, tracing deer tracks, and hauling in a sturgeon bigger than a man.

We also meet Jerry Sanapaw, an educated Vietnam vet:

> Jerry, dark-eyed and muscular, wants to remain with his people. But he is superstitious about being too successful among them. "You know, my brother LeRoy died a year ago," Jerry recalled. "His bad luck came, I know, because he was better than the rest. He was an Indian dancer, winning awards, ribbons, recognition all over. When you're a Menominee you can't stand out, you can't be better off than your brothers."

(2) Give that peoples' impact on society, perhaps their importance in history. Here's a brief excerpt from Samuel W. Matthews's "The Phoenicians: Sea Lords of Antiquity":

> They grew rich on commerce, on hewing the timber that covered their home mountains, on skillful working of bronze and iron and glass, gold and ivory, on dyeing cloth purple with an extract of sea snails. They traded with Egypt's pharaohs, brought King Solomon's gold from Ophir, fought for Xerxes against the Greeks, were beseiged by Nebuchadnezzar and Alexander the Great, and from Carthage . . . sent Hannibal to beset the Romans in their own land.
>
> From about 1200 B.C. to the razing of Carthage in 146 B.C., the Phoenicians wrote into history and legend a thousand years

of daring voyages, of tireless productivity, of sure genius in trade and diplomacy.

(3) Namedrop anyone of importance who has been associated with the place or who has been there. This is one of the techniques that enhances the style of Alec Blasco-Ibanez and qualifies him as a travel editor. Writing about Wyoming, he says:

> Charlie Russell captured the colors, shapes, moods, topography on his unforgettable canvasses. . . .
> "It looked like Spain, but it was Wyoming," wrote Papa Hemingway in his nostalgic *Wine of Wyoming.* . . .
> The others have been here too . . . Remington, Zane Grey, Lord Gore. The Irish aristocrat on one of his expeditions west, got captured by the Indians, his baggage and animals taken, and started the streaking fad—the big chief also took his clothes. He had to walk back bare to St. Louis.

Name dropping, combined with such anecdotal touches, is much more dramatic than straight description. In another feature the same author calls Istanbul, Turkey, "a Humphrey Bogart and Sidney Greenstreet world of intrigue and adventure." He adds:

> They've all been here at one time or another. That is the saints and sinners of the past 2,000 years.
> Alexander, Xerxes, the Caesars, the field marshals of Genghis Khan, the Crusaders who sacked the city far worse than the "Infidels," Richard the Lionhearted, Marco Polo, the Catalon Mercenaries, Sulyman the Magnificent, Lord Nelson, Lizst, D. H. Lawrence and Winston Churchill.

(4) Quote what some well-known person has said of the place, especially if it adds flavor and harmonizes with your angle. It's surprising, for instance, how Mark Twain and the very ill Robert Louis Stevenson got around in days when travel was really travail!

In writing about the Kentucky Derby, Peter Chew quotes Irvin S. Cobb, "the homespun philosopher of Paducah":

> . . . imagine a track that's like a bracelet of molten gold encircling a greensward that's like a patch of emerald velvet. . . All the pretty girls in the state turning the grandstand into a brocaded terrace of beauty and color such as the hanging gardens of Babylon never equaled. . . All the assembled sports of the nation going crazy at once down in the paddock. . . Until you go to Kentucky and with your own eyes behold the Derby, you ain't never been nowheres and you ain't never seen nothin'!

Travel-Related Articles

In addition to places and people, you should be on the lookout for travel-related ideas that will inform, instruct, inspire, and/or entertain the reader who is interested in going places and doing, seeing, and learning things. Humor is always a good bet. Ernest Havemann pokes hilarious fun at some globe-trotting kooks in his feature "All Right, Why *Do* the Wrong People Travel?" which is captioned: "Add to the non-book and the non-author and even more flourishing species of our time: the non-traveler."

Here are a few titles of published articles that are not straight "Where-To" pieces but are of the travel-related types of features that editors like to buy: "Applying for a Passport—Or, Your Hidden Past and What's in a Name," "Your Life Is an Open Bag," "The Customs Service—How to Protect Valuables," "A Short History of Luggage," "Freighter Travel," "Energy Conservation: Bus Travel," "The Most Scenic Trips You Can Make by Rail," "Bus Wheeling Around in Europe," "Wild-River Floating in Idaho," "Riding Mexico's Funky Old Ferrocarril," and "The New Innocents Abroad," which is captioned:

> Down Europe's airport corridors they come, flightbags packed with all the paraphernalia of youthful travel—the new breed of American tourist. Inevitably under 30 and increasingly under 20, they are changing both the face of European tourism and America's image abroad.

What travel sidelights can you think of? Perhaps you can produce several different articles about the same trip. Sometimes, if your main piece is too long, you may be able to extract a separate article from it, making two sales instead of one.

Animals are popular subjects in travel publications. Here are a few titles from *National Geographic*: "Europe's Shy and Spectacular Kingfisher," "At Home with the Bulldog Ant," "How the Decoy Fish Catches Its Dinner," "The Maligned Coyote," "The 'Lone' Coyote Likes Family Life," "Last Stand for the Bighorn," "The Heron that Fishes with Bait," "Bats Aren't All Bad," "Beavers—Master Mechanics of Pond and Stream," and "The American Lobster—Delectable Cannibal."

Maybe you can sell enough travel-related or local (that is, near to your home) articles to finance an exotic vacation!

Travel Writing Dos

(1) Start collecting and studying travel brochures to give you ideas for trips and places to write about. You can get excellent ones from the U.S. Government Printing Office, from your local and nearby Chambers of Commerce, travel agencies, and auto clubs. Writing and selling features about local places and events can finance more distant trips. A. B. Zu Tavern wrote: "By starting with trips to nearby places and radiating outward, like ripples on a pond when a stone is thrown in, travel can be made a lifelong experience with a profit."

(2) Study the colorful style of travel brochures and published articles and make your writing even more vivid. In *Playboy*, John Clellon Holmes writes:

> Down there, across the milky-green Arno at low water, Florence lay spread out in a shallow bowl of hills—its pale yellow piazzas, and walls of earthy pink, and tiled roofs in terraces of faded ocher as graphic as a high-definition photograph in the startling clarity of the Tuscan morning. "From up here, in this light, you'd never guess that it's become a madhouse," I had to admit.
>
> ("Thanksgiving in Florence")

(3) Develop the habit of breaking down published articles into the HEY! YOU! SEE! SO! YOU! form. This will help train your mind to organize your own nonfiction ideas into this accepted format before you are tempted to write an amorphous, amateurish script that will bounce. The following is analysis of "Be a Smart Traveler" by Ralph Morse, which appeared in a *Reader's Digest* reprint from *Parade*.

> CAPTION that stresses Reader Identification (the YOU):
>
> "When you fly, and things go wrong, you don't have to grin and bear it."
>
> HEY! "Poor airline passenger service—getting 'bumped,' a long pre-flight delay, lost luggage—can make a shambles of a trip."
>
> YOU! "But not for the smart traveler (you, of course). He knows he is protected by rules enforced by the Civil Aeronautics Board."
>
> SEE! (1) *Problem:* Delays caused by weather or mechanical reasons.

Solution: Ask a passenger-service representative for information on the available amenities you are entitled to. Delays of more than four hours from take-off time may entitle you to free meals, hotel, and transportation to and from the hotel.

(2) *Problem:* Interrupted flight.
Solution: Same as the first above.

(3) *Problem:* Being bumped or refused seating although you hold a confirmed reservation.
Solution: Airline is obliged to book you on the next available flight on any airline going to your destination. If you are bumped and delayed more than two hours on domestic or four on overseas flights, you may demand and receive full refund of ticket price (up to $200) plus free passage on the next available flight. (Here, also, is a discussion of being "Denied Boarding Compensation.")

(4) *Problem:* Lost baggage.
Solution: Notify airline personnel immediately. Acting quickly will probably recover it. Otherwise put in your claim. Ask airline representative about reimbursement for clothes and items you need right away. If your luggage and contents are very valuable, buy extra insurance before you board the plane.

(5) *Problem:* Damaged luggage.
Solution: Notify airline personnel so that the damaged item will be repaired, replaced, or compensated for.

SO!

and

YOU! If you're still unsatisfied, protest to the federal agency, Civil Aeronautics Board, Consumer Affairs Office, 1825 Connecticut Ave. NW, Washington D.C. 20428.

(4) Choose for your trip and travel article a little-known spot, or plan a fresh approach to a famous place. Perhaps highlight a colorful celebration, a rodeo, a fiesta, off-trail trips nearby, natural history, or interesting folklore.

(5) Read everything that has been written about the place, checking *National Geographic Index* and *Reader's Guide to Periodical Literature* as well as back issues of the magazine you want to write for.

(6) Before going away, do enough research to query ahead, presenting various ideas for the editor's approval. An editorial order can be an Open Sesame to Bigwigs and fascinating places and experiences throughout your trip.

(7) While writing your material, try to anticipate and answer all questions the average reader might ask about the place. A *Sunset* article, "Mexico City," sums up the usual questions in its caption: "What is it really like to a visitor? What can you eat, see, do,shop for? Where should you stay? When should you go? What about the weather? And what will it all cost?"

(8) Write with starry-eyed enthusiasm, not just of yourself and what you did but about the recreational, human interest, sports, or scenic attractions for the reader. Be honest and up-to-date about current prices, conditions, rent-a-car or boat facilities, side trip costs, and, in the case of foreign spots, rates of exchange.

(9) Spruce up your writing style with contrasts and comparisons. Olympics ski champ Sten Erikson writes of New Zealand's Tasman glacier: "You can visualize such formations in ice cream, but to see such tremendous walls around you! Ice-cream puffs as high as 70-story buildings!" Then he *shows* steam from a living volcano in this same frozen area, adding: "Although the icy, snowy whiteness looks like fine powder, it has a curious consistency. It's a little like skiing in cement."

From *Sports Illustrated's* article about Tokyo:

> Hard by an ancient Buddhist temple 2 miles from the middle of downtown Tokyo, the Japanese observe their newest religion: *golf*. As a result, the grounds of the Shiba Driving Range . . . look as if every cherry blossom in Japan had fallen at once.

Travel Writing Don'ts

(1) Don't write a "destination piece," that is, a blow-by-blow account of your own trip. That's suitable for a mimeo to enclose in Christmas cards to friends who know and love you, but the reader must be his own hero in your travel adventures.

(2) Don't write off the top of your head without structuring, slanting for a specific magazine, and using the T-R-A-V-E-L tips.

(3) Don't overwrite. Pack information in your photo captions so that the article will be sharply focused and brief. Some auto magazines use features as short as 300 words.

(4) Try to send the kind of photographs that the particular magazine uses and don't forget to get signed releases from people in them. Buy the releases at your stationery store or write your own.

(5) Don't whitewash the truth or misrepresent in any way. Warn

of inconveniences, but in a constructive, not griping way. Tell readers to take rain clothes and insect repellent in handy packets, spray, or liquid. That's more helpful than saying sarcastically:

> French Polynesia has 2 seasons: the rainy season and the season when it rains. . . . In some hotels the management places large, hairy spiders in the rooms to keep down the mosquitos.

Sam Johnson said, "The use of traveling is to regulate imagination by reality, and instead of thinking how things may be, to see them as they are." Prepare the reader to make the best of things, and avoid unfavorable comparisons. World-traveler Richard Halliburton said: "The bee, though it finds every rose has a thorn, comes back loaded with honey from his rambles. Why should not other tourists do the same?"

(6) Don't write dull narrative or abstract descriptions, or use nonvisual words like "breathtaking," "gorgeous," "never-to-be-forgotten," or phrases that don't paint visual pictures.

(7) Don't overlook the wider market range now that travelitis is a national—yes, an international — epidemic. Squeeze many different scripts out of each trip for different reader groups.

(8) Don't stay home. Go away and write about it, not forgetting to take along your *philoxenia* —love of the foreigner! It may also help you if you heed the advice of a sixteenth-century proverb that tells the traveler to have "a falcon's eye, an ass's ears, an ape's face, a merchant's words, a camel's back, a hog's mouth, and a stag's legs."

9

How to Tell People How-To

"How and why are words so important that they cannot be too often used." —Napoleon

A hopelessly depressed woman wanted to commit suicide efficiently so she went to the library to do research.

On the way to look up *How to Commit Suicide*, she read hundreds of happy, healthy titles like *How to Be Happy though Single, How to Be Happy though Married, How to Be Happy though Young . . . though Old*, etc., *How to Be Young 'till 90, How to Feel Great, How to Be 30 for 40 Years, How to Find the Job You Want, How to Get Land Free from Uncle Sam, How to Conquer Fears . . . Shyness . . . Worries, How to Live Joyously Twenty-Four Hours a Day*, and how to be an expert in almost every field from advertising to zymology.

These perked up her spirits so gloriously that she not only forgot about ending her life, but she wanted to live forever to read and practice all the uplifting self-help advice that is the perennial favorite fare of magazine editors and book publishers.

"We never seem to get enough good self-helps," a publisher's representative told me.

Although many other literary styles seem to come and go, the demand for do-it-yourselfs is increasing more and more as paperbacks as well as magazines are sold in drugstores, markets, dime stores, and transportation terminals. People seem to want desperately to use their new leisure and higher income to improve their knowledge, skills, and personalities. Whether the self-improvement era began with the Industrial Revolution or the American or French Revolution or Dale Carnegie's *How to Win Friends and Influence People,* it is growing undeniably stronger today with people wanting to be better, smarter, happier, healthier, more successful, and cleverer at building and doing things than they are. And they are largely depending on writers (and experts via writers) to tell them how.

A great majority of the current crop of popular nonfiction is of this self-help, utility, or promotional type. It is easy to write and sell, especially if you are an authority on the subject.

In selecting your subject matter, keep in mind that today's readers are primarily interested in *the practical*—such as "How I Became My Own Consumer Advocate," "How to Locate Your Elected Officials," "How to Fight Computers and Win," "How to Avoid a Lawsuit," "How to Live with a New Puppy," or "Quick Way to Build a Brick Patio" (or anything useful)—*the timely*—such as "How to Cope with Metrics," "Easy Home Pollution Control," "How to Survive a Heart Attack," "How to Clamp Down on Auto Repair Gyps," "How to Save Money on Gas . . . at the Produce Center . . . with a Home Freezer," "How to Stop the Smut Epidemic," or any current trend or problem—*the curious*— how to understand, make, or use oddities, as in "How to Make Dolls from Apples," or new fads or new sports like parasailing, hang-gliding, needlepoint—and *the dramatic.* Sometimes what you have done is less exciting than the accomplishments of specialists and big names. Dramatic how-tos can be a third-person feature like "How She Nailed the Highjacker . . . Rapist," "How He Outwitted the Commies," "How They Saved Twenty Thousand Lives a Year," "How Jackie Gleason Lost 65 Pounds," "How She Used Biofeedback to Select a Mate. . . Break a Bad Habit."

You can get ideas from your own experience, from your job, from talking to other people and finding out what they want to learn and what they already know, and from reading. For instance, Ben Franklin's recipe for winning an argument was:

> . . . don't pound and pummel your listener. State the facts
> accurately and moderately; then scratch your head and shake it a
> little and allow as how that's the way it seems to you but you may

be wrong. This will cause your listener to consider what you have said; and in all likelihood he will try to convince you that you are right—since you seem to be in doubt.

Doesn't this give you ideas for adding other steps, including your own ideas and perhaps those of other people?

You can obtain U.S. Department of Commerce booklets or a list of U.S. Government pamphlets by writing to the Superintendent of Documents care of the Government Printing Office, Washington D.C. 20402. These include how-tos of every kind that are in public domain, so you may use them freely, But it is always advisable to imagineer, adding your own research, anecdotes, case histories, and ideas.

Put Your Personal Expertise to Work

Your hobbies, skills, and other subjects you know well can be written up in different ways for various magazines, often for readers of both sexes and differing age groups, as I have done with graphology (handwriting analysis). Here are a few openings from the forty-plus articles I have sold on this one subject: For a woman's slick, my feature "Secrets in Your Scrawl" opened:

> You may hide dust under the carpet and bulges beneath your girdle, but you can't hide your real character from a competent graphologist (handwriting analyst). One look at your writing and he knows your vices, virtues, passions, and potentialities better than your mother, who nursed you through every crisis from measles to matrimony. There's no hocus-pocus involved. Your hand merely holds the pen. Your brain dictates the writing movements, recording your true self so accurately that the Chinese call handwriting "a portrait of the mind."

For *'Teen*, my article "Be a Handwriting Detective" started out with what concerns girls almost more than anything else, popularity:

> Wouldn't you rather be a party-popper than a party-pooper? It's easy when you know handwriting analysis. Graphology can help you find out what kind of a person you really are, and why people either like you or don't.
> According to experts in the field, by changing your pen scratches you can correct your faults and watch your popularity rating soar like a spaceship. And you'll be able to analyze the writings of the rest of the gang and be a real wheel!

I used a different approach for another girls' magazine and used entirely different material and a new angle. "You Can Change Your Personality Just by Changing Your Writing" opened:

> A pretty but puzzled Karen wondered why Jeff suddenly stopped dating her and took Marci to the prom instead. She was sure it was because her clothes and records weren't as "in" as Marci's, but she was wrong. One look at her handwriting and I knew what the real reason was.
>
> Her heavy-pressured, angular-shaped words proved that she liked to be the boss, and her down-slashing t-bars showed her domineering nature and bad temper. . . .

Since graphology proved to be popular with the men's magazines, I sold them several different features, each written from a different approach. Here are a few openings:

> In the never-ending, all-out war that is underestimatedly called the battle of the sexes, you need some help like the electronic I.F.F. black box we used in World War II. Remember how it worked? It meant "Identification: Friend or Foe," and when you sent a signal you knew from the response whether your contact was friend or foe.
>
> Now more than ever, when you're choosing a date or a mate you need an infallible way to tell which doll is for you so you won't rush in too deep with a gal you think you can't live without and then learn she's someone you can't live with.
>
> How can you tell if she's a honey or a phony? Whether her sparkling champagne humor will go flat or bubble annoyingly when you're in trouble? Will she be a gold digger, pennypincher or brilliant budgeter? . . .

> The bank said the signature on the check was valid. This was confirmed by the boss and other higher-ups. But my analysis of the handwriting proved that the man himself was *not* valid or honest in any way. My graphological hobby saved my company $60,000 . . . .

> A quipster observed:
>   "Man is something like a sausage,
>   Very smooth upon the skin.
>   But you can never tell exactly
>   How much hog there is within."
>
> Most women are even more deceptive because they have more nature -given wiles to snare men and more falsies and other tricks to embellish their looks. It's getting so we can't tell how much "hog" there is within until it's too late. . . .

> Before you tie up a night with a date or your life with a mate, don't you wish you had a way of knowing what she's really like

beneath that alluring exterior? Is she a palpitating passion-flower or a frigid statue? Will she turn out to be a builder-upper or a tearer-downer? Braggy? Naggy? You *can* tell all this and more from the pressure, slant, size, and shape of her writing. . . .

A parents' periodical started with:

> A child's handwriting, like his formative years, can be revealing, malleable and can be modified to his advantage later on. You can learn the clues to his good and bad traits as well as symptoms of inner disturbance. . . .

If there is a moral in the preceding examples, it is: Don't stop with one approach or check. Try to get reprint rights.

In addition to your favorite hobbies and/or sports, there are also marvelous ideas in local newspaper articles, such as these headlines: "Divorce Judge Lists 8 Aids for Dating Couples," "Firechief Gives Tips on Preventing Fire Tragedies," "Police Offer Bicycle Safety Rules," and "Ex-Burglar Provides Tips on Avoiding Thefts." Insurance brochures and auto club pamphlets offer nuggets that you can develop on such subjects as how to live a longer and healthier life and how to prevent heart attacks or car thefts, or what to do in case of an accident, or how to drive through snow or fog, or how to buy or sell a car.

Choose Your Title with Care

There's always an abundance of how-to material in hundreds of different periodicals and on book lists. You may not recognize them at first because they don't always use the how-to label, which was monotonously overdone for several years. Of course, you'll still see it used in such titles as *How to Be Your Own Best Friend* and *How to Be Awake and Alive* (by Mildred Newman and Bernard Berkowitz with Jean Owen), *How to Survive Your Husband's Heart Attack* (by Jane Schoenberg and Jo Ann Stichman), *How to Get Rich Using Other Peoples' Money* (by Earl S. Weinreb), *How to Grow Beautiful Houseplants* (by T. H. Everett), and the works of the how-to king Shepherd Mead, whose *How to Get to the Future before It Gets to You* followed *How to Succeed in Business without Really Trying* and *How to Succeed with Women without Really Trying*.

Many promotional or utilitarian titles avoid the overly used how-to. Dr. Norman Vincent Peale's *You Can if You Think You Can* explains how to achieve success by never quitting and by maintaining self-confidence, just as his *Power of Positive Thinking* told how to achieve by being affirmative instead of negative. Others include: *You Can Profit from a Monetary Crisis* (Harry Browne), *Shifting Gears: Finding Security in a Changing World* (Nena and George O'Neill), *The Joy of Sex* and *More Joy* (Dr. Alex Comfort), *The Memory Book* (Harry Lorayne and Jerry Lucas), *Why Did You Do That?—Be Your Own Shrink* (Dr. E. Fuller Torrey), Stay Youthful and Fit: A Doctor's Guide (Dr. Lawrence E. Lamb), *The Intimate Enemy* (Dr. George R. Bach), *Creative Aggression: The Art of Assertive Living* (Dr. George R. Bach with Dr. Herb Goldberg), and *Dr. Rubin, Please Make Me Happy* (Dr. Theodore M. Rubin).

Study phrasing in such articles as "The Right Way to Fight in Marriage," "A Good Way to Manage Your Money," "The Strategy and Tactics of Job Jumping," "A Fresh Way of Understanding Yourself," "To Scare a Thief," "You Can Avoid Being a Mental Patient," "Teaching a Child to Think," "Secrets of a Low Calorie Cook," "What Makes a Good Father," "The Fine Art of Complaining," "New Exercise Plan," and "Ways to Keep your Income Tax Down."

Plotting Your Basic Steps

Specific numbers in a title are great because they promise the reader several ways to solve a problem. A few are: "76 Ways to Save Your Life," "18 Places Where You Can Live Better for Less," "A Doctor's 7 Rules for Reducing," "11 Ways to Serve Tuna," "7 Steps to Greater Personal Freedom," "9 Ways to Beat the Heat," "35 Ways to Cut Your Cost of Living," "50 Clues to Looking Prettier," "5 Tips on Fire Insurance," "20 Ways to Save Money at the Supermarket," "8 Tips for Smart Drivers," "9 Steps to a Longer Life," "5 Ways to Solve Husband-Wife Problems Before They Arise," "10 Ways to Protect Yourself from Lightning," "41 Ways to Beat the High Cost of Living," and "14 Rules for Avoiding Unnecessary Surgery."

Such numbers promise a *complete* service article that will have for its major section *several* valuable steps. These can be presented in any of the different ways described below.

(1) They can be numerically presented: example, "How to Help Your Husband Succeed in Business," by Lloyd Watson:

1. Don't hit him with homefront problems as soon as he comes in the door.
2. Never disturb him at work with phone calls.

3. Don't visit him at the office.
4. Be understanding when job demands require him to be away from home.
5. Encourage him to attend classes to learn more about his business and help him get ahead.
6. Never shame him by comparing.
7. Be a good listener.
8. Should he lose his job, extend yourself.

Esquire's "How to Get Old and Do It Right" gives eight rules:

1. Stand up straight.
2. Mind your gerontic zones (i.e., trim hair in nostrils).
3. Never stop working.
4. Don't use cosmetic devices (no toupees, hair dyes, or facelifts).
5. Learn to narrate entertainingly (don't start "when I was young . . .").
6. Rage, don't whine. (Whining is subjective, raging is objective . . . more like the way Harry Truman did.)
7. Embrace winter. Spend two months of every year in a cold climate. "A good old person doesn't go to Florida or Arizona and perish of jungle rot or terminal suntan . . . the death rate is twice as high in Florida as in Alaska."
8. Acquire a big ego. "A good old person doesn't depend on his children or anyone else . . . he is sufficient unto himself and can spend weeks with a few books or even alone. . . . Such ego may make a brat at twenty or a tyrant at fifty, but at seventy it makes a mensch."

Johnny Carson satirized this article in the risqué style of his *Tonight* television show, adding his own tips for "How to Get Old and Do It Right":

Try to live 'till Tuesday.
Demand respect (even if you have to shove your cane at people).
If you're a woman, don't let your figure go.
If you're man, learn to zip all the way to the top.
Make old age fun: swap your teeth with a friend.
Hook up with a good pension plan . . . and a good lawyer.
Feed a stroke, starve a coma.
Be proud of bodily functions . . . when they go right.
Don't neglect sex . . . you can have sex till the day you die and if you're lucky 'till the last moment.
Hold on to your youth.
Hold on to your vitality.
Hold on to your son's arm.
Hold on to the fence.
Most of all, hold on!

(2) Sometimes there is a ten-commandment "format" as in the *Family Circle* article "Collecting Antiques on a Shoestring" by Wendell Garrett:

1. Be suspicious of bargains when shopping for antiques.
2 Do not buy antiques solely as an investment.
3. Be wary of the heavily restored and excessively refinished pieces.
4. Be wary of reproductions and fakes.
5. Do not haggle about price.
6. Study the field and learn all that you can about antiques.
7. Confine your collecting instincts within manageable bounds.
8. Resist the temptation to buy mammoth objects at great distances from home.
9. Learn to trust the first impression of your sight and touch.
10. Collect for pleasure alone.

(3) They can be given in question format, like Dr. Joyce Brothers' articles:

Are your priorities of commitment sound?
Have you developed interests of your own, or do you rely on your husband too much?
Are you attractive and desirable as a woman?
Do you face problems squarely, instead of harboring resentments?
Are you reasonably consistent in your expectations?
Are you supportive when things go wrong?

The specific questions and their presentation can give originality to a subject that has been often written about. For example, study the following three articles on the subject of good sleep.

"How You Can Sleep Better," by Thomas J. Majerski:

What about late meals and evening snacks?
What about smoking?
What about alcohol?
Is exercising good at bedtime?
What are the best evening activities?
Does it matter what kind of bed we sleep in?
What sleeping position is best?
Does a daytime nap interfere with night sleep?

"Sleep from A to ZZZZ," by Dr. Christopher Evans and Brenda Jones:

What is a daydream?
How much sleep do you need?

Do people dream in color?
Is it possible to do without sleep altogether?
How long do dreams last?
Can you sleep on your feet or with your eyes open?
Can one pay off a sleep debt with an extra-long night's sleep?
Does eating cheese bring nightmares?
Can one learn when one is asleep?
Can we dream of events in the future?
Is it possible to have too much sleep?
Are catnaps helpful?
Why is it so difficult to remember your dreams?
Why do we sleep less as we get older?

"How to Beat Insomnia without Sleeping Pills," by Barbara Yuncker:

Get a correct diagnosis of the cause.
Get plenty of exercise.
Live by your natural rhythm.
Go to bed the same way at the same time as often as you can.
Hang onto your common sense and your sense of humor.

(4) They are occasionally presented as don'ts as in "How to Get Along with Your Teenager," by Dr. Haim G. Ginott:

Don't try to be like them.
Don't invite dependence.
Don't violate his privacy.
Don't belabor the future.
Don't judge opinions and taste.

(5) A more thorough presentation gives both dos and don'ts as 'If Infidelity Strikes—What Not to Do," by Dr. S. U. Lawton:

A Dozen Don'ts

Don't touch the phone when you find out.
Don't do anything about it for 24 hours. At least!
Don't take it personally. Think: "Just like a man!"
Don't start packing. Reflect on life without him.
Don't tell him what you know.
Don't heap coals of fire on his head.
Don't deny him sex privileges. (The other woman would love you to!)
Don't mention the other woman. Ignore her and wait.
Don't be pressured by indignant relatives or friends.
Don't divorce him without giving trial separation a chance.
Don't just forgive. Work hard at forgetting.
Don't turn the children against him. Ever!

A Dozen Dos

Have a good long private cry.

Face up to your share of blame. Think of ways you may have hurt him or let him down recently.

Try to act friendly or at least normal when he comes home.

Think of his tailspin as a kind of moral flu. Rx: Sympathy!

It's time for a new negligee, hairstyle, makeup.

Try some new ideas in your lovemaking. Live a little!

Make love more often.

Multiply the number of things you do together.

Arrange more evenings with mutual friends.

Try to swing a second honeymoon. And *swing*!

Seek professional help. You'll find it a relief to talk it all out with a trained impartial observer.

Give thought and time to your decision and make it on the basis of what will be best in the long run for you, for him, for the children.

or as in Dr. Norman Vincent Peale's "If There's an Alcoholic in Your Family":

What Not to Do!

Don't regard this as a family disgrace.

Don't nag, preach, or lecture to the alcoholic.

Guard against the "holier-than-thou" or martyr-like attitude.

Don't use the "if you loved me" appeal.

Avoid any threat unless you think it through carefully and definitely intend to carry it out.

Don't hide the liquor or dispose of it.

Don't let the alcoholic persuade you to drink with him.

Don't be jealous of the method of recovery the alcoholic chooses.

Don't expect an immediate 100-percent recovery.

Don't try to protect the recovering alcoholic from drinking situations.

What to Do!

Learn the facts about alcoholism.

Understand that, to be cured, the alcoholic himself has to admit his helplessness and reach out for help.

Concentrate on the fact that your loved one can be cured.

Develop the proper attitude.

Pray for patience.

Take a personal inventory of yourself.

Strive for stability in the home, especially if there are children.

Seek out a treatment center or attend the AA meetings.

Subject the alcoholic to every possible spiritual contact— church literature, concerned people.

Pass on to others your knowledge of alcoholism.

(6) There are various other possibilities for presenting steps. Try to think up a fresh, original style. Matt Dana uses the fallacies-to-avoid technique in his article "How to Improve Your Fiscal Fitness." After enumerating the following statements, he disproves what each says:

> It's only common sense to pay your bills first and save whatever is left over.
> A nine percent interest charge means that your loan is costing you nine percent a year.
> If it's more expensive, it has to be better.
> Bonds are a safer investment than stocks.
> A penny saved is a penny earned.
> Everything costs more today, and will cost still more tomorrow.
> If you decide to buy a new home now, you can't avoid getting stuck with high mortgage rates.

Dr. Theodore I. Rubin uses a similar device in his best-seller *Dr. Rubin, Please Make Me Happy.* In the section that tells "How to Avoid Seven Fantasies that Can Make You Unhappy," there is a helpful definition and discussion of each and what should be done about it:

1. The Shangri-la Illusion
2. The Money Illusion
3. The Love Illusion
4. The Marriage Illusion
5. The Children Illusion
6. The Youth Illusion
7. The Dependency Illusion

Add Detail and Anecdote to Your Basic Outline

The steps of your basic outline are as necessary to the professional article as a skeleton is to the body, but the skeleton must be properly connected and fleshed out with anecdotes, statistics, quotes, and a definite style. When you find yourself merely teaching and preaching in straight narrative, or numbering facts, be sure to dramatize with illustrations involving researched case histories or hypothetical anecdotes that prove your point. For instance, "How to Travel for Pleasure and Find It" opens with a scene on a trans-Pacific airliner. As the west-bound plane crosses the International Date Line and the Japanese stewardess announces a change from Saturday to Monday, an American woman exclaims: "Isn't that funny? The Japanese don't have a Sunday!"

This not only opens the article with a laugh but also proves that you need mental preparation for a trip and should pack information into your head as well as clothes into your suitcase. Then the author proceeds with dramatized proof that the unprepared traveler can suffer disappointments and embarrassments. Naturally he follows with tips as to how to avoid these problems and shows the advantages of research, humor, imagination, optimism, and efforts to communicate and understand exotic cultures.

When you begin writing your article, list your steps first; then build up each step with dramatized, convincing facts and pertinent anecdotes.

Study the following different anecdote openings in articles on the same subject: protection from assault. The first tells the wrong thing to do, the second tells the right action.

"Don't Be a Crime Target," by Frank Robinson:

> She was a frail girl, perhaps 17, waiting for a noon bus on a crowded corner in San Francisco. When the bus pulled up, the girl fished a wallet out of her purse and thumbed through a sheaf of bills.
>
> A young man who had watched as she fumbled with her wallet suddenly wrenched it from her hand and disappeared into the silent crowd. The bus pulled away, and the girl was left crying on the street corner. She had broken rule number one of crime avoidance: Don't flash a large sum of money in public.

"Don't Be a Willing Victim," by P. L. Penney:

> Not long ago, a Phoenix, Arizona, housewife was walking across her own backyard when she suddenly felt strange, strong arms encircle her in a bear hug. She shifted nimbly to one side, sliced her hand swiftly downward into the man's groin, and left him moaning on the grass while she summoned the police.
>
> This woman had been trained in Judo self-defense tactics at the Phoenix YMCA. But more important than her formal training was the fact that she was mentally prepared for the attack. . . . How important is it for a woman to be prepared mentally and physically for an assault?
>
> According to the FBI . . . the U.S. has a murder every 36 minutes, a forcible rape every 14 minutes, a robbery every two minutes. . . . The crime rate, the FBI says, has increased 148 percent during the past decade. There is every indication that the increase will continue.

Types of How-tos

Building the structure and slanting and researching the steps are necessary for all three types of how-tos: (1) the physical or practical, (2) the psychological, and (3) the philosophical.

The Physical or Practical How-to

As Milton L. Zisowitz says:

> Ever since the Industrial Revolution took the worker's eye off the finished product and focused it on the time clock, Man has been groping for ways to express the creator that is in each of us. . . . Americans have turned to home carpentry, painting, decoration and handicrafts with an eagerness that has created a new multi-billion-dollar business. This . . . "do-it-yourself" industry now supplies tools and materials for the more than 15 million home workshops which form a retail sales market of about $4.5 billion dollars a year.

More and more Americans are learning to do almost everything themselves by reading books and articles, some of which you can write!

In addition to the "How to Build," "How to Fix," and "How to Make" features, you can plan, write, and sell a utilitarian article with a fresh, practical angle on hundreds of other subjects related to improvement and self-improvement such as "How to Reduce—and Stay There," or how to build a personal exercise program, choose a hearing aid, manage or save money, shop, be healthier, handsomer, or more comfortable.

To be really practical, this category should be written with the clear, no-nonsense, progressive directions you find in recipes. In most cases it's a good idea to begin with the ingredients needed to make, build, or do some thing. One example is Alma Chestnut Moore's book, *How to Clean Everything*. The introduction gives a ten-point guideline on how to "Avoid Home Accidents"; section one begins with "A List of Materials Useful in Cleaning" (and where to get them); and section two opens with a list of "Materials for Stain Removal."

The Psychological How-to

The psychological how-to can deal with any one of the many aspects of mental reconditioning, whether it be to gain popularity, happiness, love, contentment—any of the desirable states of mind that readers want help in achieving for themselves and/or others. What original ideas do you have for gaining positive goals or for conquering negative habits like worry, jealousy, temper, fear, drinking, smoking, gambling, snoring, or prejudice? Check what's been done on your chosen subject so that you will not merely repeat but originate creatively.

The psychological how-to can be done in one of several ways. You can write it as a straight second-person "How *you* can do such-and-so"; you can plan it as a first-person "How *I* did such-and-so" or third-person "How he or she turned problems into promise." An almost magical way to build a top-rate, professional feature is to plan your psychological subject, outline valuable steps, and submit questionnaires to celebrities asking their advice on the designated subject. To illustrate, most people at some time or other are victims of tenseness caused by the pressures of day-to-day living. Using a survey format, Dave Paul's feature "How the Champs Beat Tension" offers inspiration and good solid advice based on the comments of sports stars, each representing a different sport and offering a different tip, built up with dramatic anecdotes from the star's own experience. For instance, a named top golfer said: "For me, pressure exists when I'm in a slump. The only way to get out of a slump is *work* your way out of it." A specific ace jockey advises: "The secret is to *forget your mistakes.* . . . I just try to learn from my mistakes and then forget them." Be sure to use both the specific and the general and relate your examples to the reader every time! If you're writing on shyness or stage fright or some other subject people are interested in, send a questionnaire to leading entertainers, politicians, and preachers, asking their advice and tips for your readers. Whether you interview others or not, the psychological article should be outlined into steps. (See Chapter 6, "The Survey Article," for a discussion of specific techniques.)

The Philosophical How-to

The philosophical how-to quite often overlaps the psychological; the differences from a self-help and writing standpoint are very slight, as you can see when you compare the definitions of the words. Psychology is "the science of the mind . . . tries to explain why people act, think, and feel as they do. . . ." Philosophy is "the study of the most general causes and principles of the universe; system for guiding life." Although I tend to consider psychological subjects as intellectual and mental, and philosophical subjects as pertaining more to ethics and spiritual and moral values, such best-selling how-tos as those on positive thinking, peace of mind, soul power, and creativity actually include elements of both.

There are a number of markets for philosophical how-tos. In addition to the many religious magazines of every denomination, many general publications buy these inspirational "bootstrap" how-tos that give their readers a valuable pick-me-up. When writing one, follow the rules of outlining and slanting and be sure to use down-to-earth anecdotes instead of straight narrative preachment.

Just a few in my own personal library are these "oldies": David Seabury's *The Art of Selfishness*; Emmett C. Fox's many books that preceded Dr. Norman Vincent Peale's *Stay Alive All Your Life, The Power of Positive Thinking,* and *You Can If You Think You Can;* Rabbi Joshua Liebman's *Peace of Mind*; Fulton Sheen's *Peace of Soul*; Wilfred Peterson's *The Art of Living*; Maharishi Mahesh Yogi's *The Science of Being and Art of Living;* Dr. Arnold A. Hutschnecker's *Love and Hate in Human Nature* and *The Will to Live*; Dr. Erich Fromm's *The Art of Loving*; Dorothy Kopplin's *Something to Live By*; Dr. Victor Frankl's *Man's Search for Meaning*; Max Freedom Long's *Secret Science beyond Miracles*; Alice A. Bailey's *From Intellect to Intuition*; Joel S. Goldsmith's *Practicing the Present, Living the Infinite Way, The Art of Spiritual Healing,* and *The Art of Meditation*; Dr. Alexander Cannon's *The Power Within, The Invisible Influence, The Shadow of Destiny, Powers that Be,* and *Sleeping through Space;* also books by Kierkegaard, Heschel, Russell, and Buber.

If you're interested in philosophy (and every great writer is), study the thoughts of the ancients such as the Greeks—Thales, Anaximander, Anaximanes, Heraclitus, Pythagoras, Democritus, Socrates, Plato, and Aristotle; the Roman philosophies that were based on later schools of Greek pholosophy such as Sophism, Cynicism, Stoicism, and Epicurianism. Also Aurelius, and later, Descartes, Spinoza, Hegel, etc. Don't neglect ideas in Buddhism, Confucianism, Hinduism, Jainism, Shintoism, Taoism, Vedantism. I've found Baird T. Spalding's five-volume *Life and Teachings of the Far East* invaluable. You can tie "foreign" philosophies to *now!*

Since philosophical subjects tend to deal with *abstract* ideas, it's a good idea to use *concrete* imagery to enliven your presentation. In a metaphysical feature titled "Overcoming Fear Thoughts," Reverend Wayne Kintner used an apt analogy:

> One of the important departments in the motion picture industry is that of editing the film after the scenes have been photographed. Certain scenes, and perhaps a sequence of them, are deleted or rearranged so that the film as a whole will unfold a

story that has continuity and smoothness when projected on the screen.

Of course, philosophical how-tos must also have structure, as Norman Vincent Peale does in his article on conquering fear (a combination of the psychological and the philosophical):

> Step 1. *Act as if.* Many years ago the noted psychologist William James said, "If you want a quality, act as if you already have it." (This is followed by many case histories.)
>
> Step 2. *Ventilate your mind.* Another practice important to the development of enthusiasm is that of mental ventilation. A mind full of gloomy thoughts makes difficult the cheerful and spirited thinking that stimulates enthusiasm. . . .
>
> Step 3. *Tell yourself all the good news you know.* A vital element in developing enthusiasm is the manner in which you start the day. Psychologists agree that you can condition a day in the first five minutes after you wake up. . . .

Use Reversal for a Fresh Approach

A clever trick to create a fresh, often humorous, how-to is reversal. This is particularly advisable if your subject has been done frequently and you are afraid your treatment won't be different enough. For instance, if you find a plethora of pieces on improving memory, work out all the advantages of forgetting (grudges, mistakes, enemies, aches, and pains). There is not an idea that you cannot reverse, and if you do it well, you'll profit from the silver lining in the clouds. Even Dr. Norman Vincent Peale, famous for his *The Power of Positive Thinking,* authored an article "The Power of the Positive No."

A few other reversal titles are: "How to Be a Failure," "How Not to Give a Party," "How to Enjoy Being Arrested," "How to Be Late for Everything and Make Them Like It," "Worry Like an Expert." Margaret Mead's use of this technique in "Anxiety Is a Proof of Civilization" predated Joyce Lubold's *Reader's Digest* anecdote-studded article "It Pays to Increase Your Worry Power." Lubold discusses the mental pollution that characterizes our "Golden Age of Worry" and shows how to dispose of nonbiodegradable worry by following these steps:

> Concentrate your worrying.
>
> Worry creatively.
>
> Don't call it worry if it's only procrastination.

A refreshing reversal to the many how-to-get-a-man features is Mimi Sheratan's *Cosmopolitan* piece "What to Do with Leftovers— Including Men." She presents seven humorously developed steps:

(1) Invite him to dinner and serve foods he hates most: vegetable plate for a carnivorous man . . . fondue if he hates cheese . . . wear dress and hairstyle he detests.

(2) Invite him to an impromptu dinner after you've wined and dined another guy the night before. . . . Make everything unappetizingly left-over. . . . Say, "Gee, it was nice of you to help me get rid of this food."

(3) Serve horribly . . . no tablecloth . . . paperplates, messy . . . . . . olives in a can, real American white bread *that goes whoosh when you squeeze it.*

(4) Add insult to injury . . . in addition to above, look left over yourself . . . bedroom hair . . . lipstick-smeared mouth . . . curlers, cold cream, pink chenille bathrobe. (If he comes back for more, marry him . . . he'll be comfy to live with.)

(5) If he's too obtuse to take a hint, leave clues of the other man all over the place. . . . prove you're untrue to him. Say, "Guess who was here last night."

(6) Invite him to a party and ask him to bring another date since you'll have one.

(7) Palm him off on a friend . . . wine and dine the two of them while you sneak out.

Summary—Dos

(1) Steep yourself in information about a hobby, sport, or other subject until you are practically an authority and can tackle it from several angles.

(2) Check all published articles on your subject through such reference works as *Reader's Guide* and the *New York Times Index.* After studying everything that has been done, plan entirely different approaches. Query markets that haven't handled that subject recently.

(3) Be sure your facts and material are accurate and up-to-date.

(4) In writing your article, state your purpose immediately, either in the title or in the first paragraph.

(5) Briefly and brilliantly convince the reader of the advisability of learning this thing, showing how it helped someone else and what it will do for him.

(6) List the directions in the most logical sequence in step-by-step order. The only interruptions should be answers to questions he might ask along the way. In the case of a how-to-build or how-to-make, open by listing the materials and quantities needed, like a recipe.

(7) Keep your style clear, direct, and readable with short sentences, concrete terms, active verbs. Don't clutter it up with fancy writing. This is not the time to be poetic or elaborate. Humor may be an asset, depending on the market and subject.

(8) If the market you are slanting for uses charts, statistics, tables, or photographs, try to supply what seems most appropriate.

(9) Try to have your finished article checked by an expert in the field for accuracy, and by someone entirely unacquainted with it to see if it's readable and if you have interested and informed him satisfactorily. Put yourself in the place of the least informed reader and provide clear answers to all the questions that might occur to him including how, how much, why, what, where, etc.

Summary—Don'ts

(1) Don't try to write about something you don't believe in, don't care about, don't really understand, or can't do successfully.

(2) Don't write how-to directions for the reader without first following them yourself. To paraphrase Shakespeare, it is easier to tell ten what to do than to be one of the ten to follow your own instructions!

(3) Don't copy other ideas and pass them off as your own. Give credit to the sources you use, whether these are individuals, booklets you get from the government, or from insurance companies, or other previously published sources.

(4) Don't be negative, except perhaps in a humorous reversal or satire. Normally, the how-to gives affirmation and teaches the reader how to make a plus of a minus. It must inspire and encourage as well as instruct.

(5) Don't write your how-to without slanting specifically and don't stop with just one variation. Before finalizing one version, see how many different ways you can rewrite the same basic material.

(6) Don't use technical terms without defining and explaining them. Your reader will be annoyed by COIK—words that are Clear Only If Known.

(7) Don't editorialize or otherwise comment personally unless you are writing a first-person philosophical or psychological how-to, which is based on your own experience.

(8) Don't describe your steps out of order or combine more than one in the same paragraph. Don't confuse!

(9) Don't detour from the process you wish to teach or write more than is necessary for your reader to learn the process.

(10) Don't write an article longer than 1,000 words without first submitting a query letter.

(11) Don't send how-tos to magazines that do not use them or that have department editors in your subject. Most magazines with large staffs (check the list of personnel in the front of the magazine) have editors for such areas as foods, fashions, gardening, child psychology, and family problems and don't buy free-lance material on these subjects. If the magazine's how-to features have either no byline or that of an editor, save your postage.

(12) Don't stress a strictly local or limited regional appeal unless you are writing for a local market.

(13) Don't be too repetitious in a short article, although a book-length treatment might repeat vital directions and points frequently so they won't be lost in the abundance of material.

(14) Don't give up on your chosen idea because it's been done *unless* you honestly cannot come up with a brand new angle.

(15) Don't overlook the multitudinous opportunities for how-tos all around you, particularly in the newest trends, fads, styles, and predictions.

(16) Don't stop studying the published how-to books and articles. Outline the newest ones, categorize them, and analyze their structure and subject matter. This will stimulate related and reversal ideas of your own.

(17) Don't start writing your article until you have outlined it in

one of the ways described in Chapter 1—either the HEY! YOU! SEE! SO! YOU! or the ABCs of Articles.

(18) Don't think that because someone else gets away with a deviation you can, too, as George Kirgo was allowed to use the overly long title *How to Write Ten Different Best Sellers Now in Your Spare Time and Become the First Author on Your Block unless There's an Author Already Living on Your Block in Which Case You'll Become the Second Author on Your Block and That's Okay Too and Other Stories.* A probable runner-up is *How to Go to Work When Your Husband Is Against It, Your Children Aren't Old Enough and There's Nothing You Can Do Anyhow* by Felice N. Schwartz, et al. It is better to select a clever, crisp, brief title that hasn't been used, even if you omit the "How To."

10

Business Writing Is Good Business

Lucrum gaudium — To earn is joy!
Salve lucrum — All hail to profit!

These are typical inscriptions on mosaics in the mansions of wealthy businessmen in ancient Pompeii, for merchants were the pillars of the Roman Empire in its prime.

Business activity has characterized all advanced civilizations. During the long centuries before Japan became advanced by Western standards, businessmen were scorned as the lowest of the four classes into which the population was divided: (1) the Samurai and all warriors, (2) the farmers whose produce fed the nation and who paid the soldiers, (3) the artisans, and (4) the merchants. It was a rigid caste system, with the law forbidding intermarriage or any other mingling between classes. Today, when Japan has become a major world power, the order is reversed: (1) merchants and businessmen, (2) artisans (many of whom make and design the products that the merchants sell, thus increasing the nation's prosperity), (3) farmers, and (4) soldiers.

Calvin Coolidge once said, "The business of America is business." Today, he would amend it to "the business of the world is business" because of increasing international dependence stressed in such best-sellers as *Global Reach* by Richard J. Barnet and Ronald E. Muller, and such articles as *Time*'s "The Global Plague of Inflation" and *Atlantic Monthly*'s "The Russians Mean Business—About Business" by Hedrick Smith.

Now is an exciting time in the business field—a transition period between the old emphasis on profit and loss to improved quality in organizational life, partly inspired by Norwegian Einar Thorsrud, Research Director of the Work Research Institute in Oslo, and Dr. Louis E. Davis of UCLA.

Scholars are joining tycoons and laborers as heroes in business as more and more corporations recognize the importance of: Organizational Development (O.D.) that teaches personal growth within the framework of business; Continuing Educational Programs (in classes taught in adult education center, colleges, universities, and i the companies themselves) in sensitivity training, remedial reading, expression, and speech (even bartenders now study psychology so they can help their troubled customers and recommend professional assistance); and Assessment Centers that enable young aspirants to learn if they have managerial talents.

Look into these and other exciting developments, for the writer's chief business is to keep up with everything and everyone of interest to today's readers. This includes new financial developments as well as firms that offer new opportunities or products that make life healthier, happier, easier, or more interesting.

When you think you are "out of ideas," you may be wearing, eating, or sitting on one, or looking at something that could be the subject of a salable business article. This feature can be written about any item, industry, or gadget that makes a living for its originator, manufacturer, or distributor and is of use to the consumer.

This is often one of the easiest kinds of articles to write and sell because of reader identification and because publicity-minded businessmen welcome favorable articles, which are better than free advertising for them. They will cooperate with you by providing good copy and pictures—for which *you* will receive extra payment when you submit them with your article. But do not let this obligate you or make you feel that you must write a whitewashed feature; your duty is *always* to your reader and your editor.

There's a wide spectrum of markets from small magazines like *Success Unlimited* and *Good Business* and the hundreds of trade journals, house organs (that is, company magazines and newsletters), and business publications in every field, to Sunday supplements, slicks like *Reader's Digest* and *Signature*, scientific periodicals like *Science Digest*, and class magazines like *Fortune*.

Be on the lookout for a firm that has built its own success in accordance with the American Dream, whether it makes computers, cassettes, unusual toys, foods, vitamins, beauty aids, contact lenses, cleverly disguised hearing or other health aids, reducing machines, thermassagers, artificial limbs, eyes, or prosthetics . . . or hips or bosoms—or even unusual babysitting, animalsitting, housesitting, or burglar-prevention services. You can get ideas from commercial and classified ads, articles, hobby and inventors' shows, hardware and other stores, and ordinary conversations.

There are enough ideas in your supermarket to pay your food bills for years, all the way from the electric-eye door to the wire cart and the trading stamps the store may offer. Never ignore or snore through television commercials or flip by ads in magazines. They may lead you to a business article about the product, artist, packager, publicity or advertising agency involved, or the rating services or censorship medium it is controlled by.

Just as the business article has a wide range of markets, the subject matter also offers opportunities for versatility. They range from inspiring, admiring success stories about firms or people, with the emphasis on "how he or she turned adversity to advantage by doing _____, saying _____, and thinking _____, and so can you," to exposés of corruption in business and how-tos.

As with all nonfiction, the pitch must be reader identification, which you can achieve by writing about familiar things or perhaps by using snob appeal as you take the reader behind the scenes of financial success.

Start a file of categories for researching and developing. Here are some guidelines, based on the word, *business*:

B = Bigwigs of the business world
U = Unusual business, or a different angle on a usual one
S = Success secrets that will stimulate the reader
I = Intriguing inventions and ideas
N = New firms
E = Exposés of rackets, injustices, frauds, and dangers
S = Sidelights of interest in the business world
S = Structure, style, and slant

Bigwigs of the Business World

You can get ideas from interviewing people in a firm that makes a widely used product or from reading the business sections of your local newspaper or such publications as *Time, Money, Newsweek, U.S. News and World Report, Forbes, Barron's, Exchange, Fortune, Wall Street Journal, Christian Science Monitor,* or the profiles in Edwin P. Hoyt's *The Super-Salesmen.*

After choosing a subject, be sure to find out all you can about him or her, then plan fact-digging interview questions.

The most dramatic examples, of course, are the self-made moguls whose careers have soared from rags to riches. But do not emphasize the clichéd Horatio Alger formula in which the impoverished hero gains success through luck. Stress, instead, the hard work, individuality, and ingenuity angle.

For instance, you might use someone like the following: Edwin Land, whose Polaroid Land Camera empire was founded on the results of his experiments in polarizing light when he was only eighteen; Leonard S. Shoen, whose $400 million pickup trailer business was conceived when, in 1945, he was ill with rheumatic fever and looked out his navy hospital window and saw his brother's car dragging a cumbersome load on an ordinary trailer; Harland Sanders, who, broke at sixty-four and on $105-a-month Social Security because a new freeway diverted customers from his fried chicken stand, began his billion-dollar-a-year Kentucky Colonel stands that now number 5,300 stores in thirty-nine countries; ex-construction laborer Earl Gagosian, who worked his way up to become ruler of the Royal Inns empire, just as Caesar Balso rose from bellboy to become the "Conrad Hilton of Mexico" and the late David Sarnoff overcame immigrant poverty to become head of the world's largest communications organization—RCA— as well as U.S. Air Force general and adviser to five presidents.

How many interesting people can you interview like weather wizard Irving P. Krick, founder of Water Resources Corporation, a successful rainmaking outfit that produces rain by bombarding clouds with silver iodide crystals? Consider people who started new careers in later life like the many enrolled in Columbia University's New Career Program for ambitious older people who want to try something else, or Paul Klein who became a top cosmetics tycoon ("King's Men," "42" products, etc.) by hiring "overage," chemists, idea men, and controllers who had been fired from other jobs, or "The Gallos: Dynamic Duo of Winemaking."

Of course your bigwig can be a successful woman in the business field like advertising agency queen Mary Wells, who was Macy's fashion ad manager at twenty-three, Doyle, Dane, Bernbach copy head at twenty-seven, and co-owner of the Wells, Rich Greene Agency at thirty-seven. Check magazines and books published in 1975, "International Women's Year"—you'll get many ideas.

Even women's consumer magazines buy profiles of such businesswomen as: Ruth Handler, president of Mattel Toy Company; Jean Nidetch, founder of the multimillion-dollar Weight Watchers Enterprises; Evelyn Wood, discoverer of Reading Dynamics; textile designer Vera; ladies who started fabulous firms right in their own homes like Margaret Rudkin of Pepperidge Farm breads and Merrie Ann Jarvis of Kold Kist frozen foods; and movie stars with business careers (Polly Bergen, Gloria Swanson, Arlene Dahl, and Zsa Zsa Gabor in cosmetics, Cary Grant with Fabergé, Ginger Rogers with J. C. Penney, Joan Crawford of Pepsi-Cola, and Lana Turner who heads her own Health Spas).

Cash in on the belated breakthrough of women into all fields of business. This gives you latitude with timeliness, extra human interest, and psychology. Marianne Mantell and Barbara Holdridge, whose fabulous success with their Caedmon record company which featured poets reading their works, has never been equaled by its many imitators, say:

> Being women was no handicap to us in getting started. We had a lovely aura of naiveté and crusading zeal when we started. We weren't out to make a fast buck. This seemed to evoke an element of chivalry in the businessmen we dealt with. We still don't have any competition. . . . Other companies don't seem to have put it over.

Seek out members of minority groups who are making it, giving credence to the American Dream ideal. There are thousands of successful black businessmen who started their own banks and many other types of companies designed to capture the $45 billion-a-year black consumer market. Even more commendable and writeworthy are female leaders of black capitalism, who have overcome twin prejudices. Just two of hundreds who might give you an idea of the possibilities are: ex-secretary Barbara Edwards, who rose to vice-president and head of California's Northwestern Title Company, and stockbroker Victoria Lynn Sanders of Chicago's Dupont, Glore, Forgan Incorporated, who says: "When you are making money for people they don't care who you are. You could be pink with blue polka dots."

Be on the lookout for writeworthy Chicano, Indian, and Asian-American business leaders.

Be on the constant lookout for interesting business personalities to write about!

Unusual Businesses or a Different Angle on a Usual One

The newer the business, the less likely it is that it has been written up. Do so quickly, and stress *universality* so that the reader will be interested in it.

Your daily papers yield a harvest of unusual ways people make a living. Here are some headlines that should give you ideas: "Company Helps Investors Lose Enough Money to Turn a Profit," "Car Repossessors Regain 75% but Other 25% Can Kill Them," "Skytyping Clear, Fast Way to Spread Message," "Tucson Firm Finds Junk Pays Off in Airplane Business, Too," "L.A. Baker Finds Own Fortune in Chinese Cookies," "Where Money Talks in Many Languages" (about firms that sell foreign currencies at airports), "Risk Analysis May Take Some of Financial Jolt Out of Earthquakes," "Heat-Resistant Grapes to Put More Class in the Glass for the Masses," "Making Barbecue Briquets of Peach Pits Big Business," "Stock Tracer Sometimes Finds Gold in Yellowing Certificates," "He Fingerprints Taste, Aroma," and "Debt Collecting: The Art of Choosing the Right Word—Furst" (about a commercial collection agency that does more than $30 million worth of business a year). There's even a National Scent Company that manufactures scents for fishing lures, some to teach dogs to chase game and some to attract or repel humans and other animals!

Do you know or know of someone who works for an unusual type of firm? Get on the trail before another writer does!

Success Secrets

Success tips should be included in your feature to inspire and help your reader. The following are a few examples that my research has uncovered.

McDonald's Hamburger success is attributed partly to the credo of Ray Kroc, who started out in 1937 by selling the original McDonald's Multimixer, a machine that made five malts at a time, only to wind up buying the whole name and formula for $2.7 million:

> Press on: Nothing in the world can take the place of persistence. Talent will not; nothing is more common than unsuccessful men with talent. Genius will not; unrewarded genius is almost a proverb. Education will not; the world is full of educated derelicts. Persistence and determination alone are omnipotent.

Advertising executive Janet Marie Carlson operates on the principle that you must shake up your client:

> Don't be afraid to frighten him with new ideas. He likes it. He wants it. He is addicted to it as an actor is to the sweet, sweaty tremors of opening night on Broadway. That's beautiful anxiety . . . the top executive is schizophrenic. Half of him is the entrepreneur who wants to take a chance. The other half is all computer.

Here are other success tips of those who proved it:

> "Keeping a little ahead of conditions is one of the secrets of business. The trailer seldom gets far."
> (Charles M. Schwab)

> "Drop the hammer and pick up the shovel."
> (J. A. Dever)

> "The great menace to the life of an industry is self-complacency."
> (David Sarnoff)

> "The business that considers itself immune to the necessity of advertising sooner or later finds itself immune to business."
> (Derby Brown)

> "Boldness in business is the first, second and third thing."
> (H. G. Bohn)

> "Business is really more agreeable than pleasure. It interests the whole mind, the aggregate nature of man more continuously and more deeply."
> (Walter Bagehot)

> "The gambling known as business looks with utter disfavor upon the business known as gambling."

Study the "Thoughts . . . on the Business of Life" section of *Forbes* magazine, their 520-page *Forbes Scrapbook of Thoughts on the Business of Life,* and other quotations books for ideas pertinent to your specific feature. Such additions not only inspire readers but also serve to break the monotony of narrative writing with direct quotations.

When you plan and write your business feature, as well as when you conduct interviews, be sure to dig for philosophical gems that will perk up your copy, relieve dull narrative, but, most of all, give insight into the people you write about.

For instance, tire tycoon Leonard K. Firestone says:

> My two great satisfactions in life are accomplishment and doing something for someone else. It's kind of a selfish approach because you get more out of it than you put into it. What you do for somebody else pays off much greater than any effort put into it.

Multimillionaire founder of Electronic Data Systems Corporation, H. Ross Perot, warns that life is hard, always was and always will be. He says:

> Capital is like the Mississippi River. Both will flow in this country only so long as the well-springs and tributaries continue to feed them. The money to run this country must come from private, individual investors. They are the tributaries that keep the capital flowing.

Intriguing Inventions and Ideas

Can you write about an inventor or about an invention that made a business more lucrative? The how, what, who, where, and when, interestingly written, can make a salable article.

Ideas have always paid off. As John Brink says, "Ideas are the basis of every accomplishment, every invention, every new product." Frustrated by the difficulties of presenting and selling his original cocktail blender that dials the right martini for everybody, Brink set up his own firm to register and sell inventions for his clients—Research of Reality, an idea development company.

Tune in on people who convert ideas into income. For instance, someone thought up the elimination of overhead costs by selling products from private homes in a party atmosphere and giving a free product to the hostess who invited her friends to get together for fun and viewing the product. You may think Tupperware started it, but long ago, Wearever aluminum and Bakelite were sold this way. Now the lead has been followed by many other merchants selling such diverse items as jewelry, pots and pans, encyclopedias, and art prints.

You can think up other examples. Idea people are always being interviewed on television, radio, or in the newspaper; they may be among your own friends, relatives, or neighbors.

New Firms

New firms and new-old businesses are marvelous grist for the business writer's mill; you could describe, for example, solar energy, geothermal power, or windmill companies like Bill Ward's Great Plains Industries.

Become a headline hunter and look for trendy, news-related companies. When there's an increase in crime, new firms crop up that sell clever burglar alarms, window protectors, hidden cameras for catching shoplifters, and other gizmos. You could write interesting articles about protection agencies that patrol neighborhoods or kennels like Continental K-9S in Cerritos, California, which trains and rents out German shepherd guard dogs. As ecology reaches the heights of a religion, you will notice more plant boutiques and other shops and companies that specialize in the enjoyment of the environment. Pollution increases the number of smog-control products on the market, as government controls on autos inspire new companies to help the situation and to give you new ideas.

Maybe you can write something about synthetic oils, new cassettes, cable television equipment, Video-Beam Projection (life-sized television), trash compactors, microwave ovens, hot-air gas engines, revolutionary new packaging, electronic microfilm, YAG (yttrium aluminum garnets or imitation diamonds), new vending machines, boat, car, or plane accessories, briefcase phones, or pocket calculators.

Since new products and companies often break into the news, study classified and other ads and commercials. You'll probably be led on the trail of good copy by such headlines as: "Special Business Services in Braille for the Blind"; "Cruise Ships Solving Hotel Shortages"; "Space and Underseas Drilling Rigs Are Big Business"; "Automated Fingerprint Files Provide I.D.s Fast"; "Containerization May Spell End of Trucking"; "Quick-Freeze Plant on Wheels Will Trail Baja California Fishing Fleet"; "Smog-Control Firm Cures Car's Halitosis"; "Gas Pumps in Ceiling in London"; and "Japanese Forsaking Sake but Westerners Love It." With the widespread use of computers, you might develop articles along the lines of "Computers Begin to Take Over Trading on Stock Exchange" and "Computers Can Spot Forgeries," or such anti-computer articles as Fred Hapgood's *Atlantic Monthly* feature "Computers Aren't So Smart After All."

By the time you read this there will be many newer, more exciting products, firms, and bigwigs

Exposés

So many too-trusting Americans are taken in by phony schemes that you will be doing society a favor by exposing racketeers and suede-shoe con-men in any business whether it's aluminum siding, incompetent television, auto, or other appliance repair firms, phony gadgets, overpriced cemetery lots, obituary rackets, or crooked vanity or pornographic publishers. Two splendid published exposés are Don Wharton's "Five Frauds to Watch Out For" (unordered merchandise, phony photographers, money-back-guarantee rackets, earn-money-at-home schemes, and uranium stock) and Leslie Velie's "Gangsters in the Dress Business."

Never copy what has been done, but come up with a new angle, fresh examples, and include up-to-the-minute developments. For instance, you might gather information and write about how foreign clothing manufacturers hijack model-forms and secrets from American industry or how industrial spies and traitors steal American plans and sell them abroad where cheap labor can underprice our firms.

A local article entitled "Stealing of Trade Secrets Plagues Electronics Industry" exposes mercenary, unprincipled scientists and businessmen who make a fast buck by working for electronics industries long enough to learn their tricks and then strike out on their own, underselling their former employers because they've saved money on research and labor.

The most dramatic are the most interesting and salable to the right market. Probe the psychology of such successful swindlers as G. Elizabeth Carmichael, whose 20th Century Motor Car Corporation and its promised three-wheel "miracle car," the Dale (costing under $2,000 and getting 70 miles per gallon), conned thousands of wishful thinkers out of investment and franchise dollars before "she" was exposed as a "wanted" con-man (Jerry Dean Michael).

Study Chapter 7, "The Exposé Explosion," to see how to develop this type of article, and be sure to make its *raison d'être* to protect the public by specific warnings.

In the brief newspaper feature "Guard Against Schemes to Divest You of Money," Anne Taylor tells shoppers to avoid:

> Tearing up or throwing away sales checks, receipts, and other identification, such as tags that identify the materials used and the cleaning instructions.
> Failing to understand the seller's policy on exchanges, refunds, and returns for credit.

Failing to read all warranties and guarantees. . . .
Signing a contract or agreement before reading and under-
standing it thoroughly. . . .
Signing a blank contract.
Failing to request and retain a copy of any contract signed.
Handing out any money to a stranger without identification
who claims to be soliciting for charity.

Villains and plagiarists in any field affecting national security, the
American consumer, or our moral standards should be exposed and a
remedy offered, but be sure of your facts and figures and be prepared
to provide a bibliography of your source material. The subject of your
exposé, be it an individual or a corporation, may very well sue for
libel and win if you can't prove your allegations.

Every day the FTC or the FDA lowers the boom on some outfit,
so you won't run out of ideas. Here are some suggestive headlines:
"FTC Orders Pet Food Firms to Back Up Advertising Claims";
"Public Member of Pay Board Raps Labor, Business Factions"; "9
Individuals, 4 Firms Indicted in Bank Fraud"; "Back It Up or U.S.
Will Back You Down, Advertisers Told"; "IBM Case a Shocker";
"CAB Sues to Halt 100 Charter Flights Set by Travel Club"; "FTC
Claims Vending Firm's Sugary Promises Turned Sour"; and "FTC
Plans to Display Talent to Phony Acting, Modeling Agents."

Reversals can be a good idea, too: "Business Pulls Switch,
Moves Against Government Monopoly" and "New Negro Group
Attacks $3 Million Brotherhood Drive."

Sidelights and Sidelines of Business

What interesting angles can you devise concerning business-
related subjects like banking, advertising, mergers, the stock market,
Better Business Bureau or government agencies that control commerce? Money itself, inflation, and dollar devaluation are popular
because, as Finley Peter Dunne said, "The American nation loves the
eagle . . . on the back of the dollar."

You can build successful features on a wide range of subjects,
from down-to-earth tips for job getting, job holding, or job switching,
to national subjects like price control or state lotteries. You can write
about diversification or any new trends in the economy, even a
general piece like "How Daylight Savings Time Affects Business."

Research and write about government agencies that have been
recently formed to protect consumers and workers. Two interesting
ones are CPSC and OSHA.

CPSC (the Consumer Product Safety Commission) regulates advertising, labeling, and product representation. Its vice-chairperson, Barbara Hackman Franklin, explains why CPSC is needed to help in specific terms:

> There is a product safety problem in the U.S. today on a nationwide scale. An estimated 20 million persons are hurt every year in accidents associated with ordinary household and recreation products. About 110,000 are hospitalized and an estimated 30,000 persons die. The cost is $5.5 billion annually—not to mention the human anguish and suffering.

OSHA (the Occupational Safety and Health Act) was formed within the Department of Labor to promulgate and enforce safety and health standards for America's five million business concerns covering sixty-two million employees.

There are several others that you should find out about. By researching thoroughly, conducting interviews, and collecting case histories, anecdotes, and other information, you should be able to produce salable articles, perhaps some significant ones for major publications!

Perhaps you have access to interesting material of international scope, such as proof that American corporations are raising living standards and winning friends in anti-U.S. countries. Perhaps you can find material like that in an article titled "Small U.S. Businessman Finds the Way to Clean Up in Europe," which shows how Scandinavian countries are impressed by our superior cleaning products (and have become eager customers).

The following newspaper headlines may trigger ideas for you: "Do Industrial Specialists Have Inferiority Complex?"; "From Cholesterol to Cosmetics, Promoting the Avocado Pays"; "Big Board President Defends 5-Day, Shorter Hours Plan"; "Students Make the Salesmen Answer for Their Products"; "How and Why to Put Your Game on the Market"; "How Paper Work Swamps Business"; "The Banking Watchdogs" (about the Federal Reserve System); "FCC Official Fears Sponsors Will Disappear if Ads Rebutted"; "Taking the Snarls Out of Financing the U.S. Consumer" (about credit cards); and "Ralston's Purina's Business Going to the Cats, Dogs—Fortunately."

Structure, Slant, and Style

Always outline before you write anything so that you will have an invaluable roadmap to keep you aware of where you are going and help you get there. The following are two brief examples:

"The Junk Mail Boom" (*New York Times Magazine*)

HEY! Q. What do the deadbeat and dropout, and the man who died have in common?
A. They're all on mailing lists.

YOU! You are on someone's mailing lists and are a target for junk mail. You are being exploited.

SEE! This main part of the article gives methods and sources of America's third largest advertising medium — mailing lists: subscription lists, motor vehicle department lists, obituaries, new baby lists, money offers, *Reader's Digest* Sweepstakes and its use of cheap circulation gimmicks.

SO! We need legislation to stop selling mailing lists and government lists; postal service should refuse to deliver money to people operating fraudulently.

YOU! It's better to drop your check down a well. Be a hermit!

"The Troubled Brahman" *(Time)*

HEY! J. Walter Thompson, world's largest ad agency, is in trouble.

YOU! You are familiar with their catch phrases, including "There's a Ford in Your Future," "Pan Am Makes the Going Great!" etc. The article then shows how they affect American thought.

SEE! Gives statistics of their drop in profits, history, how they operate, why they're in trouble.

SO! Even the "Greats" must be willing to learn and change.
AND Try harder and keep up with trends in your field, etc.
YOU!

In addition to structuring your article, you must have the market in mind and select a suitable style. This is your greatest opportunity to add originality to the source material you use, since newspaper, trade, or factual business articles tend to be straight and journalistic, devoid of cleverness, which is what you will add. One exception is a news items about the health cereal, Granola, which opens:

It's enough to make a hardnosed marketing executive laugh—or weep:

First, the folks up in Chico, California, gave their breakfast cereal this flaky name, 'Granola,' for gosh sake.

Then they put it in a plain-Jane bag with no boxtops for the kiddies to send in.

And they neglected to tell anybody about it.

Apparently nobody told the owners of Lassen Foods Inc. that their Milquetoast selling stragtegy was bound to fail in an industry renowned for snappy names and muscular promotion.

So in no time sales were compounding by 32% per year . . . and it has become the second best profit generator among breakfast foods . . . [even though it] isn't inflated, sugar-glazed, hyped with minimum daily requirements or blasted from cannons. . . .

Not only do you have writing style here, but you have another technique that adds freshness to whatever you write—reversal. Originality always helps your work, even when you're writing what you may have thought to be the uncreative business article.

If you follow the foregoing tips, you'll have sales success and fun, so that you'll agree with Wycherley, who said, "Go to your business, pleasure, whilst I go to my pleasure, business."

11

Cash in on the
Historical Revival

"The first quality of a historian is to be true and impartial, the next to be interesting."—David Hume

"If you would not be forgotten as soon as you are dead and rotten, either write things worth reading or do things worth writing."—Ben Franklin

You don't have to be great or *make* history, you need only apply up-to-date techniques that *make history come alive* in your writing.

Today there's a growing reader and author awareness of historical events. A cynical sage wrote: "There are three classes of people: the few who make things happen, the many who watch things happen, and the majority who have no idea what happened." Recording happenings is where you come in as you join the historiographers and journalistorians who are appearing more frequently on bestseller lists and in a wide variety of magazines.

Reporting history is so important that most armies took historical writers to their wars, from long before the Conquistadores' Bernal Diaz to our current correspondents. Many participated in the events they describe, in line with Montaigne's belief that the only good histories are those written by those who had command in the events they describe. Herodotus, "The Father of History," fought in the rebellion against the tyrant Lygdamis. Julius Caesar wrote about his war in Gaul while he was there directing his troops; Theodore Roosevelt penned a four-volume *Winning of the West*; and Winston Churchill won the Nobel Prize for literature for his fine histories, including *The Second World War*, in which he played a stellar role.

Every leader usually produces a book of his life and feats, often ghost-written—this may be where *you* come in. Many people who make history are not necessarily good writers, so they pay fees and/or split royalties with professional writers. When you perfect the proper techniques, you'll have many opportunities for collaborating or ghost writing memoirs and histories.

For most people, reading is a means of escape. They have traditionally escaped into fiction, then into works about space and the future, and now, as contemporary technological pressures and problems pinch harder, there is a trend toward the past in order to better understand our present crises. All this is in line with Churchill's dictum "Without a sense of history no man can truly understand the present" and George Santayana's warning "Those who cannot remember the past are condemned to repeat it."

This is one of the main things to keep in mind—a tie-up to today—when you plan historical material for any market, from fillers to full-length books and from the supplements to the slicks, and from tabloids to television specials.

Using the following tips, you can work your way into one of the four categories of historical writers set down by Harvard historian and Pulitzer Prize and NBA winner Arthur M. Schlesinger, Jr.:

(1)   Historians with a capital H—the greats, including Gibbon, Prescott, Parkman, Carlyle, and Bancroft, who recorded human hopes and struggles with such "intellectual sensuousness" that their writings survive with undiminished luster and value long after the other literature of their day is forgotten.

(2)   The "prophetic historians" like Toynbee and Spengler who add imagination and design to historical facts, penetrating the past to predict the future.

(3)   The "popularizers" who highlight, fictionalize, and dramatize to make bygone incidents fascinating to the masses. (Irving Stone)

(4)   The "journalistic pundits" who stick to technical facts

without imaginative glossing. (These writers are not commercially fascinating today when television and movies of historical events whet the public's appetite for excitement and action.)

Carlyle wrote: "In a certain sense all men are historians." It is true that everyone is interested in the beginnings of things, the foundations of the past upon which the present and future are built. But of course not everyone can interpret history dramatically. By using the following professional techniques you will give your readers facts and ideas they want to know *the way they want to learn them.* No musty stuff, but vibrantly vital drama that takes its clues from the word *history* itself:

H = Human interest
I = Identification
S = Seasonal specialties
T = Timely tie-up to today
O = Originality and organization
R = Research
Y = Yeasty yarns of yesterday

H = Human Interest

Your historical material is only as interesting as the people who made things happen or to whom they happened, for, as Emerson said, "There is properly no history, only biography." Look for specific human interest and never write about happenings without building up pulsating characterizations of the person(s) involved.

A thoroughly researched history of Madison Square Garden with its glittering events and celebrities was unsalable until the author rebuilt it around the custodian and retitled it "Madison Square Gardener."

You wouldn't write a mere factual history of the Arab-Israeli Six-Day War without *characterizing* one of its heroes, Moshe Dayan, a Sabra (native born Israeli) who typifies the tough, tenacious desert cactus plant of that name. His father, Schmuel Dayan, helped found the first kibbutz (a communal farming settlement), on which Moshe was the first baby born, and Moshe has always been a hard-working, Arab-speaking Jewish peasant who urges peaceful coexistence with the Arabs.

Robert O'Brien's article about history-reviving Knott's Berry

Farm stars Walter Knott, whose idea in building his California tourist-luring monument to the past coincides with the promise of this chapter: "The more complex the world becomes, the more people turn to the past and the simple things in life. Here at the farm and ghost town we try to give them some of these things." History should always be used as a background for the flesh-and-blood people involved—in this case, Knott, a practical visionary; his charming, hard-working wife, who, on opening day served 65¢ chicken dinners on her wedding china; and their friend-helper Rudolph Boysen, the Anaheim park superintendent who is the creator of the boysenberry.

Always sift through facts until you find human interest angles, as David Wise did when writing about the history of the New York subway. Colorful August Belmont, chairman of the board, paid $35,000,000 to have his own private luxury train-car to take him all over his subway empire in style.

If you write the history of the Girl Scouts, you could bring to life Juliette Low, who used her deafness to ignore objections to her pleas for financing the project. Your history of the Boy Scouts might star Sir Robert Baden-Powell, who incorporated the organization in 1910, or perhaps the founders of its forerunners, Daniel Carter Beard's Sons of Daniel Boone and Ernest Thompson Seton's Woodcraft Indians. One article about the magnificent French gardens of Versailles featured the personality of Andre Le Notre, a good friend of Louis XIV ("The Gardner and the King," *Reader's Digest*).

Do not overlook unknowns if they were actors in an interesting drama—like those in "The Strange Wedding of Widow Ward" by Noel C. Stevenson with Murray Hoyt, published in *Reader's Digest*. In 1789 in Vermont, Major Moses Joy wanted to marry the widow of a man who had left astronomical debts. Under state law he would have to assume the debts if he married her in her clothes, since they belonged to the estate, and the same was true if he bought her new clothes, since these would be his gift to the estate, thus involving him legally. So Major Joy had the wedding performed with the widow nude in a closet with a heart-shaped hole cut in the door through which she could hear the minister and extend her hand for the ring. After the ceremony, new clothes were taken in to her, and Major Joy was not legally responsible for her first husband's debts.

A clever solution to an interesting problem is always writeworthy; if you can find such human interest incidents in your old family diaries, journals, or other research, try to develop them in line with the other tips discussed in this chapter.

National Geographic likes features about historical personalities like Sir Francis Drake, "Queen Elizabeths's Favorite Sea Dog. . . a freebooter who—more than any other man—started England's march toward empire. . . . The man who circumvented the globe, touching the California coast in 1579." *Smithsonian, The American Heritage, Mankind,* and other historical periodicals also publish human interest stories. Up-to-date magazines like *Reader's Digest* make room for features about the past like their *Great Moments in U.S. History* that spotlight American heroes, plus lead articles about interesting people from other countries as well. Ernest O. Hauser's "Leonardo Superstar!" is captioned: "Now, more than four centuries after his death, new legend grows around this incredibly versatile genius." "A Rebel Named Goya" is written by Kenneth Clark, the noted art historian who, through television and books, has revived much interest in the past. In "The Real Uncle Tom," Thomas Fleming tells the real life story of brilliant, hard-working, enterprising Josiah Henson who inspired but was quite different from Harriet Beecher Stowe's fictional hero. He achieved freedom for several slaves in addition to his own family and led them to Canada where he set up a successful business after graduating from "The University of Adversity."

Make people your pitch, including heavies. In our age of the anti-hero, people like to read about evil doers and hoax-perpetrators like Charles Dawson, who was credited with discovering the jawbone of Piltdown Man after staining and planting fossils to deceive scientists. You'll find many frauds in every field from art to literature, not to mention war-profiteers, thieves, swindlers, and stranglers who have played strong roles in histroy. A history of quacks in medicine would include such characters as Lucius Horatillavus, who went to Rome in the first century and advertised himself as a "Wonder-Working Healer," but whose secret potions contained a poison that killed even him. Others included Nero's personal physician, Thessalus, who ran the first diploma mill, selling "certification in the healing arts" to anyone who could afford the fee. Also the Comte Saint Germain, who soaked royalty as well as the rich with his worthless "magic" elixir of life.

I = Identification

Personal involvement with the subject is always of primary importance, although it may be more difficult to bring into historical articles than others. Your reader won't be interested in bygone happenings or long-dead persons unless you point up what they mean to him, like the warning implied in the preceding example of medical quackery. In Marshall Fishwick's article about George Washington titled "The Man in the White Marble Toga" you'll also read a message for our times:

> . . . men in gray flannel suits may learn a lot from the story of the man in the white marble toga. It is not by bending to every whim and request that we achieve real popularity, or by following every popular cause that we become great. There are times to smile, and times to scowl; to confuse occasions is an act of cowardice.

In Bruce Bliven's feature "Our Legacy from Mr. Jefferson," the reader is made to feel that this versatile genius who helped found our nation gave us timely as well as timeless advice—as you can see from the headings of the different sections: "Judge for yourself," "Act out convictions," and "Trust the future, trust the young."

One sure way to achieve identification is to relate the origins and oddities of things people use, know, and celebrate now: clothes, vehicles, perfumes, cosmetics, foods, fads, or activities. Any recurring forces that are common denominators of contemporary life and the past have automatic interest and salability if you research thoroughly and write clearly. Keep in mind the words engraved at the entrance to the National Archives in Washington—"The Past is Prologue"—as you present historical information as clues to understanding the present and the future. Almost everyone is interested in money. Any monetary angles —new coins, plastic money, or any changes in currency—can be a tip-off to an interesting feature on the history of money, not just American bills and coins but ancient mediums of exchange as well. There are other potential features within this general history of money, perhaps on such related subjects as counterfeiting, inflation, banking and the stock market.

Recreation also has universal appeal, and any new game can be traced back to historical origins. Dominos originated in an Italian monastery in the early eighteenth century when two young monks looked over the forbidden wall and were punished with a three-month confinement under the rule of silence. They gathered all the stones in their cell, which happened to be twenty-eight, marked them, and planned the game we know now. The winner couldn't speak his jubilation in ordinary conversation so he uttered the first line of the prayer "Dixit Dominus Domino Meo," which was later shortened to "Domino."

The history of any food is a good bet; for example, the whole coffee industry of the New World was developed from one single coffee plant that Gabriel Mathieu de Clieu took from Paris to Martinique in 1723. What food would you like to research and write about? Be sure to check *Reader's Guide* to see if it has been done too often—as is true of beer, pretzels, donuts, hamburgers, hotdogs, pizza, and ice cream. Seek fresher material with strong identification, human interest, and humor. For instance, waffles originated in thirteenth-century England when a crusader returned home too tired to take off his armor. He accidentally sat on some fresh-baked oat cakes. Instead of bawling him out, his wife liked the way the imprints from the armor kept the butter from running off, and thereafter she had him put on his armor once a week to sit on her cakes, now called "waffles," meaning flat honeycomb-like cakes.

Using questions and research, you can dig up and dramatize other strange names of foods, such as Welsh rabbit or rarebit, which dates back to feudal Wales when peasants were not permitted to hunt on noble estates and compensated by serving melted cheese as a substitute for the forbidden rabbit. One of my students received a large check for an article tracing the history of pomegranates, which, she argued, grew in the Garden of Eden and were the forbidden fruit Eve gave Adam. Fascinating facts can be found in Reay Tannahill's *Food in History*.

Start making a list of subjects you can write the history of—ones with plenty of reader identification.

9 – Seasonal Specialties

Seasonal material should be carefully slanted and submitted six months ahead of time. Even magazines that normally emphasize present happenings often publish historical features about subjects of interest to their readers. The traditional women's magazines like romantic pieces about White House weddings, Valentine's Day, Leap Year, and love affairs of famous people when their birthdays come up. Men's magazines buy action-packed true adventures and feats from the past and exciting histories of popular sports like skydiving, skindiving, surfing, boxing, football, baseball, or golf. Medical magazines like dramatic breakthroughs in medicine like "Saving the Brain of General Wood" by Theodore Berland in *Today's Health*.

Regional events like April cherry blossom time present an occasion for you to remind readers of how Miss Elizabeth Scidmore interested Mrs. William Howard Taft in helping her buy and plant eighty Japanese cherry trees in Washington (to which smog-bound Tokyoites come every spring).

Scour your library for books on origins of holiday customs and histories of anniversaries, and use up-dated techniques to vitalize and dramatize facts in feature articles for specific magazines.

One example is the history of Halloween, which descends from a Druid Harvest Festival celebrated centuries before Christ. According to the Druid myth, the night before, "All Soul's Eve," was when Saman, the Lord of Death, assembled all the souls of wicked people, who had been condemned to inhabit animal bodies. Saman would then decide what forms they would take the following year. The Druids believed that cats were human beings changed into animals by punishment of dire crimes. Thereafter cats became standard equipment for witches and Holloween.

The Roman invasion of Britain brought with it the harvest Feast of Pamona, adding nuts, apples, pumpkins, and other goodies to the trappings of the Druid festival. The jack-o'-lantern was added in Ireland, where legend says a stingy practical joker named Jack was barred from heaven and hell because he had played many pranks on God and Satan. He was condemned to roam the streets with a round lantern until Judgement Day. His mischievousness survives in the many tricks still played on Halloween.

Study the wide variety of markets using historical material. This includes hundreds of juveniles and Sunday supplements. One of my writers was researching her Civil War novel when she found a nugget about the origin of Memorial Day, which she wrote up and sold to a national weekly for a tidy sum. In selecting material for seasonal or any other historical features, however, it is vitally important to observe the next "must."

T = Timely Tie-up to Today

Study all news media—television, radio, newspapers and news magazines—for the latest inventions, gimmicks, and events you can use as a kickoff to a historical article along that line. When topless bathing suits and waitresses made headlines, national publications traced "topless" history back to ancient Minoan times. New liquor taxes could work back to old gin-swigging England where a national alcohol crisis was averted by high gin taxes that made the populace switch to beer. New space weapons or a gun law controversy could spike interest in gun regulations in bygone times and climes—or you could write about other ancient weapons like Greek Fire, the secret weapon of the Byzantine Empire that changed history.

Collect contemporary headlines that could lead into features about the past: "Archeology Reveals Rich Cypriot Past"; "Persepolis Rises Again" (about present excavations 2,000 years after Alexander the Great destroyed Persia's Achaemenian Empire); "U.S. Military Court Legacy from British"; "First Rose Bowl Game in 1902 Such a Disaster, Chariot Races Were the Thing until 1915"; "Lost Civilization Unearthed in Turkey," or relics or excavations anywhere from "Diggers Hope to Trace Eli Whitney's Genius by Excavating His Gun Factory" to ancient Tehuacan ruins near Mexico City (which inspired Robert Claiborne's *Harper's* article, "Digging Up Prehistoric America") to Mithridatic treasures unearthed in new building projects in London. The headline "Heart Transplant Rules Set Up—Recipient Must be Dying" could be a springboard to an intriguing study of transplants in ancient times. A new wonder drug, medicine, or oral contraceptive is an invitation to write about fascinating drug facts that go back five millenia. As Dr. Edward Brady says:

> Although this is the age of wonder drugs . . . some plant drugs described in Egyptian papyri of 3,000 B.C. are still in use. Man has been taking drugs for all the years of recorded history and some of his earliest remedies may have been as effective in antiquity as they are today.

There are interesting stories in the history of many old-time remedies we still use: digitalis was used in the fifteenth century; quinine and quinidine were brought to Spain from South America in the sixteenth century; codeine and morphine come from the same gum opium used since pre-history. Ancient roots can also be found for many of the drugs that are popular topics of discussion today—amphetamines, hallucinogens, and fads like glue sniffing. Dr. Sidney Cohen, in an article for *Vogue*, traced drugs on campuses back to the days of the first universities. You could build a historical article about the American Medical Association's drug advertising, or the formation of the Food and Drug Act in 1906. Everything in modern life has a precedent and a history that can be made salable to the proper market.

One popular device to update the past and "hook" the editor is to make it sound contemporary, as in this excerpt from the description of a campus riot:

. . . From the academy it spread to the university, where, surrounded by Hectors and Achilleses heavily armed and mounted and equipped with weapons, the students are making the following demands:
1. Complete autonomy of the universities.
2. Complete freedom of teaching.
3. Free access to the university without distinction of creed, nationality, sex and social background.
4. Freedom of assemblage and recognition of student associations.
5. Establishment of a university and student tribunal.
6. Abolition of the police function of the inspectors.
7. Lowering of fees for courses.

Sound recent or contemporary? It's from a March 9, 1890, letter Anton Chekhov wrote to newspaper editor Alexei Suvorin about campus unrest in Czarist Russia!

There's also a timely tie-up to today in this opening of a historical article:

A distinguished U.S. Senator expressed himself this way: "What do we want with this vast, worthless area—these endless mountains, deserts and whirlwinds of dust? I will not vote one cent from the public treasury for this project!" But it wasn't the moon the senator was referring to, it was California. Daniel Webster, 150 years ago, was opposing the appropriation of $50,000 to establish mail service to the Far West.

("Our Spinoff Profits from Space" by Toby Freedman)

If you are writing about pollution you could point out an ironic prediction made by a London doctor in 1902. He blamed all air pollution on the dust kicked up by horses galloping across disintegrating pavements. Confidently he forecast that the advent of motor vehicles and the banishment of horses would remove all pollution from the atmosphere. There is much material on this subject, including the fact that in 1900 in London, not modern Los Angeles, the word *smog* (for smoke plus fog) was coined; whereas the term *ecology* goes back to 1876.

You can find other startling mispredictions like this optimistic one published in 1880 by Dr. J. H. McLean, a St. Louis industrialist who claimed:

The art of war will be no more in a few years! My invention "The Annihilator" that can pump an endless volley of shells into a target 20 miles away will perfect warfare. This perfection will prevent war by making it too terrible.

O = Originality and Organization

Your own fresh angle is necessary to add a fillip to what might otherwise be musty, dusty "so what?" dates and facts. Here is the way the *Alma* (Michigan) *Record* adds a clever idea to two dates:

> The man who invented the bathtub in 1850 certainly must have been the most relaxed man in history. He wouldn't have had to get out of the tub until 1875 when the telephone was invented.

Humor is a popular way to lighten historical writing. Readers like a writer whose sense of humor increases with age, as is true of Will Durant, who added lustrous laurels to his distinguished career with his humorous style in *The Age Of Louis XIV*.

Even more hilarious are the hysterical biographies in Will Cuppy's *The Decline and Fall of Practically Everybody* which may have inspired Richard Armour's delightful series: *It All Started with Columbus; It All Started with Europa; It All Started with Marx; It All Started with Hippocrates;* and *It All Started with Sticks and Stones.* Study such humor to see how it can snowball historiography into an unending series. But—always use your own *originality* and *imagineering* ability to relate your material in a brand new way. There is always a new twist or angle to everything! Anyone who doesn't realize this is like the man who resigned his job at the Patent Office in the nineteenth century because he was sure everything had been patented and the office would soon close any way. There have been over 2,500,000 patents taken out since then!

No matter how fresh your approach to a subject, organize your facts into the reliable HEY! YOU! SEE! SO! YOU! structure, as in the following analysis of "When Lincoln Was a Bartender" by Herbert Mitgang:

HEY!   Opens with liquor license issued to Berry and Lincoln to keep a tavern in New Salem, Illinois, March 6, 1833. Follows through with identification of Abraham Lincoln and William F. Berry, his Black Hawk War buddy, and how they used their mustering-out pay to go into business.

YOU!   Reader identification is achieved by this historical situation, which is a forerunner of the modern GI Bill that helps ex-GIs set up their own business. The reader can also identify with the Lincoln-Berry type of business, in reality, a grocery store. In those days groceries included liquor.

SEE!   The ups-and-downs of the Lincoln-Berry tavern-grocery: Berry's alcoholism and Lincoln's lack of business acumen, coupled with his stronger interest in studying law and making friends, made the business unprofitable. When Berry took out a special license to sell liquor over a bar, Lincoln, a non-drinker, quit, after doubtless tending bar occasionally. With temperance in the air and Lincoln interested in votes and political achievements, he quit bartending and the tavern-business.

SO!   In politics, every item from a candidate's past pops up to haunt him, and during the Lincoln-Douglas debate at Ottawa (Illinois) on August 21, 1858, Douglas accused Lincoln of having been a "storekeeper who sold whiskey." With his usual ingenuity that often helped him convert a minus into a plus, Lincoln turned Douglas's insult to his own advantage by saying: ". . . the difference between Judge Douglas and myself is just this—that while I was behind the bar, he was in front of it."

YOU!   The implied philosophical premise: When you must do a job, do your best and don't be ashamed of it. When you know you are right, stick to your guns and don't let a pompous opponent beat you down.

R = Research

One of the greatest advantages of writing must be based on facts. Arthur M. Schlesinger, Jr., says:

> . . . the Historian unlike the novelist or poet, has a prescribed and inescapable task . . . to reconstruct the past, to present as truthful a picture as he can of events that have already taken place. In performing this task, the historian requires, above all, evidence, the more contentious his history becomes.

Whether you have already chosen your subject or whether you are browsing for ideas, you should familiarize yourself with the historical source books at the reference desk of your library as well as the special subject ones listed in the card catalogue. As a starting point, you should go to section 031 (Dewey decimal system) in either reference or general circulating books. If a tidbit catches your eye, go to the history of that period or biography of persons concerned. The following reference books may give you the start you need.

All almancs, including: *Encyclopedia Almanac;*
American Almanac; World Almanac

Allison's Guide to Historical Literature
The American Book of Days
Anniversaries and Holidays
Biography Index
Dictionary of American Biography
Dictionary of National Biography (British)
Dictionary of Dates (alphabetical under subject)
Famous First Facts (by now there are six editions)
Handy Encyclopedia of Useful Information
History: How to Gather It, Write It and Publish It
Information Roundup
Lincoln Library of Essential Information (even has
    grammar and literary style)
Parker's Local History
Putnam's Handbook of Universal History
Rapid Fact Finder
U.S. Department of State Fact Book
Who's Who (all the Marquis titles)

Don't stop with the public library. If your subject is or was in medicine or law, go to medical or law libraries. Check at historical societies, dip into old newspapers and diaries, and interview old-timers. Don't overlook the excellent books sponsored by W.P.A.— they may give you ideas or additional material for the ones you already have.

Over a century ago when the great historian William Prescott started his career, he set down rules for himself, including: "Never sacrifice truth or correct view to effect. . . . Facts, facts, whether in the shape of incidents or opinion, are what I must rely upon, by which I must stand or fall." But he added: "Never introduce what is irrelevant or superfluous or unconnected for the sake of crowding in more facts." You must research the facts carefully, outline your article according to your angle, then flavor the material with your originality.

Y = Yeasty Yarns of Yesterday

"History is what one age finds worthy of note in another" wrote Burckhardt. Readers are interested in drama, anecdotally told, that runs the gamut from heroism to hoaxes. How many examples of courage does your history research yield? Have you uncovered such acts of bravery in adversity, as President Grover Cleveland's throat cancer, which, if known to the public, would have caused a panic? Cleveland planned a secret operation on a boat, perhaps the first floating hospital. Such historical dramas often find their way to television and *Reader's Digest*, as this one did.

You can sell many features developed from researched nuggets of historical facts. One of my own published articles was about a Scottish soldier named Richard Middleton, who, centuries ago, was arrested for playing cards in a Glasgow church. "Your Honor," Middleton alibied to the judge, "our soldiers' wages barely permit us to have such luxuries as a Bible, Prayerbook or Almanac. Not to mention the impracticality of carrying a library on our various moves and maneuvers." I went on to show how Middleton escaped punishment by proving that his deck of cards was Bible, Prayerbook, and Almanac, and I had jolly fun embellishing the dialogue—all of which later appeared on a popular record that sold a million copies! My published article was based on the historical Richard Middleton; the record adapter used a first person narrative to increase identification with the American audience. Let that be a lesson to you—a lesson in identification!

In *History as the Story of Liberty*, Benedette Croce says, "Any history reveals as much of the times in which it is written as the times about which it is written." Be sure that yours does!

You'll cash in richly on the historical revival when you pack your writing with H-I-S-T-O-R-Y— human interest, identification, seasonal specialties, timely tie-up to today, originality and organization, research, and yeastiness. Dramatize, update, and humanize, and you can't miss! Keep in mind Dr. Waldemar W. Argow's words:

> History is never made in the abstract. Always it is something someone has done. History is never a solid mass achievement; it is a mosaic of countless parts, each one perfected by the sacrificial devotion of some particular person. The forces that have made history, and which will continue to make it, are the undying ideals men cherish, the strong-willed plans they discipline themselves to achieve and the daring hopes by which they activate their souls.

12

Supplement Your Sales
with the Supplements

"Were it left to me to decide whether we should have a government without newspapers or newspapers without government, I should not hesitate a moment to prefer the latter."— Thomas Jefferson

Many writers who scour their daily papers in order to keep up with the latest news, newsmakers, trends, and attitudes, often overlook these same markets that are much easier to write for and sell to than the major magazines. While you are training in these minor leagues for the major publications, your rewards will include byline credits, wide circulation, and encouraging pay.

There are more than 10,000 newspapers in the U.S. and Canada that feature Sunday supplements, most of which are looking for free-lance material. They range from hundreds of local, lower-paying markets to top-paying city supplements like *New York Times Magazine*, as well as syndicated supplements that go to several different papers (e.g., *Parade, Family Weekly*).

The trend is swinging away from the national, New York-based supplements to local markets. Ask your friends who live in other cities to send you samples from their Sunday papers. If you live in a large city with newspaper stands that carry out-of-town papers, buy and study the Sunday supplements of other cities.

There are many reasons to look into this versatile market that buys many types of articles—from ten-dollar jokes and fillers to full-length features, and from folksy family items to the sensational adventurous exploits you used to see in the pulps. They like exciting action stories like "How He Outwitted a Skyjacker," "I Lost a Leg but I'm Still a Marine Jumper," "My Leap to Freedom," "I Was a Soviet Spy for the FBI," and "I Survived for 21 Days on Barnacles and Salt Water in a Leaky Sailboat in the Pacific."

They also buy confession-type features like "I Cheated on My Tax and Paid—in Jail," "I Killed My Best Friend," "I Married a Murderer," and "I Was Married in a Coed Prison." You can often sell a tightly written feature that has a connection to any news event or seasonal subject. A plethora of assassination, gun control, and Secret Service articles always follows the assassination of a public figure because supplement stories like to give their readers a behind-the-scenes look at public figures and events, whether it be in politics, ecology, space achievements, kidnapings, airplane or ship high-jackings, or solutions to racial problems, generation gaps, style trends, or cold war action.

Start collecting and analyzing all the Sunday supplements you can get. Study, too, the ten Fs of subject matter listed later on in this chapter and plan your original ideas along those lines, but do not duplicate what has already been published. All the titles given in this chapter have been used, so yours should not be the same. Remember, all editors want "fresh and original material that conforms to our formula," as one editor told a writer.

Profit from the advantages of grooming your articles to this supplement market. There are several:

(1) The competition is not as great as in the top slicks.

(2) They work closer to the date deadline, so that Christmas or New Year's material, which must be submitted to the monthly magazines in May or June, still has a chance with the supplements as late as September or October.

(3) If you are a photographer or have access to good pictures, this is an insatiable market for photojournalism.

(4) The simple, down-to-earth, humdrum problems that lack significance for the major markets may be perfect for the homey supplements. Here is the place to practice Dr. Sam Johnson's aphorism: "The two most engaging powers of an author are to make new things familiar and familiar things new."

(5) Studying and writing for this market will help you discipline your word length, for the articles here are brief, usually around 1,000 words.

(6) Supplement research does not need to be as thoroughgoing as in the top magazines, so you have more chance of acceptance. Scientific and technical subjects are written so informally that a psychiatrist wrote in one of these features: "To me psychiatry is not a science of big words and of magic. Our job is to restore people to normal and make them happy." Since you do not have to work as hard researching, you can turn out several supplement articles in the same time you could build one for a major magazine.

The Sunday supplement reflects what people all over America are talking about, laughing at, being afraid of, doing or wanting to do right now. In a sense, each issue is such a miniature culture-capsule of Americana that foreigners and people in the future could derive an understanding of our society from it. Study the ads and how the features harmonize with them.

Like other articles, the one you write for the Sunday supplement must be carefully structured (HEY! YOU! SEE! SO! YOU!). It must build up to a strong premise or express a definite angle about your subject, and it must be slanted for one specific market, with a query letter preceding any article over 1,000 words. Usually these articles are shorter, so a query isn't necessary. Unlike other articles, it should have a universal appeal and never be directed to one limited segment of readership men, women, children, blacks, whites, rural or urban dwellers. It should, instead, interest people of both sexes, all ages, and varying mentalities, political convictions, races, and religions. The supplement article should be timely, except for the rare historical piece, and even it usually explains the origin of a current holiday or fad or hooks up with a news event.

More so than the monthly magazines, the weekly supplements are in step with the headlines and names in the news today. Since all material should be submitted three months in advance, you don't always know who will be the top name in the news or the teen idol of the moment unless you have a crystal ball. But don't worry about it. Items about national or international bigwigs are usually done on assignment by "the regulars" or staff writers; however, if you do have access to an entertainment figure or other fascinating person, don't be afraid to write about him. There's a world of material for you to write about no matter who you know. In fact, the best subjects are *not* the sensational glamour fare, but the often overlooked, everyday items with reader rapport.

You don't need to be an ESP expert to know when America will be sending valentines and Mother's Day or Father's Day cards, stuffing Thanksgiving turkeys, trimming Christmas trees, and thinking in terms of baseball, football, vacationing, or going back to school.

If you are a specialist in any field —real estate, law, education, income tax, medicine, dentistry, photography, police work, or acting—or if you have an interesting hobby—macrame, rock hounding, sportsfishing, skiing, boating, dog breeding, tropical fish—work up an angle on your subject. But of even more importance than this rich speciality is your ability to draw the reader into the material so that it does or can affect him.

The long suit of every supplement piece is *reader identification.* Almost any subject that can be beamed directly at the average American is a good bet. For instance, the space race is made identifiable in "Your Bonus from the Space Race" by Thomas J. Fleming by discussing how space satellites will benefit *your* health, *your* home, *your* weather and *your* communications. An article about the Tracer Insurance Company, which finds beneficiaries to fortunes, actually concerns the few people in their files. But reader identification is implied in the title, "Is There a Fortune Waiting for YOU?" Nuclear power scares most people through personal fears or by being scientifically over their heads, but they are drawn to the title "Nuclear Power Will Make Us All Rich." Technical items or inventions would not interest the relaxing Sunday reader, but a "YOU" title like "Uncle Sam Needs Your Help" hooks his vanity.

Watch for other reader identification titles like "You Are Never Really Alone," "Up Your Mileage and Run for Your Life," "You Can Take It With You," "What Your Teenagers Really Think of You," "How's Your Sense of Humor?" "You Are Under Arrest!" "What Your Dreams Tell about You," and "New Surgical Miracles That Can Save Your Life."

Jot down your original ideas and feelings about subjects that are apt to interest both sexes and all ages who read the supplements. How many can you think of that fit in the following categories of ten Fs: Family Matters, Finances, Fun, Fears, Folks, Fads, Faith, Fashions, Fitness, and Food?

Family Matters

You can always come up with a new angle on love, marriage, child rearing, or family problems on various subjects from dishwashing to discipline. Think of ways to iron out wrinkles in the husband-wife, parent-child, or parent-teacher relationship, or the family's interaction with in-laws, neighbors, or different racial or religious groups. Harmony is the keynote here, as in such pieces as "We Get Along Fine Now" and "We Saved Our Marriage in Advance." Occasionally the supplements use a controversial piece like "Psychiatry Wrecked Our Marriage," "Woman's Lib Is Wrong!" or "Why Parents Should (or Shouldn't) Support Teen Marriages."

Finances

You don't have to show the reader how to be a millionaire, but he does appreciate practical tips for increased success in earning, managing, spending, saving, and investing money. A few examples of published titles are: "Beating the Budget," "Money in Your Pockets," "Why Does Money Wreck Marriages?" "The Nuts and Bolts of Auto Repairs," "Credit Card Pickpockets," "How to Put the Brakes on Gyp Artists," "How to Save Money on Your Income Tax," and "How to Save Money on Your Christmas Shopping."

Fun

It's easy to sell clever articles on humor, games, quizzes (see Chapter 13), travel—anything the family can enjoy doing together. Animal antics are a good bet, especially when accompanied by good action pictures. Vacation features in season are popular as are related subjects like: "How to Travel with Pets and Children," "Fun for Kids," "Take A Diplomat's Tour of America," or "How to Enjoy . . . anything."

Fears

Whenever you write about things people fear, you should suggest a feasible remedy or offer some upbeat hope, for instance: "The Energy Crisis Can Be Solved," "A Little Less Noise, Please," "Ear Pollution is Creating a New Kind of Slum," "Garbage Could Be Hazardous to Your Health" (about radioactive waste), "Wrap Up Your Cares and Go Fishing," and "Dug in for Doomsday" (about the

ABM Missile Command Control Center, a bomb-proof, fast-reacting headquarters for defending our nation). You can write about a whole gamut of affairs, including crime, pollution, delinquency, mental and physical disease, unemployment, wildlife shortage, racketeers, and death, or lighter concerns like snoring, obesity, insomnia, or talking in your sleep. Whatever fears you write about, don't be too morbid or violent for the relaxing Sunday reader. In fact, he'll be happy if you help him avoid unnecessary operations or divorce and if you alleviate his fears on any negative subject.

Folks

If you know or have access to a celebrity or anyone in the public spotlight, this might be your best bet for a quick sale. You may not know royalty or the president's family or celebrities in sports, television, or motion pictures, but perhaps you can write a profile of someone who has done something interesting or is affiliated with a timely subject (see Chapter 4 on interviewing technique).

The local boy or girl who made good is always attractive to his or her hometown paper. Published supplment articles concern "The Soul Savers" (evangelists), "King and Court" (about tennis champ Billie Jean King), "Patrons of Pop," "The Titled Teamster," "Bill Lear and His Amazing Steam Machine," and "The Mixed Marrieds." The premise of the latter is: "The best thing about intermarriage is that you don't have trouble with your in-laws because you don't see them for the first year."

You might even write about an interesting nonhuman like Smokey the Bear, Fritz, the X-rated cat, or a clever animal. A feature about the Queen Mary luxury liner was titled "A 100 Million Tons of Trouble, But What a Woman!"

Fads

You have to be so up-to-the-minute with these that the newest fads at this writing may be old hat by the time you read this. They include hang-gliding, needlepoint, water beds, the occult, mobile homes, personalized license plates, zany bumper stickers, bottlemania, biofeedback, and Alpha waves. Be alert and follow through on any new-fangled fads your kids bring home from school or currently popular sports and styles. One West Coast supplement article titled "California Is a Faddist State" (by Jerry Hopkins) opens:

Scene 1: San Gabriel, California. An engineer for a toy manufacturer hears about a 3-foot bamboo ring used in Australian gym classes. A friend sends him one and soon he has it spinning around his waist. Everyone who sees it wants one.

Scene 2: Los Angeles. A mother watches her daughter cut out and dress paper dolls, wonders if her wardrobes could be designed for 3-dimensional dolls. She tells her daughter, Barbie, about it.

Scene 3: Pasadena. A high-school boy shows his pals a rough piece of wood with roller skate wheels bolted to the bottom, on which he practices surfing around his neighborhood. His friends go home to make their own versions.

Scene 4: High above California, two San Francisco executives, flying home from Los Angeles, discuss a diet suggested by a third. Sipping their drinks, they wonder aloud, "Wouldn't it be great if somebody came up with a drinking man's diet?" So they did.

Thus, rather haphazardly, four fads were born—the hula hoop, the Barbie doll, the skate board, and The Drinking Man's Diet—four of perhaps hundreds born in California in recent years.

Faith

Since the Sunday supplement comes out on what is the sabbath for most Americans, religious articles can go if they are nondenominational, cleverly helpful but not saccharine or sermonizing, and if you have a new angle with great timeliness and reader identification.

When a leading supplement polled readers on what subjects they preferred for sermons, the heaviest votes went to "How Can I Make Prayer More Effective?" "How Can Religion Eliminate Worry and Tension?" "How Can I Make the Greatest Contribution to Life?" "Happier Families through Religion," "What Can the Individual Do for World Peace?" "Religious Approach to Social Problems," "Religious Approach to International Problems," "How to Love the Unloved," "Judging Ourselves Rather Than Others," and "How to Find Peace within Ourselves." Readers want faith related to everyday situations and beliefs that solve problems.

Fashion

If there's a fashion editor on the supplement's staff, you'll have a harder time breaking in, but a relevant subject superbly handled should sell. Try a fresh angle on the latest style in beachwear, work clothes, eveningwear, or weird get-ups. Some recent titles include:

"Clothes to Match the Job," "Fall Fashion Report: Plaid is Part of the Classic Revival," "A Spring Fashion Golf-In," "Choked Up— How to Collar Fashion," "Here Comes the Groom—A Man's Last Opportunity to Let Himself Go Clothing-Wise," "Shaping Up" (new bodyline styles for men), "Fashions That Boom in the Spring," "New Look from the Old World," "A French Look at American Styles," "What Waders Are Wearing," "Suited for Spring," "Why the New Home Sewing Craze?" "Flattering Fashions for Over-40's," and "British is Beautiful." This last-named feature shows how:

> Britannia waives the rules. The young of London are throwing out all fashion commandments in favor of wearing exactly what they want, when and where they want.

Fitness and Health

Readers love self-improvement and any new medical or psychological discoveries that will make them more salubrious. Published features include: "Comebacks from Heart Attacks," "Six Secrets of a Good Night's Sleep," "A 100-Virus Vaccine—How to Fight Infection," "Royal Road to Beauty," a number of articles about safe contraceptive methods, and exercise features like "Wake Up and Walk!"

Food

Food articles may be hard to sell if the publication has a food editor, but you'll make it if you develop a new angle like "Menu from Mars" or "How Space Age Research Helps Nutrition," or if you tie up a food subject with your knowledge of a specific job, travels, hobbies, or a seasonal pitch like "Fun Making Halloween Cookies." Here are the titles of some published free-lance food features: "Rules for Dieting on Auto Trips" (there are a number of published features involving traveling), "Kosher Burritos," "The Formica Gourmet" (about short-order eating), "Fabulous Foods from Faraway Lands," and "Desserts That Sound Fattening But Aren't."

An Alternate Method of Categorization

If the above ten Fs haven't started your mind perking, try categorizing published supplement article titles according to How, What, Where, Why, When, Who, and If. Here are a few:

How

"How America Eats," "How Parents Should Behave," "How to Talk to Your Dog," "How I Changed My Life," "How Will We Treat Foreign Tourists?" "How I Beat " (some top athlete or pop champ), "How to Eat Like an Epicurean in the Wilderness," "How to Dress with Confidence," "How It Feels to Get Clobbered" (Namath), "How Much Do You Know about Being a Parent?" "How Canadians Keep Fit," "How Good a Driver Are You?" "How to Be Your Age and Look Great," "How a TV Boast Trapped an Arsonist," "How to Find Yourself There By Work," "How Do Honest People Differ from Criminals?" "How You Can Make a Cheese Log," "How Can Your Pet Find Happiness?" "How I Picked Up the Pieces," and "How *Not* to Let Frustration Get You Down."

What

"What Makes a Driver Reckless or 'Wreckless'?" "What Psychiatrists Say About Woman's Lib," "What Price Paradise?" "What Foreign Countries Can Do for Us," "What the Dollar Devaluation Means to You," "What Breaks Up a Marriage after 20 Years?" "What Food Will Keep Me Young?" "What Makes People Lucky?" "What Makes Men Appeal to Women?" (or the reverse), "What a Psychiatrist Would Like to Know About You," "What Women Think of Men's Manners," "What Ever Happened to—" "What You Don't Know About Dreams" . . . or anything else.

Where

"Where the Flower Children Went," "Where Do Storks Come From?" "Where You Should Spend Your Weekends," "Where Good Guys Finish First," "Where in the World Are You?" and "Where to Buy 1,000 Things You Don't Need But Might Get Anyway If Only You Could Find Them," and "Where Clowning Around Is a Serious Matter."

When

"When It's Just Too Hot to Cook," "When You Should Clamp Down on Teenagers," and historical items with a current or seasonal tie-up like "When Kentucky Went Broke on the Derby," "When It Was Darkness at Noon," "When Pocahantas Saved John Smith,"

"When You Should Look for a Job," "When You Want to Hit Your Kids," and "When You're Alone You Get to Know Yourself."

Why

"Why Some People Live Such Long Healthy Lives," "Why ——Is Afraid of Marriage," and "Why Women Outlive Men."

Who

Any interesting profile that reveals little-known sidelights of well-known people or introduces the reader to an unknown person who overcame an obstacle or did something commendable. A few are: "He Knows Hollywood's Hottest Secrets," "Who Put the Zip in Zippers?" "Who Starts the Fights in Your Family?" and "Who Really Invented the H-Bomb?"

If

Anything suppositional that casts a new light on the current scene or history like "If the South Had Won the Civil War" or "If Lincoln Were Alive Today." Other "If" titles include "If They Call Your Child 'Chicken'" and "If I'd Bought the Land."

Summary—Don'ts

(1) Don't forget to slant, which means leaning or inclining toward specific readers. The articles you find in a magazine like *Vogue* are not usually appropriate for the supplements. For instance, one sophisticated *Vogue* issue contains an article differentiating various types of mink coats from the emba lutetia to the emba cerulean. (The average supplement reader is more interested in fake furs.) There's also "A Culinary Guide for Imbeciles Who Like to Eat." (The supplement's advertisers consider food sacrosanct!) *Vogue* also features swanky travel articles to jet-set glamour spots, whereas most supplements want their readers to stay home, read their pages, and buy their advertised products from diachondra to diapers. A shorter trip within the contintental U.S. is more appropriate for the supplements.

(2) Don't be pro one segment of readership: pro-men, women, or children, or pro one political party or religion. One of my students wrote an article about the streamlined Episcopalian Sunday school in which she taught. I suggested that she broaden the subject to include

changes in Sunday schools of all denominations. She interviewed other ministers, priests, and rabbis and sold the subsequent article to a top supplement.

(3) Don't forget that the Canadian supplements are excellent markets, are hospitable, and pay high rates.

(4) Don't overwrite. Brevity is the keynote. Heed Arnold Glasgow's words: "Many who have the gift of gab do not know how to wrap it up!" Study the lengths as well as the angles and subjects of published articles. If yours is longer, either cut it or perhaps break it down into two features.

(5) Don't be too controversial or sensational for a market that is for all the family from junior to grandma. Sex subjects may be handled in good taste with a sincere help-the-reader-keep-up-with-the-times style. A few are: "What Sex Education Means to You and Your Child," "Sex and the Single Teenager," and "Stop VD!"

(6) Don't write material that conflicts with the ads and policies of the newspaper. For instance, don't send a piece exposing the dangers of smoking or white sugar and flour to a paper that carries cigarette and cake-mix ads.

(7) Don't forget to highlight human interest in articles about events or things. One editor said, "We'll usually pass up a story about a new bridge, expressway, or skyscraper, but we're always on the lookout for something new about people."

Always keep in mind Thomas Jefferson's definition: "The press is the best instrument for enlightening the mind of man and improving him as a rational, moral and social being."

13

Quick Checks for Quizzes

"No man really becomes a fool until he stops asking questions."—Charles P. Steinmetz

"Who questioneth much shall learn much and contend much. . . . A prudent question is half of wisdom." —Francis Bacon

You can have informative fun by capitalizing on one of human kind's strongest traits—curiosity.

People of all times and climes have taken the riddle or quiz so seriously that prizes were often as valuable as life and property long before our television game shows (to which you can sell). Long ago, the losers were often punished so severely that Homer is said to have died of disgrace and humiliation because he didn't know a right answer. Many Thebans were killed by the Sphinx when they failed to guess the solution to this: "What goes on four feet in the morning, then on two feet in the afternoon, then on three feet at night?" When Oedipus solved it by saying "Man," the monster threw herself to her death and Thebes was freed from the evil spell.

The fascination of the quiz has not dimmed even though we don't spill *red* blood over them. In fact, by learning to write and sell them, you can often keep "out of the *red*" and receive welcome checks to balance a depressing article-reject that may come in the same mail.

To understand perennial quiz-appeal, let's examine why quizzes are, always have been, and always will be popular:

(1) A question intrigues with its built-in challenge. You can be sure of attracting a person by arousing his curiosity, teasing it, and satisfying it.

(2) Man likes to think . . . or at least he likes to think he thinks. That's why *sapiens* (thinking) is added to *homo* (man). Sherlock Holmes (S as in *sapiens*, H as in *homo*) is a most popular fiction character because he reasons, figures out, solves puzzles, *thinks*. With our current renewed interest in learning, this is even more true than ever before. Today, with our learning explosion, more people are being educated, hoping to show off their knowledge and add to it; after all, they see other people's intelligence rewarded with color televisions, refrigerators, washers, and with the thinking person's prize, a higher position.

(3) A quiz appeals to the ham that lurks in everyone . . . the showoff.

(4) Quizzes appeal to people's sense of play.

(5) The dictionary defines quiz as "informal examination." Most people like to be examined if it gives them a chance to exhibit their wit. If it reveals stupidity instead of sagacity, they consider the whole thing sort of a joke, "all in fun." The informality of most quizzes is a face-saver; the lack of seriousness gives people a graceful out if, perchance, they cannot appear as smart as they'd like to.

(6) Perennially popular is the quiz that gives the reader a crack at self-analysis. It makes him a hero because it concerns him and his interests.

The "you" pitch—especially in your quiz title—hooks the reader's vanity and increases his or her sense of participation. No wonder it's so ubiquitous!

You must consider these psychological factors when you plan and write your quiz. It must never make the reader feel inferior or stupid; if possible, it should begin with easy questions and lead him to some right answers, puffing up his pride rather than exposing his lack of knowledge.

You can collect welcome checks for quizzes if you master the technique. A quiz should be built on the principle of association, that is, having a common denominator: different people with the same name, profession, or hobby; different book titles containing the same color, animal, flower, or other word; fiction lovers who never marry; or humble but indispensible servants in different books.

Your quiz must be slanted for a specific magazine and age group, have an eye-catching title, a clever, appropriate opening, an interesting, informative set of answers, and a satisfactory scoring system. The questions should be brief and simple with any necessary explanations incorporated in the answers. There should be from ten to twenty-one questions.

In fact, every quiz should have strong reader rapport, no matter which type it is or for what market. Consider these published titles from a wide range of magazines: In *Reader's Digest,* "What's Your Energy I.Q.?" and "Are You a Genius?"; in *Modern Maturity,* "Trick Your Memory to Remember," "Do You Remember These Ads? . . . the Year?"; in the tabloids, "Test Yourself—Are You a Slave to Habit?" "How to Tell If You're in Danger of Having a Nervous Breakdown," "How Sexy Are You?" "Do You Have Charm?" "How Much Do You Know about Men? . . . about Women?" "Can You Grab an Opportunity?" "Test Your Feelings about Money," "What You Should Know about Yourself," "What Do You Think of Yourself?" "Are You a Good Wife? . . . a Good Husband?"; and a few "you" titles of quizzes from the Sunday supplements, "How Much Do You Know about Being a Parent?" "Is There a Secret to Living beyond Your Years?" "Are You Really What You Eat?" "The Way You See Yourself—Does It Affect How Others See You?" "Do You Know Your Own Levels?" "Do You Know about Your Sense of Smell?" "Little-Known Ways You Can Influence People," "Do Your Neighbors Consider You a Good Neighbor?" "Are You in Danger of Becoming a Neurotic?" "Are You a Good Loser?" and "How Much Do You Know about (Grrrrr) Hostility?" Some of Dr. Joyce Brothers' test titles are: "What Does a Friend Mean to You?" "How Much Do You Know about Love? . . . Marriage?" "How's Your Data on Women's Lib?" and "Are You a Good Parent?"

The Basic Structure of Quizzes

Usually there is a brief, sparkling introduction that states the idea and mood of the quiz in terms that fit the subject matter. For instance, a quiz about dogs asks you to identify canines who have left indelible pawprints on the pages of literature. A medical quiz calls for a medical check-up "for patient people." It asks you to "study all clues and symptoms, then fill in your prescriptions . . . with diagnoses verified on page____." Questions about the West are introduced with "Saddle up, pardner, for a ride through the wild and Woolly West . . . Set your sights on these questions and fire when ready. Check your aim on page____."

The middle and major portion is devoted to the questions themselves; after which there is a list of answers and a well-planned scoring system. The questions are as brief as possible, with necessary elaboration, documentation, and facts given in the answers rather than in the questions. In John Gibson's true-false battle of the sexes quizzes, the burden of explanation is in the answer, not in the question:

> Q. Women tend to be more cheerful and optimistic than men.
> A. FALSE. Studies conducted by University of Southern California psychologists show that women are more subject to feeling depressed and "down in the dumps" than men.

The question-answer method of dispensing information is popular because it involves the reader personally and avoids narrative (which can be dull and preachy); for this reason, it is frequently used in ads. A pharmaceutical company presents a true-false quiz "How Much Do You Know about VD?" with such questions as: "Once you are cured of VD, you are immune to it" (false); and "Damage from untreated syphillis may not show up for five to twenty years" (true). An insurance company ad gives a quiz on insurance that you're sure to flunk, but they'll gladly send a representative to straighten you out about the facts of insurance life.

A floor-covering firm runs a colorful ad-quiz titled "What Kind of Man Are You Married To?" with such questions as: "When the water pipe breaks, my husband: (A) calls the plumber; (B) fixes it himself; (C) asks me to fix it; (D) puts on his water wings." The ad then explains how their product makes (B) the easy and, of course, correct answer.

More and more columnists vary their narrative format with quiz presentations. Art Buchwald's satirical "Quick Quiz for Students of the World Monetary Crisis" contains such questions as:

> Q. If I have five French francs and you have three West German deutschemarks, what will we have all together?
> A. One of the damndest money messes since World War II.

Q. What can the average American do until the money crisis blows over?
A. Take an Englishman to lunch.

Dr. Joyce Brothers and Elizabeth L. Post are more serious in their informative quiz columns. From the former's "Effects of Environment" quiz:

> The constant noise in most urban areas seems to act as a kind of stimulant to many people and it generally increases their sexual activity. True ( )   False ( )
> FALSE. Dr. Maurice Schiff feels that too much noise tends to lead to infrequent sexual activity, and that sexual incompatibility may be caused by noise. The country person seems to be better off sexually because of less noise and fewer distractions.

Dr. Brothers's worry quiz asks several questions, carefully authenticated in the answers. Here are two samples:

> Time seems to go more slowly when you're worried and anxious. True ( )   False ( )
> TRUE. Studies at Clark University reveal that nothing makes time pass more slowly than anxiety. The greater the anxiety or worry, the more time seems to stand still.

> The truly healthy person rarely experiences anxiety or worry. True ( )   False ( )
> FALSE. The person who never worries and never is anxious is probably in serious trouble. Any sensitive, mature individual in today's world worries. If he does not, something is wrong.

Mrs. Post lets you play quiz games while learning rules of etiquette . . . and the subject is less stuffy:

> Taking leftover food home from a restaurant in a "doggy bag" is, and always has been in the poorest of taste.
> FALSE This used to be so, but today restaurants encourage the practice and it would seem foolish to leave a large, untouched portion of "dry food" which you have paid for.

> Children whose parents are divorced should not attend their mother's or father's second wedding.
> FALSE. Unless they are strongly opposed to the marriage, they should certainly be there as part of a new family unit.

Since an unusually large number of free-lance markets offer opportunities for your quiz features, it is wise to begin making a list of magazines that publish quizzes—all the way from the juveniles to the adult avant garde.

As you become more proficient in quiz technique, you may someday sell a collection of your quizzes in paperback or hardcover, so ask your purchasing editor to revert book rights to you after publication. Naturally, to achieve such success you must structure and slant.

Quizzes for the Juvenile Market

There's a plethora of juvenile markets, from those enjoyed by the tiny tots to rather sophisticated teenagers interested in current events, dating, drugs, politics, sports, words, literature, arts, crafts, history, and natural history. Know your age group (and in the case of the many hospitable religious juveniles, the dogma and taboos, even though your subjects do not have to be religious.)

Parents like to buy magazines that have puzzles, quizzes, and "fun things to do" to occupy young minds on rainy days and during sickness—and to rescue them from mentally-stultifying television. And most kids love to learn when it's fun and when they can participate with you, the author. They like brainbusters, acrostics, mazeword puzzles . . . you can even invent your own forms.

Word jumbles are popular. From a longer list of words, each of which makes three others, we have:

> BARG—brag, garb, grab
> TOSP—stop, post, spot
> CEAM—came, acme, mace

> Bird word jumbles contain:

> WOLSLAW—swallow
> WROC—crow
> CHINGFOLD—goldfinch
> LOW—owl.

Children's editors like silly riddles like "What did the bird say when the cage broke?" "Cheep! Cheep!"; "How would you describe a bull that swallowed a bomb?" "Abombinable"; "Where did Columbus go on his 21st birthday?" "Into his 22nd year."; "Is there a word in the dictionary that contains all five vowels?" "Yes, unquestionably." Silly or serious mathematical problems are also popular.

Quizzes for the Men's Market

Men's quizzes are concerned with subjects of male interest, with high-paying *Playboy* liking wacky, satirical humor like Craig Vetter's "The Great American Authors Test"—captioned "A quiz to determine whether your psyche is sufficiently wounded to qualify you as a serious writer." It opens:

> Everybody knows writers are crazy. They jump off bridges and boats, finally, or drown in gutters, and before that they shoot themselves in the legs with machine guns, stab their wives on purpose and are pretty much the heaviest juicers at the cosmic party.
>
> Since the debaucheries and the general misfortune of spirit that it takes to be a truly great American writer aren't the sorts of things you can measure in journalism classes, we've devised a snappy quiz that should protect you from the agony of actually sitting down to a typewriter before you're sure you have the deep and chronic head problems the job demands.

Even more bitter and unconventional is "Bah! Humbug!"— captioned "A puppy-kicking 20-questions quiz designed to measure your Scrooge-worthiness" (David Stevens and Alfred De Bat, *Playboy*). It starts:

> G. B. Shaw put it rather nicely when he called Christmas "an indecent subject; a cruel, gluttonous subject; a drunken, wicked, cadging, lying, filthy, blasphemous and demoralizing subject, concluding that if he had his way, "anyone who looked back to it would be turned into a pillar of greasy sausages." Ebenezer Scrooge, however, was a bit more succinct. "If I could work my will," said Scrooge indignantly, "every idiot who goes about with 'Merry Christmas' on his lips should be boiled with his own pudding and buried with a stake of holly through his heart."
>
> So now that the holidays are once again upon us, here's a quiz.designed to plumb the depths of your own acid content. . . ." (followed by directions for taking the quiz and scoring, to discover surprising things about yourself!)

Psychological subjects are popular here, often along the line of "What's your S.Q. (Sexual Quotient)?" and authentic self-analyses like "What's Your Intimacy Quotient?" (by Gina Allen and Clement Martin, M.D.). These often reflect subjects that are currently popular at the time of publication. See how this quiz opening promises self-information in relationship to the subject of many best sellers:

> Psychologists have variously and gloomily diagnosed our society as neurotic, emotionally plagued, armored, flattened, one-

dimensional, contactless, repressed, robotic and addicted to game playing. These are ways of saying that intimacy is lacking in human relationships—that it is the missing link between our rationality and our emotions, between men and women, between love and sex. Without a sense of intimacy, interpersonal contact becomes a worrisome job of guarding our psychic territory against invaders. . . .

Since *Playboy* readers aspire to financial as well as bedroom-success, one of their inevitable self-exams was titled "Playboy's Executive Quiz" and was captioned,: "Here's a mirror at the top of the promotional ladder to help see yourself as your superiors see you." All the techniques are used here—reader identification, with style and subject matter slanted to the specific reader of a particular magazine.

Quizzes for the Women's Market

Quizzes for the women's magazines stress subjects of current interest. But as strong as Woman's Liberation, equal rights, job hunting, and job keeping are, there is and always will be a preference for quizzes that test and improve the reader's self-improvement, popularity, and the man-woman relationships. Many publications for women, like *Cosmopolitan*, *Glamour*, and teen-magazines like *Mademoiselle* publish lots of quizzes with such titles as "How Feminine Are You?" "Why You Hate Housekeeping," etc.

Notice how the necessary quiz techniques spark these openings: "Are You a Threat to Men?" (by David S Viscott, M.D.) opens:

> Do you ever have the feeling that you sometimes turn men off . . . some subtle thing flows from you to them that they don't *like*—even though you feel you *adore* the male sex? This quiz is designed to help you discover how threatening (castrating) you appear to men. . . .

"How Well Do You Know Him?" (by Ernest Dichter, Ph.D.) starts:

> You may think you know how your man would behave in all circumstances, but do you really? This test is designed to help you find out for sure . . . . Try to visualize him in each situation described, then check how you think he would act. . . . After you've finished, get him to answer also (without seeing yours) . . . This test *does* need to be taken with a man, for its purpose is not to establish whether he is poised, neurotic, or attractive but how well *you* know him.

"Your Ideal Man" (by Roy Bongartz) also begins with an intimate you-the-woman approach:

> Have you ever given serious thought to the qualities your perfect man should have? Well, you can do that right now by answering a series of questions that will help pinpoint the sort of male you find attractive. We can't give you his name and address, but we can tell you what profession he's apt to be in. (People of similar temperament, interests and characteristics do congregate in specific jobs, researchers have found.) And we'll also give you some hints on where to *locate* members of that profession. The rest is up to you!

This is an ideal opening because it is a promissory note that is paid off after the scoring section in a conclusion labeled "Man-finding hints." Here the quiz-taker is told which cities and states have the most men who are actors, athletes, commercial artists, ad men, doctors, teachers, farmers, pilots, diplomats, bankers, brokers, chemists, and others. A fair warning is given regarding millionaires:

> Sorry, but statistically your chances aren't good. Of the 60,000 American millionaires, nearly half are women, and 25,000 of the men are married. This leaves about 5,000 single or widowed male plutocrats, and most of them are over 50! If you just want someone who makes good money, try the states that rank highest in personal income: Connecticut, New York, Alaska, California and Illinois. . . .

No matter what your subject or market, you need researched facts and statistics to bag those big checks! This is true of almost all quizzes, including those that sell to the supplements, the general slicks, in-flight and special magazines like *Family Health*. Recent ones give valuable information about insurance, the stock market, health, the space program, seasonal and historical subjects, as well as general psychology. Some use questionnaires that the whole family can take, probably on the assumption that "the family that plays together stays together." Some are serious funfests like "The Zoo Game," which opens: "What kind of a beast are you? Could be you're a squirrel, rhino, or heaven forbid, a hippo or . . . read on. . . ." Naturally your typical reactions or actions in given situations categorize you!

Some quizzes are more sophisticated, but preferably helpful, like "How's Your Current Knowledge on Electricity?" by Lillian Borgeson. This is so chockful of vital, possibly life-saving information that it should be required reading! (Try to make your quiz that urgent on a subject you either know well or have researched thoroughly.) This quiz opens:

> Electricity is like most forms of power: the more you know about it, the less likely you are to be bothered by it. To gauge your own insulation against everyday electrical hazards, see how well you score in this safety quiz. Answers on Page_____.

Types of Quizzes

A quiz can be built on any subject—physical fitness, psychology, philosophy, health, history, human nature, science, the stock market, or any phase of life or literature. You can translate pedantic facts into commercial scripts by converting technical information into quizzes that let the reader participate and play guessing games while he is learning. There are many possible forms for quizzes. Decide on the best one for your subject matter and market, then stay with that one pattern throughout the quiz. The most popular are the following.

True-False

The true-false quiz is always popular because the reader has a guessing-chance to be right, then he learns the full facts in the answer section. Your true-false statements can range from the juvenile simplicity of "The Milky Way is a method of fertilizing vegetables" to John Gibson's battle of the sexes questions "Men are more egotistical than women" and "Women are better at solving complicated problems than men" (with authenticated explanations in the answers).

Even in the case of difficult questions, the true-false format gives the reader a chance to get a decent score, and he gleans *more* information than he knew before in the answer, which is often verified by authorities or statistics.

Crane Evans's "Who Works Harder?" quiz contrasts man-work against woman-chores:

> Ironing takes as much energy as plowing with a tractor.
> TRUE. An hour's ironing and an hour's plowing both use 252 calories of energy.
>
> Cleaning windows is harder work than carpentry.
> FALSE. Cleaning windows takes 222 calories an hour. Carpentry takes 408 calories an hour.

John Eppingham's "What Your Sense of Humor Reveals about Your Personality" cites authorities in the answers:

> Intelligence and a well-developed sense of humor go hand in hand.
> TRUE. Studies at Purdue University and Vassar College have shown conclusively that a keen appreciation of wit and humor indicates a corresponding keen intelligence. Persons scoring highest on I.Q. tests showed the greatest ability to see the humorous side of things. . . .
>
> A sense of humor is an important factor where physical health and well-being are concerned.
> TRUE. Findings of the Michigan State University studies and others elsewhere make it clear that humor. . . provides a safety valve for the discharge of tensions.

John E. Gibson's "People Quizzes" testify to the fact that he keeps up with psychological research. Here are a few examples: "So You Think You're an Expert on Love!":

> Women are more inclined than men to believe in the starry-eyed love of pure romance.
> FALSE. Sociological studies at the University of California and elsewhere have shown that men are much more idealistic in their attitude toward love. Women may *appear* to be more romantically oriented, but personality tests show that they are more realistic.

"Do You Know What Tricks Your Memory Plays?":

> You can't remember as well when you're cold.
> TRUE. University of California studies have shown that chilling temperatures impair our recall abilities.

Another true-false quiz, "How Much Do You Know About Your Hair?" gives facts and motivation in the answers:

> Redheads are always sensitive and have explosive tempers.
> FALSE. This myth originated in ancient England where an aversion to the red-haired Danish invaders prevailed."
>
> Hair and fingernails do not grow after death.
> TRUE. Hair and nails depend on blood circulation for growth.

From a general information quiz:

> A. Your hair can be raised by intense fright.
> B. Robert Fulton invented the steamboat.
> C. Cats always land on their feet when tossed in the air.

Answers:

A. TRUE. Each hair on your body is equipped with a tiny muscle capable of pulling the hair erect when stimulated by sudden fear.

B. FALSE. Fulton's steamboat was first demonstrated in 1803. He was preceded by steamboats built by John Fitch in 1787 and by James Rumsey in the same year.

C. TRUE. A Dutch scientist proved that even when that part of a cat's brain controlling all voluntary acts is removed the animal will still land on its feet.

Yes-No

The yes-no is similar in form to the true-false:

Do moles have eyes?
Yes, but skin over the eyeballs protects them. Moles can distinguish light from darkness, but that's about all.

Are oysters poisonous in months without the 'r'?
No. But summer is the spawning season and their meat has an inferior flavor.

Sometimes a third answer, uncertain, is added to the simple yes or no, as in this job-happiness quiz:

Are you usually irritable when you come home from work?
Yes____ No____ Uncertain____
Do you suffer from a nervous stomach while at work?
Yes____ No____ Uncertain____
Do you often envy your friends?
Yes____ No____Uncertain____

Multiple Choice

Each question in a multiple-choice quiz is followed by several answers, one of which is either the only correct one or the choice that merits the highest score. These can be either factual or psychological, as demonstrated by the examples that follow.

From "How Well Do You Know Your Famous Sisters?" by Abby Adams and Sue Ristine:

If you decide to keep your maiden name after marriage, you can said to be a disciple of:
A. Alix Kates Shulman
B. Gloria Steinem
C. Lucy Stone
D. Susan B. Anthony

The first woman to be elected to the U.S. Senate was:
A. Margaret Chase Smith, Maine, 1948
B. Frances Perkins, Massachusetts, 1932
C. Hattie Caraway, Arkansas, 1932
D. Helen Gahagan Douglas, California, 1944
E. Suzanne LaFollette, New York, 1920
Which of these designers is *not* a woman?
A. Schiaparelli
B. Vionnet
C. Cardinali
D. Balenciaga
E. Grès
F. Callot
Correct answers: C; C; D.

From Mark J. Appleman's "Are You a Good or Bad Investor?":

Buying at the low, selling at the high
A. is the only way to invest
B. is a desirable goal
C. can't be done except by liars
The best stock to buy is one
A. other people you respect are in
B. you have inside information about
C. that seems to meet your objective better than any other
D. that's priced low enough to fit your budget

From a feminine "How Sexy Are You?" quiz by Jeannie Sakol:

A boyfriend has just phoned to say he'll be over in 10 minutes.
You:
A. take a 3-minute bubble bath
B. straighten the living room and get rid of that half-eaten sandwich
C. straighten the bedroom and see that the lighting is warm and flattering.
Which of the following most closely matches your food preference?
A. icy-cold melon
B. strawberry shortcake with mountains of whipped cream
C. crisp, pungent pepperoni pizza—spicy and sharp

From a general quiz, "Do You Get the Most Out of Life?" by Robert Glenton (notice the wide appeal of the opening):

Is there an adventurous gleam in your eye? Are you really alive and *living*? Do you find each day exciting, or is it just something with 24 hours in it?
This quiz will tell you just how receptive you are to life's

challenges and perhaps awaken you to its interesting and infinite possibilities.

Would you like: (a) more sleep (b) less sleep? (c) or are you getting enough?

How many really idle hours (watching TV or such) do you have in an average week? (a) none. (b) 10 or less. (c) 25 or less. (d) more than 25.

If you inherited $10,000 but with the proviso that it must not be used to pay bills or add to your household possessions, would you: (a) invest it? (b) invest half of it and spend the other half on a vacation? (c) buy something that would give you some fun—a boat, for instance?

Another psychological quiz that tests a man's calibre as a husband is appropriately titled "Are You a Better Spouse than a Louse?" It consists of three different solutions for given situations, with a scoring system that puts the husband-reader in his proper niche. A few are:

1. You are on your way to a cocktail party, and nearly there, when you notice a sizable stain on the back of your wife's dress. Would you
    A.   tell her?
    B.   not tell her and do nothing?
    C.   not tell her but try and stand around behind her to act as a screen?

2. At the party you observe that your wife is in the clutches of the biggest bore in the place, while you have just been introduced to a ravishing glamour girl. Would you
    A.   drop the G.G. and rush over and rescue your wife?
    B.   rush to rescue taking G.G. with you?
    C.   decide she's out of luck?

3. "Man's work lasts till set of sun/But woman's work is never done . . ." Do you consider that this adage is
    A.   100% correct?
    B.   somewhat overstated?
    C.   ridiculously exaggerated?

4. You have stayed on at the office local, drinking with the boys. Do you
    A.   ring up your wife and say you're sorry?
    B.   stay out till all hours hoping she'll be asleep when you get home?
    C.   not give a damn?

This quiz has a humorous closing that tells the husband whether he is a better spouse than a louse. If he is a good spouse, his answers would be: 1—A; 2—B; 3—A; 4—A.

Comparison or More or Less

Like the true-false, any information in addition to the correct answer should appear in the answer section, *not* the question.

In "Calorie Countdown," the reader checks the less fattening food:

> apple or tangerine
> cup of canned fruit cocktail or a cream puff
> big slice of watermelon or half a cantaloupe
> cup of applesauce or a cup of fresh strawberries
> Camembert cheese or Roquefort cheese
> one anchovy or one shrimp

> *Answers:*
> A tangerine has 35 calories; an apple, 75
> A a cream puff has 125 calories; a cup of canned fruit cocktail, 175 . Surprise!
> Half a cantloupe has 35 calories; a big slice of watermelon, 120
> A cup of applesauce has 185 calories; strawberries, 55
> An ounce of Camembert has 85 calories; Roquefort, 111
> A shrimp has 2 calories; an anchovy, 10.

Fill in the Blanks

All ages like fill in the blanks, from tots to adults. However, be sure that there is a common denominator.

A simple, fun juvenile quiz is titled "Lost on the Prairie":

> These Indians have lost all their vowels (a,e,i,o,u). Can you help them find their tribes? Fill the blanks with the right vowels to spell the tribes' names.

N__V__H__	NAVAHO
CH__CK__S__W	CHICKASAW
P__WN____	PAWNEE
__A__CH__	APACHE
S__N__C__	SENECA

"Man Hunt" is constructed along the same principle:

1. Man _____. Musical instrument.
2. General _____ man. Marched through Georgia during the Civil War.
3. Man _____. Sold by the Indians for $24.
4. Ethel _____ man. Broadway singer.

Aswers: 1. Mandolin. 2. Sherman. 3. Manhattan. 4. Merman.

From a *Good Housekeeping* quiz in a romantic Valentine issue

> Give these famous lovers their proper mates:

Tristan and _____
Romeo and _____
Pelleas and _____
Ophelia and _____

Answers: Isolde, Juliet, Melisande, and Hamlet.

From a more complex quiz, "Bels, Bells, Belles!"

Belle _____ was a Confederate spy.
Acton Currer and Ellis Bell were the pseudonyms of these famous writing sisters:_____, _____ and
_____ _____.
The deadly nightshade is the bell _____
Belle _____ was a notorious American outlaw.
This "Belle" is a famous New York hospital.

Answers: Boyd; Anne, Charlotte and Emily Bronte; belladonna; Starr; Bellevue

Mix and Match, Association, or Scrabble

In any of these formats, the questions (words or phrases) are in the left column, answers in the right.

"Blackstone in Brief" by Dr. Raymond J. Murphy is a helpful legal terminology quiz that opens:

Pity the poor man in court for the first time, who thinks that *damnum infectum* means a nasty illness . . . when it really means that he may be endangering somebody's property or reputation. How good are you at deciphering other common and important legal phrases?

Lawyers' Language	*Translation*
1. a priori	a. suit pending
2. bona fide	b. deductive
3. caveat emptor	c. produce the body
4. habeas corpus	d. in good faith
5. ipso facto	e. let the buyer beware
6. sui generis	f. at first view

Answers: 1-b; 2-d; 3-e; 4-c; 5-f; 6-a

From a literary quiz that asks the reader to match title and author:

1. "The Moon and Sixpence"	( ) Jack London
2. "Valley of the Moon"	( ) Lady Gregory
3. "The Rising of the Moon"	( ) Somerset Maugham

Answers: 3, 2, 1.

Also popular are word quizzes:

1. bumpkin   ( ) small cucumber
2. gherkin   ( ) term of endearment for girl or woman
3. jerkin   ( ) awkward fellow; lout
4. manikin   ( ) close fitting jacket, of leather
5 minikin   ( ) little man; pygmy, or dwarf

Answers: 2, 5, 1, 3, 4

Straight Answer

The reader must rely on his own knowledge with no help from the author in straight answer quizzes. Either the questions are individualized so that only the reader knows them—as in self-analysis memory-tests with such questions as "What was your first favorite song or movie star?"—or they are beamed at an intelligent reader who is particularly versed in this field.

One quiz asks you to name writers who were doctors:

1. A popular lecturer in anatomy and physiology for forty years and a founder of the Tremont Medical School in Boston, this M.D. is best remembered as an essayist and writer of light verse.

2. An eminently successful novelist and playwright for over fifty years, this writer recorded some of his experiences as a medical student in Liza of Lambeth (1897).

Answers: Oliver Wendell Holmes (Senior, not his son, the Supreme Court judge) and Somerset Maugham

In a *Health* quiz:

1. What metallic element is essential to good, red blood?
2. What is the cause of scurvy?
3. When you suffer from parotitus what do you have?

Answers: Iron, lack of Vitamin C, mumps

One Word Common to All

This type of quiz uses the familiar word association. One example asks "What word fits in front of these quintets?":

Seas, Jump, Hat, School, Treason
Circuit, Cut, Story, Wave, Stop
Cross, Herring, Tape, Light, China
Verse, Lance, Enterprise, Port, Will

Answers: High; Short; Red; Free

See how many of these eight types of quizzes you can find, then select the best form for your quiz idea(s). There are many others: photoquizzes, anagrams, riddles, and tricky ones like Charles Rice's "World's Cussedest Quizzes," in which the obvious answer is wrong, and a reverse "Diabolical Quiz" (by Thomas Sharkey in *Reader's Digest*) in which the ridiculously obvious answers are right!

An in-flight magazine features a free-lance department titled "Games Passengers Play," which is captioned:

> An astounding Assortment of Perplexing Puzzle Pages, Quixotic Quizzes, Conceptual Competitions and Enigmatic Oddities—all for the Intellectually Inclined.

Whether intellectually-oriented or not, your quiz should provide informational entertainment to brighten your reader's journey through life, help him avoid daily tedium, and encourage his adventure into reading. Fun and play should be your goals when you write quizzes, which can be a welcome change of pace from your serious writing, sharpen your mental discipline, and perhaps even inspire you with a valuable gimmick for a more ambitious work.

No matter whether your quiz writing leads to a column, paperback collection, or just quick checks— Enjoy! Enjoy!

You'll enjoy more success in this field if you observe the tips in the following acrostic:

Q = Questions that are clear, concise, and meaty, beginning with easy-to-answer ones that become more difficult.

U = Urgency of subject with ubiquity of appeal so that it concerns a large percentage of the readers of a specific magazine.

I = Insight into the quiz-taking reader's character, behavior patterns, and knowledge, with help as to how he can improve them.

Z = Zeal in researching and presenting your material in a zestful way. Be sure to zoom into your subject in the title or first paragraph so that the reader is not misled or confused.

14

Writing Book Reviews

"A wise skepticism is the first attribute of a good critic."
—James R. Lowell

"The rule in carving holds good as to criticism: never cut with a
knife what you can cut with a spoon."—Charles Buxton

A book review is a double interview: you must conduct a thorough
analysis and evaluation of a book (the same is true of a play or movie)
plus its author and relay the essence of both to your specific readers.
You are permitted to inject more of yourself than in the average
interview, since you are acting in the capacity of critic and your
opinion will score points in turning others toward or away from the
work in question.

Every author should be a book reviewer (and many famous ones
are).

You cannot write in a vacuum if your works are going to be
worthwhile. In addition to the research and perhaps experience you
synthesize in your own and related fields of interest, you must keep
up with recent publications in unrelated fields in order to know what
readers and publishers want.

What better way to keep abreast of what's new, build your own
library, and stimulate your mind than by becoming a reviewer? You
will receive the newest books free plus many bonus advantages:
sharpening your critical awareness so that you can be more objective

about your own work and therefore improve it; getting "inside the heads" of successful authors; and perfecting your concentration, since you must ingest and digest several hundred pages of information and relay their substance to the reader in a few hundred words.

Good book (or play) reviewing, like every other type of success, requires specific techniques. It must do much more than prove that you read the book (or saw the play or movie) and liked it or did not.

Whether you're writing a short or long report for a local or national publication, you should answer the following questions:

1. What does the work as a whole say?
2. Can I offer a capsule statement of the author's premise?
3. How well does the book accomplish the author's purpose?
4. What effect, if any, will the work have on the reader (or viewer)?
5. If I like and recommend it, can I offer reasons?
6. If I don't like it, can I offer reasons?
7. Can I offer a well-balanced critique, pointing out both pluses and minuses?
8. Can I use appropriate imagery, adding style and punch?
9. Am I thinking of my readers and slanting specifically for them?

In the sections that follow, a number of examples are offered to show you how these questions could be answered.

What Does the Work as a Whole Say?

The opening paragraphs of a review often offer a summary of the content of the work as a whole. To be most effective, you should develop the habit of concentrating the essence of the work in as few words as possible. The content summaries that follow are not meant as finished copy for your review but as the outline from which you would develop two or three tightly written paragraphs. The actual length of your summarizing paragraphs will depend upon your specific market; the reviews in *Library Journal* are often shorter than 100 words.

Raising Children in a Difficult Time by Dr. Benjamin Spock:

"In the eternal war between the generations, it is the initial battles over trivia that are important in achieving a stable balance of power." When it is necessary to achieve that balance of power the author favors "firm if moderate discipline." The present deplorable situation of children refusing to grow up and remaining kids interminably (prefering their own fads, music, clothes, etc.) is due to the fact that adults do not really mature themselves and even compete with their children in dress, sports, and faddishness.

Death By Choice by Daniel C. Maguire:

"The problem of willful death-dealing is as old as man. What makes it a matter of new and insistent urgency are: (1) revolutionary developments in medical science; (2) the laggardly state of the law; and (3) important shifts in moral outlook." The author approves of euthanasia in certain cases.

Sexual Suicide by George F. Gilder:

Reversing the Victorian concept that women are too delicate and spiritual to be subjected to contact with the vulgar realities of nondomestic life, the author argues that men are so inferior sexually and so terrified of this fact that without the domesticating control and encouragement of women they would all collapse into madness, murder, sloth, and/or suicide. Women should remain domesticated for the protection of men and for the balance of society.

Saved, the shocker play by Edward Bond:

[Without giving away all the action (except the world-famous horror scene in which a gang of delinquents stone a baby to death) reviewer Edith Oliver informs us of the mood and substance of this drama.]

". . . it is about the compromises that the characters are forced to make, and their submission to circumstances, partly out of inertia of defeat and partly out of the instinctive knowledge that changing those circumstances, even if that were possible, wouldn't make much difference."

Economics and the Public Purpose by John Kenneth Galbraith:

Insatiable consumption—the American addiction—causes more problems than it pretends to solve, and the market system of supply-and-demand is controlled and unbalanced by an all-powerful corporate technostructure. Galbraith sums up his indictment thus: "Unequal development, inequality, frivolous and erratic innovation, environmental assault, indifference to personality, power of the state, inflation . . . are part of the system as they are part of reality."

Working: People Talk About What They Do All Day and How They Feel About What They Do by Studs Terkel:

> With the exception of workers who feel that what they do is meaningful, the "work ethic" is a myth and "pride in work for work's sake" a misconception. The deterioration of goods and services is not due to laziness, but to the exploitation of workers. The real culprits are the snooping and harassment business uses to control its employees.

The American Condition by Richard N. Goodwin:

> This book reiterates Reich's *Greening of America* but adds that we are *all* the "oppressed." There is no ruling class to blame, there is only a ruling force—the impersonal but seductive power of the great public and private bureaucracies. "Freedom is the use and fulfillment of our humanity—its powers and wants—to the outer limits fixed by the material conditions and capacity of our time."

Can I Offer a Capsule Statement of the Author's Premise?

Since readers of reviews often look for capsule statements, or handles, to decide whether a book might interest him, practice writing one or two sentence statements like the following:

His Picture in the Papers by Richard Schickel: We punish our idols mercilessly after raising them too high.

A Different Woman by Jane Howard: An unmarried woman can live a full, rich life. The more a woman talks, the more mysterious and complex she proves to be.

The Beginning Was the End by Oscar Kiss Maerth: Once an ancient ape discovered that eating the brain of another ape increased his intelligence and potence; whereupon he created the human race with all its follies.

The Big Change by Max Nicholson: "Our inherited culture is dying and can no longer be serviceable to us. We must find a global view of man's life and function on earth.

The Last Butterfly by Michael Jacot: Humor can help to alleviate inconceivable misery. In this poignant story of a Pagliacci in prison, clown Antonin Karas cheered up children in Terezin concentration camp before they were murdered in the gas ovens.

How Well Does the Book Accomplish the Author's Purpose?

One reviewer explained that, in his *Denial of Death*, Ernest Becker tried to show

> how mankind tries to transcend death in culturally standard ways—through heroism, narcissism, charisma, religion, and even neuroses. He examines the works of Kierkegaard, Rank, and Freud, and the personality of Freud in light of his theory. And he ventures into the first full-scale confrontation and interpretation of the thought of Otto Rank, the important but neglected disciple of Freud.

Becker succeeded so well that he was awarded a posthumous Pulitzer Prize, and his book was acclaimed by theologians as well as psychologists, doctors, and other scientists.

What Effect, if Any, Will the Work Have on the Reader (or Viewer)?

Of Becker's *The Denial of Death* , Dr. Elisabeth Kubler-Ross, M.D., wrote: "One of those rare masterpieces that will stimulate your thoughts, your intellectual curiosity, and last but not least, your soul."

Playboy pays tribute to Lillian Hellman's autobiography, *Pentimento* because it "summarizes and examines her own rich life so thoroughly and meaningfully that it makes the reader feel he has somehow missed the boat." How can you tell what effect the work will have on readers? Obviously, you can't always, since tastes, intellectual backgrounds, moods, and reader needs and interests vary so widely. You can only do your best at evaluating the material and sincerely state your own reaction to it. You can play a fascinating game of comparing and contrasting different reviewers' critiques of the same work.

Cosmo's book reviewer Mary Ellin Barrett has nothing but praise for James Baldwin's sixteenth novel, *If Beale Street Could Talk,* which she considers "the author's sharpest battle cry yet." On the contrary, John W. Aldridge (in *Saturday Review*) considers it a namby-pamby "cop out" of false sentimentality and unreality. He says:

> It is extremely sad to see a writer of Baldwin's large gifts

producing, in all seriousness, such junk. Yet it has been evident for some time that he is deteriorating as a novelist and becoming increasingly a victim of the vice of sentimentality.

You will find many contradictory reviews of the same book, depending upon the readership of the magazines in which the reviews were published. There is room for different opinions in the democracy of book reviewing, which is why there will always be a need for good reviewers who conscientiously peruse a work, distill its essence for the reader, and then honestly pass judgment on its merits or demerits.

If I Like and Recommend It, Can I Offer Reasons?

Edward Weeks praises Edwin O. Reischauer's *Toward the 21st Century* for its clarity and "its calm assessment of the imponderables and its hope, based on the experience of Japan, that West and East can meet."

Playboy calls *Jonathan Livingston Seagull* "ornithology's answer to *Lost Horizon* and *Love Story*. In an age of cynicism and moral slippage, a languid little hymn to positive thinking can justly lay claim to equal time."

Herbert Gold writes of Carolyn See's *Blue Money: Pornography and the Pornographers:*

> As to style and form, this book is a model of what the best New Journalism can do to a subject. Second of all, pick the right and appropriate pop subject; first of all, attack with delicacy, discretion, ample but not overflowing information, genuine involvement but not abandonment (emotion recollected in busy tranquility). Dr. See . . . is good-humored throughout, not earnest or prurient.
> . . . The reader grows to like the observer as he takes a ride with her which could have seemed a little, uh, icky.

Gold also is impressed by the theme of the book:

> . . . These men, since they owe their riches to the fantasies of millions, aren't cut off from those millions, but are their representatives, as much as any governor or congressman or movie star. . . . They are often outlaws in the best sense . . . . They are extraordinarily free. . . .

If I Don't Like It, Can I Offer Reasons?

Reviewer Richard Todd says *The Fan Man* by William

Kotzwinkle is "so cute it could hug itself"; *Death, Sleep and the Traveler* by John Hawkes is "too narrow, gamelike and self-protective to justify the formidable claims that are made for him"; and Lois Gould's *Final Analysis* is:

> . . . amusing stuff, but pat and romantic: It glamorizes more than it satirizes the plight in question. Its ideal reader is the girl from a small mining town out West who'd love to suffer the way they do Back East.

Harold Clurman criticizes Edward Albee's glibness in writing of human torment (*Who's Afraid of Virginia Woolf?*):

> What I object to is that its disease has become something of a brilliant formula, as slick and automatic as a happy entertainment for the trade. . . The pessimism and range . . . are immature. Immaturity coupled with a commanding deftness is dangerous.

Malcolm Muggeridge feels that the biography *Solzhenitsyn* by David Burg and George Feifer is unnecessary and superfluous, piecing together "scraps of information without any access to the man himself or to any authentically personal documents." He considers the book inexcusably inferior to the self-portraits in the author's works.

Playboy often objects to the device of stringing articles together to make a book. Two examples are John Sack's *The Man-Eating Machine* and George Plimpton's *Mad Ducks and Bears*, which, "like some other books cobbled together from leftover notes and tapes and previously published magazine pieces . . . could have been a zero." It is saved by the author's insights and characterizations.

Playboy also finds Emma Rothschild's *Paradise Lost* too viciously critical of the U.S. auto industry. "She presents every fact, every supposition, every quote as if she were a prosecuting attorney going for the death sentence." Robert Kirsch faults Richard Condon's *Winter Kills* thus:

> In his effort to expose the American penchant for regarding news, however tragic or somber, as entertainment, he has fallen into the same trap. In his search for sensation he has gone into the orbit of paranoid fantasy.

Victor Lieberman criticizes the emotionlessness of Brown Meggs' *Saturday Games:*

. . . the events are arranged as if programmed by a computer. The screenplay-like style suggests the sterile language of a machine. The characters don't live outside the printed page. There is no life to what they do. In the book, a crime occurs. We are introduced to the people involved. The characters conflict. The crime is solved. That's it. There's no mystery, no imagination.

Edward M. White says of Kurt Vonnegut, Jr.'s *Wampeters, Foma & Granfalloons:*

My objection to Vonnegut, particularly in this collection of superficial journalism, is similar to his objection to the Maharishi: All the while he proclaims his visionary and prophetic function as a writer (and he does, steadily), he takes his single, pat stance toward the world. . . . A sardonic shrug . . . allows all of us frauds to get by in a fraudulent world.

Can I Offer a Well-Balanced Critique, Pointing Out Both Pluses and Minuses?

If accurate, this is preferable to all-good or all-bad review. The following are a few examples of good, well-balanced reviewing.

Richard Todd writes of Merle Miller's *Plain Speaking: An Oral Biography of Harry S. Truman:*

If you can stand the crackerbarrel prose, you can find some enjoyable and even illuminating things. . . . *Plain Speaking* is politically a lightweight and emotionally an untidy book. It is tantalyzing though. . . .

Newsweek says Peter Lyon's *Eisenhower: Portrait of the Hero* has:

. . . disturbing lack of material on the inner Eisenhower, his thoughts, feelings and motivations. . . . Yet this is a worthwhile book. What it lacks in intimacy, it makes up for in scope and breadth. If it does not astonish, it does inform.

Playboy zeroes in on the vices and virtues of Richard Price's *The Wanderers* by saying:

The characters are about as memorable as the thugs who snapped the aerial off your car. They never really grow anything but older. But some of the scenes are riveting and the dialog simply carries the book.

The same magazine calls Christopher Elias's *The Dollar Barons:*

. . . a comprehensible. if less than delectable diatribe by an outsider of the banks whose financial power is unrealized. . . . Most of his arguments against credit cards, against the independence of the Federal Reserve Board, against the "usurious" interest charges on mortgages seem weak and in some cases rather simple-minded. . . . But Elias does a creditable job of tracing the history of banking in this country through one conflict of interest to another and has given the reader some sense of what banking power is all about—and of how it is often at odds with the social good. . . . It is informative and a good place to start to learn about the "real" financial power in the U.S.—the banks.

Can I Use Appropriate Imagery, Adding Style and Punch?

Be creative in evaluating the work, using a vivid style instead of slapdashing off your impressions in a dull way. Remember: appropriate imagery can add color to a review. Ruth C. Ikerman begins her critique of *Bachelor Fatherhood* by Michael McFadden with:

> Reading this relaxed, practical book is like shaking a child's kaleidoscope and watching the segments of family life rearrange themselves into new patterns, even as the changing pieces of the ancient toy constantly shift to form new pictures.

Peter S. Prescott begins his review of the fifteenth edition of *Encyclopaedia Britannica* by writing:

> Encyclopedias are like loaves of bread: the sooner used the better, for they are growing stale even before they reach the shelf. In search of that perfect blandness most acceptable to the uncritical masses, the busy bakers bleach their flour, editors winnow authoritative articles and the nutritious elements fall away. Never fear. We'll throw in a penny's worth of vitamins to replace our more obvious losses and call our product new, enriched. Who will know what else is missing unless he once ate real bread, or read an old encyclopedia?

Prescott adds that this new encyclopedia reflects the fashion our times: to know more and more about less and less, which is the *Britannica's* fault. He then cites several examples of compressions and omissions.

Am I Thinking of My Readers and Slanting Specifically for Them?

The above review performs a service to readers of *Newsweek* by telling them to think twice before unloading their old *Britannica* and buying a new edition for $598 plus tax. You must always be your readers' trustworthy guide and serve their interests. The following is one of my own reviews aimed at golfers.

"GAMES DOCTORS PLAY"
Edited by Claude A. Frazier, M.D.

A Medic's eye-view of recreational sports that has genuine universal appeal; variety's the byword here

Perhaps physicians are under more pressure than most people. A good one never stops studying and learning the newest, most sophisticated medical advances, adding work and strain to a heavy schedule boobytrapped with life-and-death decisions, performance and incredible responsibility.

But *Games Doctors Play* isn't just for physicians. *Everyone* needs what this book offers: relief from stress, emotional tensions and boredom. The latter is defined as "deprivation of stimuli." The games described here offer enough stimuli to banish boredom for a lifetime!

Games Doctors Play is more reassuring than the best seller *Games People Play* by the late Dr. Eric Berne. Dr. Claude Frazier uses the word "games" positively and literally to show how work-pressured M.D.s relax at a wide spectrum of sports which are available to most of us, in contrast to the neurotic-interactive deceptions people use to mask their true motives and emotions in the earlier psychological work.

Dr. Frazier's book is an enlightening compendium of different doctors' favorite sports ranging from expensive (flying, soaring, sailing, horsemanship and quail-shooting) in which you need costly equipment, to moderately expensive (golf, mountain climbing, tennis), to inexpensive (table tennis, handball, volleyball) to costless (jogging, calisthenics, rope-jumping and running. An Indian proverb is quoted: "Running in a sense is like medicine—it is most useful when taken properly; too much or none at all may be potentially harmful.")

The sports also range from highly skilled to skilless and from competitive (fencing, tennis, golf, etc.) to relaxing and restful. Like fishing and sailing, which Dr. H. W. Virgin Jr. defines as "a sport in which the physician can become buried in his entirety; and it can thereby prevent him from thinking about his busy practice, the ringing telephone and the social engagements."

Don't we all—non-doctors as well—need some sort of refuge from routine and change of pace?

As Kay Frazier writes in her chapter, "Love Game" which describes how her husband taught her tennis:

"Creative play is not a sin, nor is it a luxury as some would have us believe. It is a companion and helpmate of work and just as necessary a part of everyday living."

This embodies the premise of the book in which separate chapters cover different sports: tennis, table tennis, volleyball, golf (the most interesting for *Country Club Golfer* readers), lawn bowling, curling, handball, fencing, sprinting, skeet and trapshooting, mountain climbing, water skiing, wild-water paddling, soaring, sailing, ballooning, horsebackriding, swimming, hunting and fishing. The concluding chapter is "Immediate Care of Athletic Injuries" by Dr. H. Royer Collins, but the whole tone of the volume is positive and practical, never negative.

You'll learn much more about these sports from a variety of M.D.s (each writing with know-how and affection) than you could from a one-man-show. There's a variety of styles of writing interspersed with fact tidbits. Some chapters offer a glossary of terms, instructional tips, sources and addresses of specific sports headquarters and equipment supplies. Some list bibliographies for further reading. It would be better if they all did.

You can't read *Games Doctors Play* without increasing your knowledge of your own sport(s) and—what's more important—without gaining interest and insight into new ones you may not have considered before. How vital today when lifespans are increasing, workspans decreasing and countless Americans plagued by leisure time they don't know what to do with!

We especially liked the way the following myths are exploded:

1. "You have to be young and healthy to engage in sports." In several different parts of the book authorities prove the reverse and cite the international Coronary Curling Club of which President Eisenhower was an honorary life member and case histories of handicapped, aged fencing champs.

2. "Doctors don't exercise although they warn patients of the dangers of a sedentary life."

3. "The athlete's heart is abnormally enlarged." Dr. Delano Meriwether says that sports activity "makes the heart a stronger and more effective organ to provide oxygen and remove metabolic wastes from body tissues." In truth, *the loafer's heart is abnormal!*

4. "Dieting alone is the best way to lose weight." Dr. James P. Harnsberger reaffirms what we believe: all the while fat-

conscious therapy groups are worriedly weighing each ounce of food and counting each calorie, they could be *enjoying* a recreational game that burns up calories and feel *great* as well as slim!

5. "Americans are the flabby overweight society whom TV is converting into broadening-bottomed, snack-munching, dull-witted spectators."

We gleaned these exploded myths from throughout the different chapters, but they could comprise a book in themselves!

Another reassuring quality is the welcome thread of patriotism that runs throughout the pages. Most of the sports are U.S.-oriented and American-adapted, even though our ancestors brought them from other lands. These historical touches are especially welcome as we march toward our Bicentennial in 1976. Handball was introduced by an Irish immigrant from Britain where it was called "fives," similar to squash. Golf was recommended by Dr. Benjamin Rush, signer of the Declaration of Independence, before we were a nation! In 1772 in his book, *Sermons to Gentlemen Upon Temperance and Exercise,* he wrote:

"Golf is an exercise which is much used by the Gentlemen of Scotland. A large common in which there are several little holes is chosen for the purpose. It is played with little leather balls stuffed with feathers, and sticks somewhat in the form of a handy wicket. He who puts a ball into a given number of holes, with the fewest strokes, gets the game. The late Dr. McKenzie . . . used to say that a man would live ten years longer for this exercise once or twice a week."

Unfortunately, Dr. Frazier's recent book is almost as male-oriented as Dr. Rush's volume of 200 years ago. At least one woman doctor should have been included. The only chapter written by a member of the fair sex is by a non-doctor, his wife, and it is one of the best!

It might also have been better to add more bibliographies and sports-helping foods and supplements (Dr. August F. Daro is the only one who does and his enthusiasm seems confined to Vitamin E). Much of the repetition could have been cut, especially of clichés like "All work and no play makes Jack a dull boy" (p. 4) and "All work and no play makes John a dull boy" (p. 95).

But the virtues far outweigh the vices. What Dr. John B. Gramlich says of mountaineering is true of all sports and of *Games Doctors Play:* "The joy of climbing is the pleasure of discovery of being able to see farther and from a greater height." Thanks, doctors, for helping us rediscover the physiological, psychological and philosophical benefits of recreational sports!

Don'ts of Reviewing

(1) Don't sell out and overpraise a work (even if you're pressured by the author or publisher). Your first duty is to your reader. It isn't true that "flattery will get you everywhere." On the contrary, "all sunshine makes a desert." Be objective and honest in your evaluating.

(2) Don't be too general or use abstract descriptions like "brilliant," "stimulating," "dull," or "pedestrian." Explain why and how specifically. Don't be like Parker Ballentine, the critic-protagonist of Ira Levin's play, *Critic's Choice*, who kept a boxfull of form criticisms and pulled out what seemed to fit a production. Approach each work individually and give it the criticism it deserves, never using an "interchangeable" description that might fit several different books.

Here's an example: "A beautiful book . . . seldom does one encounter such a combination of basic knowledge, insight, humor and poetry." What does that tell you about the contents? Almost nothing.

(3) Don't forget to include the premise of the work. Although Donald E. Westlake's *Help, I Am Being Held Prisoner* is a humorous piece of entertainment, reviewer Dick Lochte points out its social consciousness by relaying its pithy premise:

> The rebels (in prison) are radicalizing the criminals, which is why there've been so many prison riots and strikes recently, but at the same time the crooks are criminalizing the radicals. A college student who enters prison for smoking marijuana . . . comes out knowing how to jimmy apartment doors and crack safes. A few years from now the world in general may be in for an unpleasant surprise.

Dorothy Hughes, in reviewing Francis Clifford's *Another Way of Dying*, says he insists that coincidence is inevitable and can play havoc in the life of an ordinary man.

(4) Don't be afraid to be original without overshadowing the author's style. Use imagery to heighten your impression.

Of Thomas S. Klise's *The Last Western*, reviewer V. S. Lieberman says its "pace is like a visual alarm clock: When the introspection gets sluggish, we get great buzzes of action." Of the characters he writes:

> If major, we see them complete and detailed, like a widescreen movie of our imagination. If minor, we see their strength and weaknesses instantly, like a Polaroid picture of their souls.

Melvin Maddocks calls Charles Reich's *The Greening of America* "Evangelistic pop sociology" and "a melting pot of Zen, Marcuse and vintage *Catcher in the Rye*, brought to a boil by acid rock."

Playboy compares the lukewarm affair between the lovers in the film *The April Fools* to "a rendezvous between Dagwood Bumstead and Madame Bovary."

(5) Don't be *too* cute, exhibiting your own cleverness at the expense of the author you are reviewing.

(6) Don't, under any circumstances, give away a surprise ending. You may indicate that it is a blockbuster or worth hanging around for, or incredible, or whatever is your honest opinion, but don't tip it off. A theater strike was averted in London when strikers threatened to carry placards announcing the surprise ending!

(7) Don't be vitriolic in panning a work. In a constructive way, point out the shortcomings and perhaps suggest improvements. Some critics are so acerbic and petty they seem to be spoilsports. Unable to construct the edifice of a successful script, they specialize in tearing down those that make it. No wonder a critic has been defined as a man whose wife ran away with a writer!

Many thespians agree with Bette Davis in wanting to take their shows on tour for six months before bringing them to New York "where one man can kill a show in one night and wash out any chances of profit."

You may be able to carve a worthwhile career for yourself as a critic, but you do not have to be nasty and destructive to do so. The most respected and successful reviewers are those who are fair and honest in their evaluations, which must be valid and in line with what the specific audiences will think and feel. Don't be like the ninnies described by O. W. Holmes: "Nature, when she invented, manufactured and patented her authors, contrived to make critics out of the chips that were left."

A local Iowa book reviewer, Mary Ann Riley, seems to think there are just two extremes of reviewers. She writes:

It is often implied that book reviewers are persons of influence, presumption and malevolence who can make or break a potential best-seller. How about the thousands of reviewers around the country who write for local dailies? Pathetically, they read every review copy sent to them by publishers in search of something, anything that will make the book sell . . . we small-time volunteers in the heartland are poised to give most any author 150 words of nonderogatory notice.

Wow! As if praising a bad book isn't as reproachable as panning a good one! By now you realize that there's much more to book reviewing than serving as an omnipotent schoolmaster whose only task is to stamp "pass" or "fail" on each victim. You must instruct, enlighten, and protect your reader as fairly and constructively as you can. Don't fall into either of the preceding mentioned traps: condemning or condoning in a superficial, naive way.

If you must criticize negatively, be specific and constructive. If you recommend the book highly, explain why, preferably in a way that proves your in-depth knowledge of the subject and related fields. It is not necessary to have a hero-worshiping attitude toward a work that has proved itself worthy of being published or produced, but some respect is advisable. As the much-criticized Racine said: "The critics have vanished. The plays remain."

Afterword

Be a Stimulating Cerebral Spelunker

03/08/07

Successful authorship is the result of spelunking into places, people, experiences, reading—everywhere—for ideas to develop into original scripts.

As you know, a spelunker is a cave-explorer, but more than one who just walks in and out of caves. A spelunker is a person interested in speleology—the *science* of exploring caves.

To be a professional author, you must approach writing as a *science*, which the dictionary defines as "systematized knowledge derived from observation, study and experimentation . . . establishing and systematizing facts, principles, and methods." *1, 2, 3*

Before you write anything (fiction, nonfiction, poetry, drama . . for juveniles or adults) be sure to:

(1) Establish the market slant and write with acute awareness and *who* understanding of the specific reader you are writing for. The amateur pours words on paper then asks, "Where shall I send this?" The pro has his market and readers firmly in mind and slants everything he writes for them.

> "Cheshire Puss," [Alice] began . . . "Would you tell me, please, which way I ought to go from here?"
> "That depends a good deal on where you want to get to," said the Cat.

227

"I don't much care where—" said Alice.
"Then it doesn't matter which way you go," said the Cat.

To get someplace, you must know where you're going. You'll sell what you write only if it's beamed toward your customers and written the way they want it.

(2) Plan the emotional reaction you want to arouse—laughter, tears, disgust, admiration, wonder, etc. Don't hold back with cold objectivity unless you're writing for technical or trade journals or scientific periodicals. Best-selling Poet Rod McKuen's timely message is "Be sentimental. . . . Don't stay cool, stay warm." One of his popular books is even titled *Listen to the Warm*. Most people do . . . they've had enough of the "cool" and "cool it!"

(3) Write out the premise or premises you wish to convey. Plan these in your mind in harmony with your individual philosophy. Try to represent opposite philosophical viewpoints in your script, then work out a teetertottering conflict that will culminate in a strong overall premise that coincides with your thinking.

What is your general outlook? Optimistic? Pessimistic? Middle of the road? "Know Thyself" and be true to your beliefs and you can't be false to your writing.

Study the premises of professional works and observe how the author works out the action or outline-development to prove his belief. Categorize premises into the three following major categories . . . not just the themes of professional fiction, drama, and nonfiction (also poetry) but ideas and proverbs that interest you and that may inspire your future works.

Positive Optimistic Premises

"Nothing is too wonderful to be true."
Farady

"Thou, O God, dost sell unto us all good things at the price of labour . . . as a well-spent day brings happy sleep, so life well -used brings happy death."
Leonardo de Vinci

"If you really know what things you want out of life, it's amazing how opportunities will come to enable you to carry them out."
John M. Goddard

You can add all the old standby "uplifts" like: "Hope springs eternal in the human breast", 'Every cloud has a silver lining"; "Sweet are the uses of adversity"; etc.

All of Saroyan's works reflect his optimistic faith in the goodness of man and the wonder of life. How many more positive premises can you find and concoct? How are premises dramatized in fiction? Nonfiction? Although *A Night of Watching* by Elliot Arnold is certainly not a happy-go-lucky novel—it is permeated with true-life tragedies during the Nazi occupation of Denmark—its premise is a promise of hope: Man's evil can be reduced when confronted by human courage and good.

Negative Pessimistic Premises

"We are all sinful; and whatever one of us blames in another each one will find in his own heart."
Seneca

"Man is a useless passion"; "Life is meaningless"; "The bourgeoisie are swine."
Jean Genêt

"Open not thy heart to every man lest he repay thee with an evil turn."
Ecclesiastes 8:22

"For even saintly folk will act like sinners. . . . Unless they have their customary dinners."
(Brecht . . . quoted as a prologue to Langdon Gilkey's *Shantung Compound*, which exposes the moral decay of missionaries under stress of imprisonment.)

"Death is the only coming in from the cold there is."
John Le Carré

"I am a man alone. A lone hell. . . . Men are the lice of Christ."
Salvatore Quasimodo

Eugene O'Neill's consistent pessimism reiterates the negativism of his master, Strindberg . . . both assert the idea that men are pitiable, disgusting creatures, totally maladjusted to the universe. Such negativism permeates the Theatre of the Absurd as well as a great number of other downbeat plays, books, and poetry. See, for example, the work of Samuel Beckett, who states that the major sin is the sin of being born.

Neutral Middle-of-the-Road Premises

"It is not what you have lost, but what you have left that counts."
    Harold Russell

"Some of the people are good and some of them are bad—just like the fruit on a tree."
    Gordon Parks in *The Learning Tree*

Courage
Courage is the price that Life exacts for granting peace
The soul that knows it not
Knows no release from little things:
Knows not the livid loneliness of fear,
Nor mountain heights where bitter joy can hear
The sound of wings.

How can Life grant us boon of living, compensate
For dull, gray ugliness and pregnant hate
Unless we dare
The soul's dominion? Each time we make a choice, we pay
With courage to behold resistless day,
And count it fair.
    Amelia Earhart

"If you can't make light of troubles, keep them in the dark."
    Cheerful Cherub

"Life is a quarry out of which we are to mould and chisel and complete a character."
    Goethe

"The trouble with Life: You're halfway through before you realize it's one of those do-it-yourself deals."
    Fletcher Knebel

When writing nonfiction, it's a good idea to take the Rotary International Four-Way Test:
    First—Is it the truth?
    Second—Is it fair to all concerned?
    Third—Will it build goodwill and better friendships?
    Fourth—Will it be beneficial to all concerned?
    Add your own goals of correct slant, reader identification, premise, and your very best writing style.
    In *What Is Literature?* Jean Paul Sartre wrote: "The function of a writer is to call a spade a spade. If words are sick, it is up to us to cure them . . . I distrust the incommunicable; it is the source of all violence."

Index

231